# Language Technology for Cultural Heritage, Social Sciences, and Humanities 2012

# (LaTeCH 2012)

AA005980

**Held at the 13th Conference of the European Chapter of the Association for Computational Linguistics (EACL 2012)**

## Avignon, France
## 23 – 27 April 2012

ISBN: 978-1-62276-493-8

**Printed from e-media with permission by:**

Curran Associates, Inc.
57 Morehouse Lane
Red Hook, NY 12571

**Some format issues inherent in the e-media version may also appear in this print version.**



Printed by Curran Associates, Inc. (2012)

For permission requests, please contact the Association for Computational Linguistics at the address below.

Association for Computational Linguistics
209 N. Eighth Street
Stroudsburg, Pennsylvania 18360

Phone: 1-570-476-8006
Fax: 1-570-476-0860

acl@aclweb.org

**Additional copies of this publication are available from:**

Curran Associates, Inc.
57 Morehouse Lane
Red Hook, NY 12571 USA
Phone: 845-758-0400
Fax: 845-758-2634
Email: curran@proceedings.com
Web: www.proceedings.com

# Preface

The LaTeCH (*Language Technology for Cultural Heritage, Social Sciences, and Humanities*) annual workshop series aims to provide a forum for researchers working on aspects of natural language and information technology applications that pertain to data from the humanities, social sciences, and cultural heritage. The LaTeCH workshop series, which started in 2007, was initially motivated by the growing interest in language technology research and applications to the cultural heritage domain. The scope quickly broadened to also include the humanities and the social sciences.

Advances in information technology and web access of the past decade have triggered a multitude of digitisation efforts by museums, archives, libraries and other cultural heritage institutions. Similar developments in the humanities and social sciences have resulted in large amounts of research data becoming available in electronic format, either as digitised or as born-digital data. The natural follow-up step to digitisation is the intelligent processing of this data. To this end, the humanities, social sciences, and cultural heritage domains draw an increasing interest from researchers in NLP aiming at developing methods for semantic enrichment and information discovery and access. Language technology has been conventionally focused on certain domains, such as newswire. These fairly novel domains of cultural heritage, social sciences, and humanities entail new challenges to NLP research, such as noisy text (e.g., due to OCR problems), non-standard, or archaic language varieties (e.g., historic language, dialects, mixed use of languages, ellipsis, transcription errors), literary or figurative writing style and lack of knowledge resources, such as dictionaries. Furthermore, often neither annotated domain data is available, nor the required funds to manually create it, thus forcing researchers to investigate (semi-) automatic resource development and domain adaptation approaches involving the least possible manual effort.

In the current sixth edition of the LaTeCH workshop we have again received a record number of submissions, a subset of which has been selected based on a thorough peer-review process. The submissions were substantial not only in terms of quantity, but also in terms of quality and variety, underlining the increasing interest of NLP and CL researchers in in this exciting and expanding research area. A central issue for a substantial part of the contributions to this LaTeCH workshop is the development of corpora, lexical resources and annotation tools for historical language varieties. Some contributions focus on two other recurrent issues, namely the description and classification of cultural heritage objects and the problems related to noisy and handwritten text. Most importantly, the research presented in this edition of the LaTeCH workshop showcases the breadth of interest in applications of language technologies to a variety of social sciences and e-humanities domains, ranging from history to ethnography and from philosophy to literature and historical linguistics.

We would like to thank all authors for the hard work that went into their submissions. We are also grateful to the members of the programme committee for their thorough reviews, and to the EACL 2012 organisers, especially the Workshop Co-chairs, Kristiina Jokinen and Alessandro Moschitti for their help with administrative matters.

*Kalliopi Zervanou and Antal van den Bosch*

**Organizers:**

Kalliopi Zervanou (Co-chair), Tilburg University (The Netherlands)
Antal van den Bosch (Co-chair), Radboud University Nijmegen (The Netherlands)
Caroline Sporleder, Saarland University (Germany)
Piroska Lendvai, Research Institute for Linguistics (Hungary)

**Program Committee:**

Ion Androutsopoulos, Athens University of Economics and Business (Greece)
David Bamman, Carnegie Mellon University (USA)
Toine Bogers, Royal School of Library & Information Science, Copenhagen (Denmark)
Paul Buitelaar, DERI Galway (Ireland)
Kate Byrne, University of Edinburgh (Scotland)
Milena Dobreva, HATII, University of Glasgow (Scotland)
Mick O'Donnell, Universidad Autonoma de Madrid (Spain)
Claire Grover, University of Edinburgh (Scotland)
Ben Hachey, Macquarie University (Australia)
Jaap Kamps, University of Amsterdam (The Netherlands)
Vangelis Karkaletsis, NCSR Demokritos (Greece)
Stasinos Konstantopoulos, NCSR Demokritos (Greece)
Barbara McGillivray, Oxford University Press
Joakim Nivre, Uppsala University (Sweden)
Petya Osenova, Bulgarian Academy of Sciences (Bulgaria)
Katerina Pastra, CSRI (Greece)
Michael Piotrowski, University of Zurich (Switzerland)
Georg Rehm, DFKI (Germany)
Martin Reynaert, Tilburg University (The Netherlands)
Herman Stehouwer, Max Planck Institute for Psycholinguistics (The Netherlands)
Cristina Vertan, University of Hamburg (Germany)
Piek Vossen, Vrije Universiteit Amsterdam (The Netherlands)
Peter Wittenburg, Max Planck Institute for Psycholinguistics (The Netherlands)
Menno van Zaanen, Tilburg University (The Netherlands)
Svitlana Zinger, TU Eindhoven (The Netherlands)

# Table of Contents

# Conference Program

**Tuesday April 24, 2012**

9:00–9:05 *Welcome*

***Poster Boaster Session: Tools & Resources***

9:05–9:10 *Lexicon Construction and Corpus Annotation of Historical Language with the CoBaLT Editor*
Tom Kenter, Tomaž Erjavec, Maja Žorga Dulmin and Darja Fišer

9:10–9:15 *A High Speed Transcription Interface for Annotating Primary Linguistic Data*
Mark Dingemanse, Jeremy Hammond, Herman Stehouwer, Aarthy Somasundaram and Sebastian Drude

9:15–9:20 *BAD: An Assistant Tool for Making Verses in Basque*
Manex Agirrezabal, Iñaki Alegria, Bertol Arrieta and Mans Hulden

9:20–9:25 *Toward Language Independent Methodology for Generating Artwork Descriptions – Exploring FrameNet Information*
Dana Dannélls and Lars Borin

9:25–9:30 *Harvesting Indices to Grow a Controlled Vocabulary: Towards Improved Access to Historical Legal Texts*
Michael Piotrowski and Cathrin Senn

9:30–9:35 *Ontology-Based Incremental Annotation of Characters in Folktales*
Thierry Declerck, Nikolina Koleva and Hans-Ulrich Krieger

9:35–10:30 Poster session & Coffie break

***Oral Session 1: Applications in Humanities & Social Sciences***

10:30–11:00 *Advanced Visual Analytics Methods for Literature Analysis*
Daniela Oelke, Dimitrios Kokkinakis and Mats Malm

11:00–11:30 *Distributional Techniques for Philosophical Enquiry*
Aurélie Herbelot, Eva von Redecker and Johanna Müller

11:30–12:00 *Linguistically-Adapted Structural Query Annotation for Digital Libraries in the Social Sciences*
Caroline Brun, Vassilina Nikoulina and Nikolaos Lagos

12:00–12:30 *Parsing the Past – Identification of Verb Constructions in Historical Text*
Eva Pettersson, Beáta Megyesi and Joakim Nivre

**Tuesday April 24, 2012 (continued)**

# Lexicon construction and corpus annotation of historical language with the CoBaLT editor

**Tom Kenter[1], Tomaž Erjavec[2], Maja Žorga Dulmin[3], Darja Fišer[4]**

[1] Institute for Dutch Lexicology
Matthias de Vrieshof 3, gebouw 1171, 2311 BZ Leiden
tom.kenter@inl.nl
[2] Department of Knowledge Technologies, Jožef Stefan Institute
Jamova cesta 39, SI-1000 Ljubljana
tomaz.erjavec@ijs.si
[3] maja.zorga@gmail.com
[4] Department of Translation, Faculty of Arts, University of Ljubljana
Aškerčeva 2, SI-1000 Ljubljana
darja.fiser@ff.uni-lj.si

**Abstract**

This paper describes a Web-based editor called CoBaLT (Corpus-Based Lexicon Tool), developed to construct corpus-based computational lexica and to correct word-level annotations and transcription errors in corpora. The paper describes the tool as well as our experience in using it to annotate a reference corpus and compile a large lexicon of historical Slovene. The annotations used in our project are modern-day word form equivalent, lemma, part-of-speech tag and optional gloss. The CoBaLT interface is word form oriented and compact. It enables wildcard word searching and sorting according to several criteria, which makes the editing process flexible and efficient. The tool accepts pre-annotated corpora in TEI P5 format and is able to export the corpus and lexicon in TEI P5 as well. The tool is implemented using the LAMP architecture and is freely available for research purposes.

## 1 Introduction

Processing tools as well as linguistic studies of historical language need language resources, which have to be developed separately for each language, and manually annotated or validated. The two basic resource types are hand-annotated corpora and lexica for historical language, which should contain (at least) information about the modern-day equivalent of a word form and its lemma and part-of-speech (PoS). The first of these is useful for easier reading of historical texts, as well as for enabling already developed modern-day PoS tagging and lemmatisation models to be applied to historical texts. PoS tags make for a better environment for linguistic exploration and enable further levels of annotation, such as tree-banking. They also facilitate lemmatisation, which is especially useful for highly inflecting languages as it abstracts away from the inflectional variants of words, thereby enabling better text searching.

To develop such resources, a good editor is needed that caters to the peculiarities of historical texts. Preferably it would combine the production of annotated corpora and corpus-based lexica. This paper presents CoBaLT, a Web-based editor which has already been used for developing language resources for several languages. We describe it within the framework of developing a gold-standard annotated reference corpus (Erjavec, 2012) and a large lexicon of historical Slovene.

This paper is structured as follows: in the next section we describe the implementation and functionality of CoBaLT. In Section 3 we present the input and output corpus and lexicon formats, in particular from the perspective of our project. In Section 4 we compare existing tools serving a similar purpose to CoBaLT and discuss the advantages and disadvantages of the CoBaLT environment. The last section summarizes and lists our conclusions.

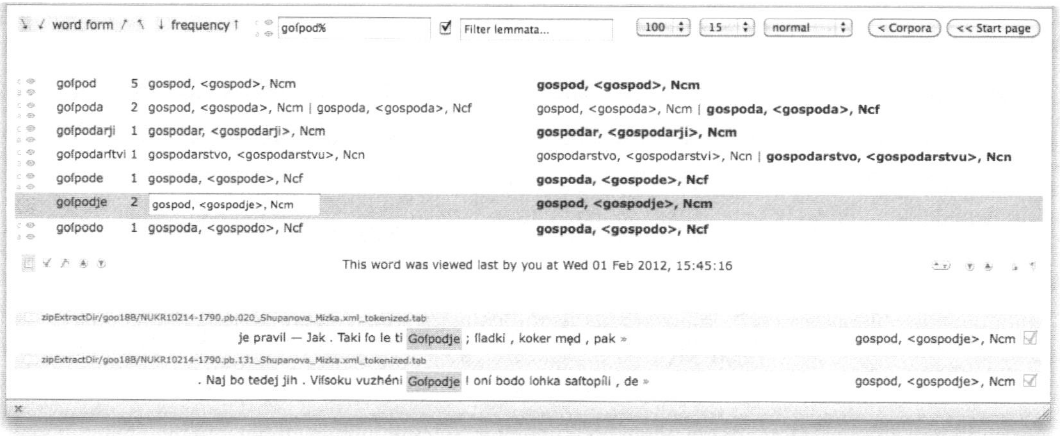


Figure 1. CoBaLT interface

## 2 The CoBaLT tool

### 2.1 Implementation

CoBaLT is a Web-based editor using the classic LAMP architecture (Linux, Apache, MySQL and PHP). Ajax (Asynchronous JavaScript and XML) technology is used extensively as it enables updating only relevant parts of the screen which increases speed and usability. The code is optimised to work with large datasets and comes with documentation on various settings for MySQL and PHP that enhance handling large data collections. System, project, language-specific details (e.g. the list of valid PoS tags to enable their validation during editing) and some interface settings are encapsulated in a PHP file, making the adaptation of the tool to other environments very easy. However, some knowledge of MySQL is still required, e.g. to add new users to the system which is performed directly in MySQL.

Apart from an Internet browser, no additional software is required at the user side. The interface can be used from various browsers on all major operating systems, although it has been tested primarily on Mozilla Firefox.

### 2.2 User interface

Apart from logging into the tool and selecting the corpus or file to work on, the CoBaLT user interface is always contained on a single screen. The icons and fields on the screen have associated tool-tips.

As shown in Figure 1, the screen is divided in four parts:

1. The upper, "dashboard" part enables ways of organizing the displayed information, i.e. how to sort the word forms, which ones to select, whether to hide certain less interesting word forms (such as numerals), the number of word forms shown, and links back to start pages.
2. The left side of the middle part shows the (selected) historical word forms with their corpus frequencies. This is followed by an editable window giving the modernised word form, lemma, PoS and potential gloss; if the corpus contains distinct annotations for the word form, they are all shown, separated by a pipe symbol. Finally, on the right-hand side, all the possible lexical annotations of the word form are given; those in bold have been validated.
3. The separator between the middle and lower parts shows who has worked last on the selected word form, and gives icons for sorting the word forms in context in the lower part according to a number of criteria: word form, right and left context, analysis and verification.
4. The lower part of the screen shows the selected word form tokens in context together with their analyses in that context and a tick box for validation next to each. Also displayed is the name of the document in which they appear. The arrows next to a context row allow for expanding the context. Clicking on the camera icon at the left side of the row opens the facsimile image.

The separator bar in the middle can be dragged for relative resizing of the middle and lower part.

### 2.3 Editing in CoBaLT

There is more than one way of editing the analyses assigned to a word form in CoBaLT. The user can work on a specific word form either in the middle screen or in the lower screen, with keyboard shortcuts making the process very efficient. Multiple rows of a word form in context can be quickly selected with the mouse. The user can assign the analysis to selected word form tokens a) in the middle part either by writing it in the editable window or by clicking on a proposed analysis; b) in the lower part by clicking on the word token, which opens a drop down menu. Further options are available, explained in the user manual.

A special feature is the ability to assign analyses to a group of word tokens, e.g. when multiple word tokens in the historical text correspond to a single modern word. Multiple analyses can also be assigned to a single word token, e.g. if one historical word form corresponds to several modern ones.

Working on historical language, the need occasionally arises to correct the transcription. This can be done by Ctrl-clicking the word form in context in the lower screen. An editable box will appear in which the user can correct a typo or separate merged words.

## 3 Data import and export

### 3.1 Corpus import and export

CoBaLT input corpus files can be in arbitrary formats, as long as the tokens, and possibly their annotations, are indicated in the texts, and appropriate import routines are in place. The tool currently accepts plain text and a parameterisation of TEI P5 XML (TEI Consortium, 2007). The latter option is more interesting for our case, as TEI files can already be structurally and linguistically annotated. Zip files are also supported, which enables uploading large datasets with many separate files.

The Slovene corpora are encoded in TEI, and each corpus file contains the transcription of a single page, together with the link to its facsimile image. The page is also annotated with paragraphs, line breaks, etc. Such annotation is imported into CoBaLT but not displayed or modified, and appears again only in the export.

The texts in our project were first automatically annotated (Erjavec, 2011): each text was sentence segmented and tokenised into words. Punctuation symbols (periods, commas, etc.) and white-spaces were preserved in the annotation so the original text and layout can be reconstructed from the annotated text. Each word form was assigned its modern-day equivalent, its PoS tag and modern day lemma.

Such files, a number of them together constituting one corpus, were then imported into CoBaLT and manually edited, with CoBaLT supporting the export of the annotated corpus as TEI P5 as well. In the export, each validated token is additionally annotated with the annotator's username and time of annotation.

One particular facet of the annotation concerns the word-boundary mismatch between the historical and modern-day word forms. As mentioned, CoBaLT supports joining two words in the transcription to give them a common annotation, as well as giving several successive annotations to a single word, and this is also reflected in the exported TEI annotation.

### 3.2 Lexicon export

While it is of course possible to produce a direct SQL dump of the lexicon, CoBaLT also supports lexicon export in TEI P5 using the TEI dictionaries module. This lexicon is headword (lemma) oriented. The lemma entry in the export consists of a headword, part of speech and optionally a gloss. The entry also contains all the modern word forms of the lemma as annotated in the corpus. For each modern word form one or more historical word forms are listed, including their normalised and cited forms. The difference between normalised and cited forms is that cited forms are the exact word forms as they appear in the corpus, while the normalised ones are lower-cased, and, in the case of Slovene, have vowel diacritics removed as these are not used in contemporary Slovene and are furthermore very inconsistently used in historical texts. These normalised forms are also what is listed in the left column of the middle part of the CoBaLT window. As illustrated in Figure 2, one cited form with examples of usage is "gláſnikam", the normalised form "glaſnikam", the modernised one "glasnikom" and the lemma form "glasnik", which is a common noun of masculine gender. This word does not exist anymore, so it is assigned a gloss, i.e. its contemporary equivalent "samoglasnik" (meaning "vowel").

The cited forms also contain examples of usage together with the file they occurred in. The export script can be limited as to how many usage examples get exported, as in the case of a fully annotated corpus the number of attestations for high-frequency words (typically function words) can easily go into the thousands, and there is little point in including all of them in the lexicon.

```
<entry>
 <form type="lemma">
  <orth type="hypothetical">glasnik</orth>
  <gramGrp>
   <gram type="msd">Ncm</gram>
   <gram type="PoS">Noun</gram>
   <gram type="Type">common</gram>
   <gram type="Gender">masculine</gram>
  </gramGrp>
  <gloss>samoglasnik</gloss>
  <bibl>kontekst, Pleteršnik</bibl>
  <lbl type="occurrences">1</lbl>
 </form>
 <form type="wordform">
  <orth type="hypothetical">glasnikom</orth>
  <form type="historical">
   <orth type="normalised">glaſnikam</orth>
   <form type="cited">
    <orth type="exact">gláſnikam</orth>
    <cit>
     <quote>kadar beſeda, ktira naſléduje,
        sazhénja s' enim <oVar>gláſnikam</oVar>
      al tudi s' enim/quote>
     <bibl>NUK_10220-
        1811.pb.007_Pozhetki_gramatike.xml
     </bibl>
    </cit>
   </form>
  </form>
 </form>
</entry>
```

Figure 2. Example of a TEI dictionary entry

The export script also accepts parameters that determine which word forms should be exported – all, or only the attested or verified ones.

As in the corpus, the special case of multiword units and split words arises in the lexicon as well. Multiword units have the lemma and modern day forms composed of multiple words, and multiple grammatical descriptions, one for each lemma, while split words have the historical word forms composed of two or more words.

Also included with CoBaLT is a script to merge two TEI lexica (e.g. derived from different corpora) into a single TEI lexicon and to convert the TEI lexicon into HTML for web browsing. We extended this script for the case of Slovene to also give direct links to several on-line dictionaries and to the concordancer that hosts our corpora.

# 4 Discussion

## 4.1 Strengths and weakness of CoBaLT

First, it should be noted that CoBaLT is not limited to working with corpora of historical language – it could also be used for non-standard language varieties (e.g. tweets) or for standard contemporary language, by slightly modifying the import/export and the parsing of the word annotation in the editor. Nevertheless, it incorporates several features that make it particularly suitable for handling historical texts:

- CoBaLT supports both corpus annotation and corpus-based lexicon construction; extensive lexica are, at least from the point of view of good processing of historical language, much more important than annotated corpora.
- The texts of historical corpora are typically first produced by optical character recognition (OCR) software and then manually corrected. In spite of corrections, some errors will invariably remain in the text and will be, for the most part, noticed during the annotation process. While not meant for major editing of the transcription, CoBaLT does offer the possibility to correct the transcription of individual words. This is a rare functionality in other annotation editors, which typically take the base text as read-only. The current version of CoBaLT offers support for editing, splitting, and joining word tokens. Deleting word forms altogether, however, is not supported – an option that should be added in the future.
- Related to the previous point is CoBaLT's feature to display the facsimile of a particular page, making it possible to check the transcription or OCR result against the original image of the page.

As regards the functioning of the tool, it is important to note that almost all linguistic processing occurs outside of CoBaLT making it more light-weight as well as more language independent. In previous work (Erjavec et al., 2010) a different editor was used which had linguistic processing built in and proved to be more difficult to adapt to Slovene than CoBaLT.

In this particular project we decided to organise the files around the concept of a facsimile page. This has a number of advantages, in particular a straight-forward mapping between files and facsimile images, a simple unit of sampling for the corpus, and small files, which makes it easier to manage the work of annotators. However, this arrangement causes some problems from a linguistic point of view, namely that the page will often start or end in the middle of a paragraph, sentence or even word. We decided to start and end each page with a paragraph or sentence boundary, while split words are marked by a special PoS tag. It should be noted that this is used only at page-breaks – split words at line-breaks are joined before importing the texts into CoBaLT.

From a user-interface perspective, a distinguishing feature of CoBaLT is that there is a single editor window, with keyboard shortcuts making the jumps between the parts of the screen faster than moving a mouse, allowing for quick and efficient editing. Adding or deleting a number of analyses is also just a click away. This again makes the tool very efficient but also means that the user has to be quite careful not to accidentally destroy already existing annotations – this proved to be a problem in the annotation round.

From an implementation standpoint, we should note that the level of security offered by CoBaLT is limited. Only a user name is needed to log in and have access to the data. While this can be easily circumvented by placing the entire interface behind a secure page, a higher level of security, e.g. just adding passwords to the login procedure, should be implemented in the future. On the other hand, access should not be too restricted, as simple access does allow for easy crowdsourcing.

### 4.2 Related work

Historical corpora have been compiled, annotated and made available for searching in a number of projects, such as Corpus of Historical American English (Davies, 2010), Penn Corpora of Historical English (Kroch et al., 2004), GermanC historical corpus (Durrell et al., 2007), Historical Corpus of the Welsh Language (Mittendorf and Willis, 2004) and Icelandic Parsed Historical Corpus (Wallenberg et al., 2011), etc. Surprisingly few of these initiatives have developed or discussed the need for a historical text platform that would enable manual correction of pre-annotated corpora, facilities for lexicon building, and a standardized annotation format.

As the simplest solution, some of the projects used general-purpose XML. However, human annotators usually have a hard time working in XML directly to revise word-level annotations and transcription errors. This is one of the reasons why automatic and manual corpus-development tasks were integrated into the same environment in the GermanC project (Scheible et al., 2010), where the GATE platform (Cunningham et al., 2002) was used to produce the initial annotations and to perform manual corrections. However, GATE does not provide explicit support for texts encoded according to the TEI P5 guidelines, which is why the GermanC team spent a lot of time on writing scripts to deal with formatting issues. As GATE has automatic processing integrated into it, it is also not trivial to adapt it to a new language.

The only special-purpose tools for historical corpus development we could find is E-Dictor, a specialized tool for encoding, applying levels of editions and assigning PoS tags to ancient texts for building the Tycho Brahe Parsed Corpus of Historical Portuguese (de Faria et al., 2010). It is similar to CoBaLT in that it too has a WYSIWYG interface and allows annotators to check transcriptions and assign several layers of annotations to the tokens. E-Dictor enables export of the encoded text XML and the lexicon of editions in HTML and CSV. This is an interesting tool although it does not seem to support a lexical view of the data or merging and splitting word forms, and it is not quite clear how it interacts with automatic processing of the texts, or if a user manual is available.

As the review of related work shows, there is a general lack of tools such as CoBaLT which can significantly simplify and speed up most historical corpus and lexicon development projects. We believe CoBaLT has a number of qualities that will make it attractive for other researchers.

## 5 Conclusions

The paper presented CoBaLT, an editor for constructing corpus-based lexica and correcting word-level annotations and transcription errors in corpora. The editor has been extensively tested in a project in which a historical corpus was manually annotated and used to produce a lexicon, with the lexicon being further extended on the basis of a much larger corpus. Seven annotators have worked on the resources for over half a year, which put the tool through a good stress test. CoBaLT has also been used in several similar projects for other languages, in particular in producing historical lexica for Czech, Polish, Dutch and Spanish (de Does et al., 2012).[1]

With the help of CoBaLT Slovene now has two essential historical language resources, both encoded in TEI P5. The resources will be used to build better models for (re)tokenisation, transcription, tagging and lemmatisation, and to facilitate corpus-based diachronic language studies. We also plan to continue using CoBaLT to further extend the hand-annotated corpus and lexicon.

CoBaLT is freely available for research use from the Web site of the Impact Centre of Competence, http://www.digitisation.eu. The distribution contains the code, user manual, and associated scripts mentioned in this paper.

## Acknowledgements

The authors would like to thank the anonymous reviewers for their helpful comments and suggestions. The work presented in this paper has been supported by the EU IMPACT project "Improving Access to Text", http://www.impact-project.eu.

## References

Mark Davies. 2010. *The Corpus of Historical American English (COHA): 400+ Million Words, 1810–2009.* http://corpus.byu.edu/coha

Jesse de Does, Katrien Depuyd, Klaus Schulz, Annette Gotscharek, Christoph Ringlstetter, Janusz S. Bień, Tomaž Erjavec, Karel Kučera, Isabel Martinez, Stoyan Mihov, and Gilles Souvay. 2012. *Cross-language Perspective on Lexicon Building and Deployment in IMPACT.* Project Report. IMPACT.

Tomaž Erjavec, Christoph Ringlstetter, Maja Žorga, and Annette Gotscharek. 2010. Towards a Lexicon of XIXth Century Slovene. In Proceedings of the Seventh Language Technologies Conference, Ljubljana, Slovenia. Jožef Stefan Institute.

Tomaž Erjavec. 2011. Automatic linguistic annotation of historical language: ToTrTaLe and XIX century Slovene. In *Proceedings of the 5th ACL-HLT Workshop on Language Technology for Cultural Heritage, Social Sciences, and Humanities*, ACL.

Tomaž Erjavec. 2012. The goo300k corpus of historical Slovene. In *Proceedings of the Eight International Conference on Language Resources and Evaluation, LREC'12*, Paris, ELRA.

Anthony Kroch, Beatrice Santorini, and Lauren Delfs. 2004. *The Penn-Helsinki Parsed Corpus of Early Modern English (PPCEME).* Department of Linguistics, University of Pennsylvania. CD-ROM, first edition. http://www.ling.upenn.edu/hist-corpora/

Martin Durrell, Astrid Ensslin, and Paul Bennett. 2007. The GerManC project. *Sprache und Datenverarbeitung,* 31:71–80.

Ingo Mittendorf, and David Willis, eds. 2004. *Corpws hanesyddol yr iaith Gymraeg 1500–1850 / A historical corpus of the Welsh language 1500– 1850.* http://people.pwf.cam.ac.uk/dwew2/hcwl/menu.htm

Joel C. Wallenberg, Anton Karl Ingason, Einar Freyr Sigurðsson, and Eiríkur Rögnvaldsson. 2011. *Icelandic Parsed Historical Corpus (IcePaHC).* Version 0.9. http://www.linguist.is/icelandic_treebank

Silke Scheible, Richard J. Whitt, Martin Durrell, and Paul Bennett, 2010. Annotating a Historical Corpus of German: A Case Study. *Proceedings of the LREC 2010 Workshop on Language Resources and Language Technology Standards*, Valletta, Malta.

Hamish Cunningham. 2002. GATE, a General Architecture for Text Engineering. *Computers and the Humanities*, 36:223–254.

Pablo Picasso Feliciano de Faria, Fabio Natanael Kepler, and Maria Clara Paixão de Sousa. 2010. An integrated tool for annotating historical corpora. *Proceedings of the Fourth Linguistic Annotation Workshop*, ACL'10, 217–221.

TEI Consortium, eds. 2007. *Guidelines for Electronic Text Encoding and Interchange.* http://www.tei-c.org/P5

[1] For more information on these projects please see the Impact Centre of Competence: http://www.digitisation.eu/

# A high speed transcription interface for annotating primary linguistic data

**Mark Dingemanse, Jeremy Hammond, Herman Stehouwer,**
**Aarthy Somasundaram, Sebastian Drude**
Max Planck Institute for Psycholinguistics
Nijmegen
{mark.dingemanse, jeremy.hammond, herman.stehouwer,
aarthy.somasundaram, sebastian.drude}@mpi.nl

## Abstract

We present a new transcription mode for the annotation tool ELAN. This mode is designed to speed up the process of creating transcriptions of primary linguistic data (video and/or audio recordings of linguistic behaviour). We survey the basic transcription workflow of some commonly used tools (Transcriber, BlitzScribe, and ELAN) and describe how the new transcription interface improves on these existing implementations. We describe the design of the transcription interface and explore some further possibilities for improvement in the areas of segmentation and computational enrichment of annotations.

## 1 Introduction

Recent years have seen an increasing interest in language documentation: the creation and preservation of multipurpose records of linguistic primary data (Gippert et al., 2006; Himmelmann, 2008). The increasing availability of portable recording devices enables the collection of primary data even in the remotest field sites, and the exponential growth in storage makes it possible to store more of this data than ever before. However, without content annotation for searching and analysis, such corpora are of limited use. Advances in machine learning can bring some measure of automation to the process (Tschöpel et al., 2011), but the need for human annotation remains, especially in the case of primary data from undocumented languages. This paper describes the development and use of a new rapid transcription interface, its integration in an open source software framework for multimodality research, and the possibilities it opens up for computational uses of the annotated data.

Transcription, the production of a written representation of audio and video recordings of communicative behaviour, is one of the most time-intensive tasks faced by researchers working with language data. The resulting data is useful in many different scientific fields. Estimates for the ratio of transcription time to data time length range from 10:1 or 20:1 for English data (Tomasello and Stahl, 2004, p. 104), but may go up to 35:1 for data from lesser known and endangered languages (Auer et al., 2010). As in all fields of research, time is a most important limiting factor, so any significant improvement in this area will make available more data and resources for analysis and model building. The new transcription interface described here is designed for carrying out high-speed transcription of linguistic audiovisual material, with built-in support for multiple annotation tiers and for both audio and video streams.

Basic transcription is only the first step; further analysis often necessitates more fine-grained annotations, for instance part of speech tagging or morpheme glossing. Such operations are even more time intensive. Time spent on further annotations generally goes well over a 100:1 annotation time to media duration ratio[1] (Auer et al., 2010).The post-transcription work is also an area with numerous possibilities for further reduction of annotation time by applying semi-automated annotation suggestions, and some ongoing work

[1]Cf. a blog post by P.K.Austin http://blogs.usyd.edu.au /elac/2010/04/how_long_is_a_piece_of_string.html.

to integrate such techniques in our annotation system is discussed below.

## 2 Semi-automatic transcription: terminology and existing tools

Transcription of linguistic primary data has long been a concern of researchers in linguistics and neighbouring fields, and accordingly several tools are available today for time-aligned annotation and transcription. To describe the different user interfaces these tools provide, we adopt a model of the transcription process by (Roy and Roy, 2009), adjusting its terminology to also cover the use case of transcribing sign language. According to this model, the transcription of primary linguistic data can be divided into four basic subtasks: 1) *find* linguistic utterances in the audio or video stream, 2) *segment* the stream into short chunks of utterances, 3) *play* the segment, and 4) *type* the transcription for the segment.

Existing transcription tools implement these four steps in different ways. To exemplify this we discuss three such tools below. All three can be used to create time-aligned annotations of audio and/or video recordings, but since they have different origins and were created for different goals, they present the user with interfaces that differ quite radically.

Transcriber (Barras et al., 2001) was "designed for the manual segmentation and transcription of long duration broadcast news recordings, including annotation of speech turns, topics and acoustic condition" (Barras et al., 2001, p. 5). It provides a graphical interface with a text editor at the top and a waveform viewer at the bottom. All four subtasks from the model above, FSPT, are done in this same interface. The text editor, where Segmenting and Typing are done, is a vertically oriented list of annotations. Strengths of the Transcriber implementation are the top-to-bottom orientation of the text editor, which is in line with the default layout of transcripts in the discipline, and the fact that it is possible to rely on only one input device (the keyboard) for all four subtasks. Weaknesses are the fact that it does not mark annotation ends, only beginnings,and that it treats the data as a single stream and insists on a strict partitioning, making it difficult to handle overlapping speech, common in conversational data (Barras et al., 2001, p. 18).

BlitzScribe (Roy and Roy, 2009) was developed in the context of the Human Speechome project at the MIT Media Lab as a custom solution for the transcription of massive amounts of unstructured English speech data collected over a period of three years (Roy et al., 2006). It is not available to the academic community, but we describe it here because its user interface presents significant improvements over previous models. BlitzScribe uses automatic speech detection for segmentation, and thus eliminates the first two steps of the FSPT model, Find and Segment, from the user interface. The result is a minimalist design which focuses only on Playing and Typing. The main strength of BlitzScribe is this streamlined interface, which measurably improves transcription speed — it is about four times as fast as Transcriber (Roy and Roy, 2009, p. 1649). Weaknesses include its monolingual, speech-centric focus, its lack of a mechanism for speaker identification, and its single-purpose design which ties it to the Human Speechome project and makes it unavailable to the wider academic community.

ELAN (Wittenburg et al., 2006) was developed as a multimedia linguistic annotation framework. Unlike most other tools it was built with multimodal linguistic data in mind, supporting the simultaneous display and annotation of multiple audio and video streams. Its data model is tier-based, with multiple tiers available for annotations of different speakers or different modalities (e.g. speech and gesture). Its strengths are its support for multimodal data, its handling of overlapping speech, its flexible tier structure, and its open source nature. Its noted weaknesses include a steep learning curve and a user interface that was, as of 2007, "not the best place to work on a 'first pass' of a transcript" (Berez, 2007, p. 288).

The new user interface we describe in this paper is integrated in ELAN as a separate "Transcription Mode", and was developed to combine the strengths of existing implementations while at the same time addressing their weaknesses. Figure 1 shows a screenshot of the new transcription mode.

## 3 Description of the interface

From the default Annotation Mode in ELAN, the user can switch to several other modes, one of which is Transcription Mode. Transcription Mode displays annotations in one or more columns. A column collects annotations of a single type. For

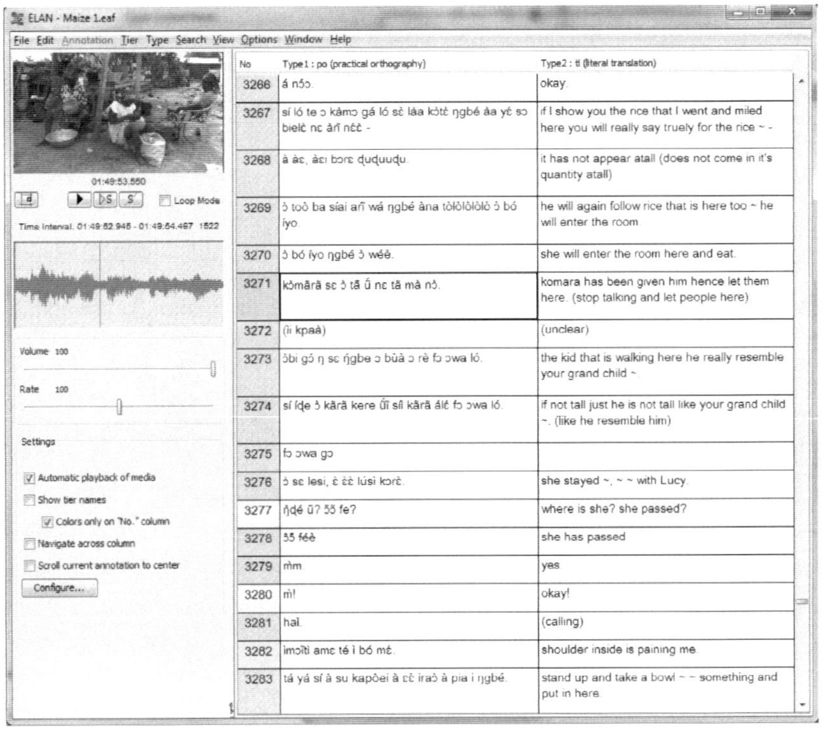

Figure 1: The interface of the transcription mode, showing two columns: transcriptions and the corresponding translations.

instance, the first column in Figure 1 displays all annotations of the type "practical orthography" in chronological order, colour-coding for different speakers. The second column displays corresponding, i.e., time aligned, annotations of the type "literal translation". Beside the annotation columns there is a pane showing the data (video and/or audio stream) for the selected utterance. Below it are basic playback parameters like volume and rate, some essential interface settings, and a button "Configure" which brings up the column selection dialog window. We provide an example of this preference pane in Figure 2.

The basic organisation of the Transcription Mode interface reflects its task-oriented design: the annotation columns occupy pride of place and only the most frequently accessed settings are directly visible. Throughout, the user interface is keyboard-driven and designed to minimise the number of actions the user needs to carry out. For instance, selecting a segment (by mouse or keyboard) will automatically trigger playback of that segment (the user can play and pause using the Tab key). Selecting a grey (non-existent) field in a dependent column will automatically create an annotation. Selection always opens up the field for immediate editing. Arrow keys as well as user-configurable shortcuts move to adjacent fields.

ELAN Transcription Mode improves the transcription workflow by taking apart the FSPT model and focusing only on the last two steps: Play and Type. In this respect it is like BlitzScribe; but it is more advanced than that and other tools in at least two important ways. First, it is agnostic to the type of data transcribed. Second, it does not presuppose monolingualism and is ready for multilingual work. It allows the display of multiple annotation layers and makes for easy navigation between them.Further, when transcription is done with the help of a native speaker it allows for them to provide other relevant information at the same time (such as cultural background explanations) keeping primary data and meta-data time aligned and linked.

Some less prominently visible features of the user interface design include: the ability to reorder annotation columns by drag and drop; a toggle for the position of the data streams (to the left or to the right of the annotation columns); the ability to detach the video stream (for instance for display on a secondary monitor); the option to show names (i.e. participant ID's) in the flow of anno-

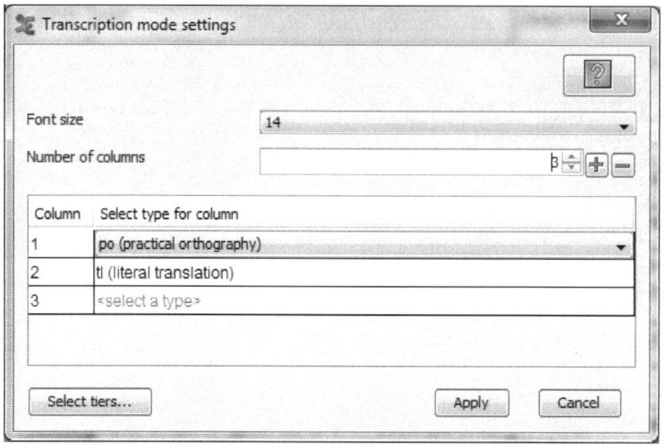


Figure 2: The interface of the transcription mode; the configuration dialog.

tations or to indicate them by colour-coding only; the option to keep the active annotation centered; and settings for font size and number of columns (in the "Configure" pane). These features enable the user to customise the transcription experience to their own needs.

The overall design of Transcription Mode makes the process of transcription as smooth as possible by removing unnecessary clutter, foregrounding the interface elements that matter, and enabling a limited degree of customisation. Overall, the new interface has realised significant speedups for many people[2]. User feedback in response to the new transcription mode has been overwhelmingly positive, e.g., the members of mailing lists such as the Resource Network for Linguistic Diversity[3].

## 4 A prerequisite: semi-automatic segmentation

As we noted in the introduction, the most important step before transcription is that of segmentation (steps Find and Segment in the FSPT model). Segmentation is a large task that involves subdividing the audio or video stream in, possibly overlapping, segments. The segments each denote a distinct period of speech or any other communicative act and each segment is commonly assigned to a specific speaker. This step can potentially be sped up significantly by doing it semi-automatically using pattern recognition techniques, as pursued in the AVATecH project (Auer et al., 2010).

In the AVATecH project, audio and video streams can be sent to detection components called 'recognisers'. Some detection components accept the output of other recognisers as additional input, next to the audio and/or video streams, thus facilitating cascaded processing of these streams. Amongst the tasks that can be performed by these recognisers is the segmentation of audio and video, including speaker assignment.

A special challenge for the recognisers in this project is the requirement of language independence (in contrast to the English-only situation in the Human Speechome project that produced Blitzscribe(Roy et al., 2006)). The recognisers should ideally accommodate the work of field linguists and other alike researchers and therefore cannot simply apply existing language and acoustic models. Furthermore, the conditions that are encountered in the field are often not ideal, e.g., loud and irregular background noises such as those from animals are common. Nevertheless, automatic segmentation has the potential to speed up the segmentation step greatly.

## 5 Future possibilities: computational approaches to data enrichment

While a basic transcription and translation is essential as a first way into the data, it is not sufficient for many research questions, linguistic or

[2]Including ourselves, Jeremy Hammond claims that: "*Based on my last two field work trips, I am getting my transcription time down below that of transcriber (but perhaps not by much) but still keeping the higher level of data that ELANs tiers provide - probably around 18-20 hours for an hour of somewhat detailed trilingual annotation.*"

[3]www.rnld.org

otherwise. Typically a morphological segmentation of the words and a labelling of each individual morph is required. This level of annotation is also known as basic glossing (Bow et al., 2003b; Bow et al., 2003a).

Automatically segmenting the words into their morphological parts, without resorting to the use of pre-existing knowledge has seen a wide variety of research (Hammarström and Borin, 2011). Based on the knowledge-free induction of morphological boundaries the linguist will usually perform corrections. Above all, a system must learn from the input of the linguist, and must incorporate it in the results, improving the segmentation of words going forward. However, it is well known from typological research that languages differ tremendously in their morphosyntactic organisation and the specific morphological means that are employed to construct complex meanings (Evans and Levinson, 2009; Hocket, 1954).

As far as we know, there is no current morphological segmentation or glossing system that deals well with all language types, in particular inflectional and polysynthetic languages or languages that heavily employ tonal patterns to mark different forms of the same word. Therefore, there is a need for an interactive, modular glossing system. For each step of the glossing task, one would use one, or a set of complementary modules. We call such modules "annotyzers". They generate content on the basis of the source tiers and additional data, e.g. lexical data (or learnt states from earlier passes). Using such modules will result in a speedup for the researcher. We remark that there are existing modular NLP systems, such as GATE(Cunningham et al., 2011), however these are tied to different workflows, i.e., they are not as suitable for the multimodal multi-participant annotation process.

Currently a limited set of such functionality is available in Toolbox and FLEX. In the case of both Toolbox and FLEX the functionality is limited to a set of rules written by the linguist (i.e. in a database-lookup approach). Even though the ELAN modules will offer support for such rules, our focus is on the automation of machine-learning systems in order to scale the annotation process.

Our main aim for the future is to incorporate learning systems that support the linguists by improving the suggested new annotations on the bases of choices the linguist made earlier. The goal there is, again, to reduce annotation time, so that the linguist can work more on linguistic analysis and less on annotating. At the same time, a working set of annotyzers will promote more standardised glossing, which can then be used for further automated research, cf. automatic treebank production or similar (Bender et al., 2011).

## 6 Conclusions

The diversity of the world's languages is in danger. Perhaps user interface design is not the first thing that comes to mind in response to this sobering fact. Yet in a field that increasingly works with digital annotations of primary linguistic data, it is imperative that the basic tools for annotation and transcription are optimally designed to get the job done.

We have described Transcription Mode, a new user interface in ELAN that accelerates the transcription process. This interface offers several advantages compared to similar tools in the software landscape. It automates actions wherever possible, displays multiple parallel information and annotation streams, is controllable with just the keyboard, and can handle sign language as well as spoken language data. Transcription Mode reduces the required transcription time by providing an optimised workflow.

The next step is to optimise the preceding and following stages in the annotation process. Preceding the transcription stage is segmentation and speaker labelling, which we address using automatic audio/video recogniser techniques that are independent of the language that is transcribed. Following transcription, we aim to support basic glossing (and similar additional annotations based on transcriptions) with a modular software architecture. These semi-automated steps lead to further time savings, allowing researchers to focus on the analysis of language data rather than on the production of annotations.

The overall goal of the developments described here is to help researchers working with primary language data to use their time more optimally. Ultimately, these improvements will lead to an increase in both quality and quantity of primary data available for analysis. Better data and better analyses for a stronger digital humanities.

## References


Eric Auer, Peter Wittenburg, Han Sloetjes, Oliver Schreer, Stefano Masneri, Daniel Schneider, and Sebastian Tschöpel. 2010. Automatic annotation of media field recordings. In *Proceedings of the ECAI 2010 Workshop on Language Technology for Cultural Heritage, Social Sciences, and Humanities (LaTeCH 2010)*, pages 31–34.

Claude Barras, Edouard Geoffrois, Zhibiao Wu, and Mark Liberman. 2001. Transcriber: Development and use of a tool for assisting speech corpora production. *Speech Communication*, 33(1-2):5–22, January.

Emily M. Bender, Dan Flickinger, Stephan Oepen, and Yi Zhang. 2011. Parser evaluation over local and non-local deep dependencies in a large corpus. In *Proceedings of the 2011 Conference on Empirical Methods in Natural Language Processing*, pages 397–408, Edinburgh, Scotland, UK., July. Association for Computational Linguistics.

Andrea L. Berez. 2007. Review of EUDICO linguistic annotator (ELAN). *Language Documentation & Conservation*, 1(2):283–289, December.

Catherine Bow, Baden Hughes, and Steven Bird. 2003a. A four-level model for interlinear text.

Cathy Bow, Baden Hughes, and Steven Bird. 2003b. Towards a general model of interlinear text. In *Proceedings of EMELD Workshop 2003: Digitizing and Annotating Texts and Field Recordings*. Lansing MI, USA.

Hamish Cunningham, Diana Maynard, Kalina Bontcheva, Valentin Tablan, Niraj Aswani, Ian Roberts, Genevieve Gorrell, Adam Funk, Angus Roberts, Danica Damljanovic, Thomas Heitz, Mark A. Greenwood, Horacio Saggion, Johann Petrak, Yaoyong Li, and Wim Peters. 2011. *Text Processing with GATE (Version 6)*.

Nicholas Evans and Stephen C. Levinson. 2009. The myth of language universals: Language diversity and its importance for cognitive science. *Behavioral and Brain Sciences*, 32(05):429–448.

Jost Gippert, Nikolaus P. Himmelmann, and Ulrike Mosel, editors. 2006. *Essentials of language documentation*. Mouton de Gruyter, Berlin / New York.

Harald Hammarström and Lars Borin. 2011. Unsupervised learning of morphology. To Appear in Computational Linguistics.

Nikolaus P. Himmelmann. 2008. Reproduction and preservation of linguistic knowledge: Linguistics' response to language endangerment. In *Annual Review of Anthropology*, volume 37 (1), pages 337–350.

Charles F. Hocket. 1954. Two models of grammatical description. *Word 10*, pages 210–234.

Chris Rogers. 2010. Review of fieldworks language explorer (flex) 3.0. In *Language Documentation & Conservation 4*, pages 1934–5275. University of Hawai'i Press.

Brandon C. Roy and Deb Roy. 2009. Fast transcription of unstructured audio recordings. In *Proceedings of Interspeech 2009*, Brighton, England.

Deb Roy, Rupal Patel, Philip DeCamp, Rony Kubat, Michael Fleischman, Brandon C. Roy, Nikolaos Mavridis, Stefanie Tellex, Alexia Salata, Jethran Guinness, Micheal Levit, and Peter Gorniak. 2006. The human speechome project. In Paul Vogt, Yuuga Sugita, Elio Tuci, and Chrystopher Nehaniv, editors, *Symbol Grounding and Beyond*, volume 4211 of *Lecture Notes in Computer Science*, pages 192–196. Springer, Berlin / Heidelberg.

Michael Tomasello and Daniel Stahl. 2004. Sampling children's spontaneous speech: How much is enough? *Journal of Child Language*, 31(01):101–121.

Sebastian Tschöpel, Daniel Schneider, Rolf Bardeli, Peter Wittenburg, Han Sloetjes, Oliver Schreer, Stefano Masneri, Przemek Lenkiewicz, and Eric Auer. 2011. AVATecH: Audio/Video technology for humanities research. *Language Technologies for Digital Humanities and Cultural Heritage*, page 86.

Peter Wittenburg, Hennie Brugman, Albert Russel, and Han Sloetjes. 2006. ELAN: a professional framework for multimodality research. In *Proceedings of LREC 2006*.

# BAD: An assistant tool for making verses in Basque

**Manex Agirrezabal, Iñaki Alegria, Bertol Arrieta**
University of the Basque Country (UPV/EHU)
maguirrezaba008@ikasle.ehu.es, i.alegria@ehu.es, bertol@ehu.es

**Mans Hulden**
Ikerbasque (Basque Science Foundation)
mhulden@email.arizona.edu

## Abstract

We present work on a verse-composition assistant for composing, checking correctness of, and singing traditional Basque *bertsoak*—impromptu verses on particular themes. A performing *bertsolari*—a verse singer in the Basque Country—must adhere to strict rules that dictate the format and content of the verses sung. To help the aspiring *bertsolari*, we provide a tool that includes a web interface that is able to analyze, correct, provide suggestions and synonyms, and tentatively also sing (using text-to-speech synthesis) verses composed by the user.

## 1 Introduction

In the Basque Country there exists a long-standing live performance tradition of improvising verses—a type of ex tempore composition and singing called *bertsolaritza*. Verses in *bertsolaritza* can be seen as discourses with strict rules governing the technical structure of them: verses must contain a certain number of lines and each line must have a defined number of syllables, certain lines have to rhyme in certain patterns, and so forth.

In this paper we present a web-based assistant tool for constructing verses (*bertsoak*) according to the rules of *bertsolaritza* (Garzia et al, 2001).

If the reader is interested in this topic, we recommend watching the 2011 film *Bertsolari*[1] [2], directed by Asier Altuna.

[1] IMDB: http://www.imdb.com/title/tt2058583

[2] Trailer on: http://vimeo.com/9355066

## 2 Relationship to earlier work

There exist some prior works dealing with Basque verse-making and computer technologies, such as BertsolariXa (Arrieta et al., 2001), which is a rhyme search tool implemented as finite-state automata using the two-level morphology formalism. The tool also contains other features, including semantic categorization of words, narrowing word-searches to certain themes, etc. While BertsolariXa focuses mostly on the word-level, the current work also includes constraints on overall verse structure in its implementation as well as a synonym search tool, a melody suggestion system, and possibilities for plugging in text-to-speech synthesis of verses.

### 2.1 The *Bertsolari* tradition

*Bertsolaritza* is very ingrained in the Basque Country and championships, competitions and get-togethers on *bertsolaritza* are quite common. Usually the competitors in such event, called *bertsolaris*, are given a theme to produce a verse on under some very limited time constraints.

But the Basque Country is not the only place that hosts such troubadour traditions—similar customs are present in many other countries such as Cuba, Brazil, Argentina, etc. The goal of the current tool is to be generalizable, and so applicable to various strategies of verse improvisation, and possibly be useful not only for Basque speakers, but also for others.

Below we briefly present an example of a verse made in the Basque Country. In 1986 Andoni Egaña (a well-known *bertsolari*) was asked to sing a *bertso* and assigned a topic. In the verse, he was asked to play the role of an old person who lived alone, and who realized that he could not even tie his shoes. Within a few seconds he composed and sang three verses. Here, we analyze the first verse.

Verse:
Gazte aroan ibili arren
gustora tirriki-tarra,
denbora honen joan etorriak
ederki jo dit gitarra,
gorputza daukat ximeldurikan
ta eskuen punta zaharra,
denborarekin seko galdu det
gazte aroko indarra,
ez al da pena gizon mardul bat
hola ibili beharra.

Translation:
Even when I was young
I was always on a spree
over time
I have been punished
I have a crumpled body
and the tip of the hands very old,
Over time I lost
the strength I had when I was young,
It's a shame that a strong man
has to end up like me.

The special charm of *bertsolaritza* improvisation is that people proficient in the art can quickly express a variety of ideas, although they are working with very restrictive rules concerning the number of syllables in words they use, and how the words must rhyme. We must take into account that Andoni Egaña was able to sing this verse within a few seconds of being given the topic, and also, that it complies exactly with a certain metric. In this case, the verse contains eight lines, each odd line consisting of ten syllables, and each even line of eight syllables, with the even lines rhyming.

Formal training in the *bertsolari* tradition also exists in the Basque Country. In the last 20 to 30 years, an important movement has developed that aims to provide instruction to upcoming generations on how to create verses (orally or in writing). This kind of instruction usually takes place in learning centers called *bertso-eskolak*, which in English roughly means, "verse-making schools." The proliferation of this movement has produced a strong base of young *bertsolaris*, of whom many achieve an outstanding level of improvisation skills.

## 3 The BAD tool

BAD is the acronym for "*Bertsotarako Arbel Digitala*", roughly "Digital verse board." The aim of the tool is to serve as a general assistant for *bertsolari*-style verse composition and help verse-making learners in their learning process.

This tool has been developed using the PHP programming language, but it contains certain parts developed using finite-state technology. The main functions of this tool, which will be discussed in more detail in the next five sections, are the following: visualization of the verse structure, structure checking, rhyme and synonym searching and verse singing.

### 3.1 Verse structure

The main rules of the *bertsolari* verse are that a verse must consist of a certain predefined number of lines and each line in turn, of a predefined number of syllables. Traditionally, about a hundred different schemes are used, and the tool provides support for all these patterns. For example, the structure called "*Hamarreko handia*" has ten lines and ten syllables in the odd-numbered lines, and eight syllables in the even-numbered lines. In this structure, the even-numbered lines have to rhyme. Selecting this scheme, the tool will mark the corresponding lines with their requirements.

The web interface can be seen in figure 1, which shows the general layout of the tool, illustrated with the example verse referred to above—we see that each line has been approved in terms of line length and syllable structure by the tool.

We have designed a database in which the main verse structures are saved so that when the user selects one verse schema, the system knows exactly the number of lines it must contain, where must it rhyme and how many syllables each line should have. Those schemata are also linked to melodies, each melody corresponding to one possible structure.

### 3.2 Structure checking

After writing the verse, the system can evaluate if it is technically correct, i.e. if the overall structure is correct and if each line in the form abides by the required syllable count and rhyming scheme. The syllable counter is implemented using the *foma* software (Hulden, 2009), and the implementation (Hulden, 2006) can be found on the homepage of

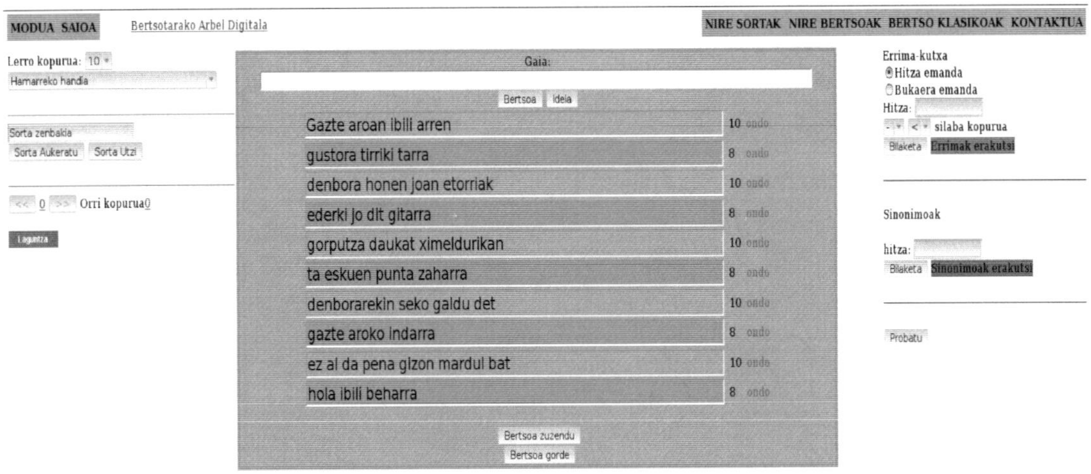


Figure 1: A verse written in the BAD web application.

*foma*.[3]

Separately, we have also developed a rhyme checker, which extracts special patterns in the lines that must rhyme and checks their conformity.

These patterns are extracted using *foma* (see section 3.4) after which some phonological rules are applied. For example, an example rule *era* $\rightarrow$ {era, eda, ega, eba}, models the fact that any word ending in *era*, for example, *etxera*, will rhyme with all words that end in *era*, *eda*, *eba* or *ega*. These rhyming patterns have been extracted according to the phonological laws described in (Amuriza, 1981).

### 3.3 Synonym search

Usually, people who write verses tend to quickly exhaust their vocabulary and ideas with to express what they want to say, or encounter problems with the number of syllables in various tentative words they have in mind. For example, if the verse-maker wants to say something containing the word "family," (*familia* in Euskera, a four-syllable word) but is forced to use a three-syllable word in a particular context, the interface provides for possibilities to look for three-syllable synonyms of the word *familia*, producing the word *sendia*— a word whose meaning is otherwise the same, and made up of three syllables.

For developing the synonym search, we used a modified version of the Basque Wordnet (Pociello et al., 2010), originally developed by the IXA group at the University of the Basque Country. Within Wordnet we search the synsets for the incoming word, and the words that correspond to those synsets are returned.

### 3.4 Rhyme search

The classical and most well-known problem in *bertsolaritza* concern the rhyming patterns. As mentioned, various lines within a verse are required to rhyme, according to certain predefined schemata. To search for words that rhyme with other words in a verse, the BAD tool contains a rhyme search engine. In the interface, this is located in the right part of the BAD tool main view, as seen in figure 2.

The rhyme searcher is built upon finite-state technology, commonly used for developing morphological and phonological analyzers, and calls upon the freely available *foma*-tool, to calculate matching and nonmatching rhyme schemes.

Its grammar is made up of regular expressions that are used to identify phonological patterns in final syllables in the input word. The result of the search is the intersection of these patterns and all the words generated from a morphological description of Basque (Alegria et al., 1996)—that is, a list of all words that match both the required phonological constraints given (rhyming) and a morphological description of Basque.

Based upon figure 2, if we search rhymes for the word *landa* (cottage), the system proposes a

[3] `http://foma.googlecode.com`

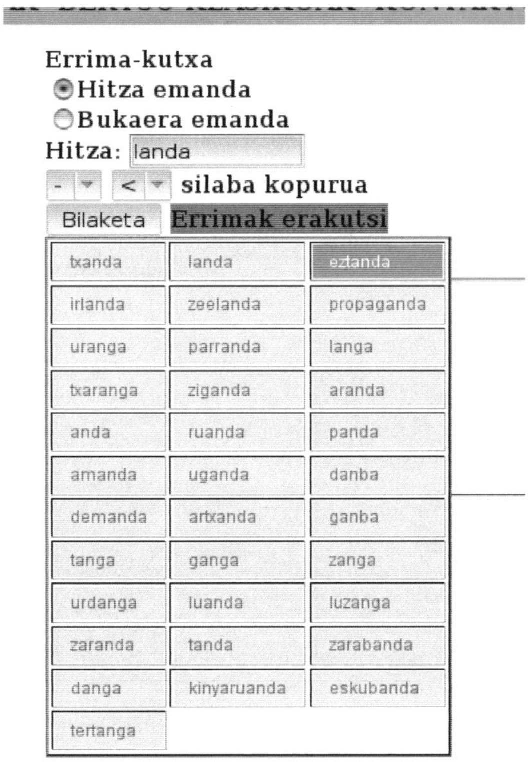


Figure 2: The response of the rhyme search engine.

set of words that can be filtered depending on the number of syllables required. Among this list of words, we can find some words that end in *anda*, such as, *Irlanda* (Ireland) or *eztanda* (explosion), but through the application of phonological equivalency rules we also find terms like *ganga* (vault).

### 3.5 Singing synthesis

Another characteristic, as mentioned, is that, in the end, the verses are intended to be sung instead of only being textually represented. Based on other ongoing work in singing synthesis, we have designed a system for singing the verses entered into the system in Basque.

This is based on the "singing mode" of the Festival text-to-speech system (Taylor et al., 1998). The advantage of using this is that Festival is open-source and has given us ample opportunities to modify its behavior. However, as Festival does not currently support Basque directly, we have relied on the Spanish support of the Festival system.[4]

Based on current work by the Aholab research team in Bilbao—a lab that works on Basque speech synthesis and recognition—we have implemented a singing module for BAD, based on the text-to-speech HTS engine (Erro et al., 2010). Our application is able to sing the composed verses entered into the system in Basque, with a choice of various standard melodies for *bertsolaritza*.[5]

## 4 Discussion and future work

Now that the BAD tool has been developed, our intention is to evaluate it. To make a qualitative evaluation we have gotten in touch with some verse-making schools (*bertso-eskola*), so that they can test the system and send us their feedback using a form. Once the evaluation is made, we will improve it according to the feedback and the system will be made public.

Our ultimate goal is to develop a system able to create verses automatically. To achieve this long-term goal, there is plenty of work to do and basic research to be done. We have in our hands a good corpus of 3,500 Basque verse transcriptions, so we intend to study these verses from a morphological, syntactical, semantical and pragmatic point of view.

In the short term, we also plan to expand the synonym search to be able to provide searches for semantically related words and subjects (and not just synonyms), like hypernyms or hyponyms. The Basque WordNet provides a good opportunity for this, as one is easily able to traverse the WordNet to encounter words with varying degrees of semantic similarity.

Another feature that we want to develop is a system that receives as input a verse together with a MIDI file, and where the system automatically sings the verse to the music provided.

Finally, in order for the system to be able to provide better proposals for the verse artist—including perhaps humorous and creative proposals—we intend to work with approaches to computational creativity. We are considering different approaches to this topic, such as in the work on *Hahacronym* (Stock et al., 2005) or the *Standup* riddle builder (Ritchie et al., 2001).

[4]While morphologically and syntactically, Spanish and Basque have no relationship whatsoever, phonetically the languages are quite close, with only a few phonemes, syllabification rules, and stress rules being different enough to disturb the system's behavior.

[5]However, this functionality is not available on the web interface as of yet.

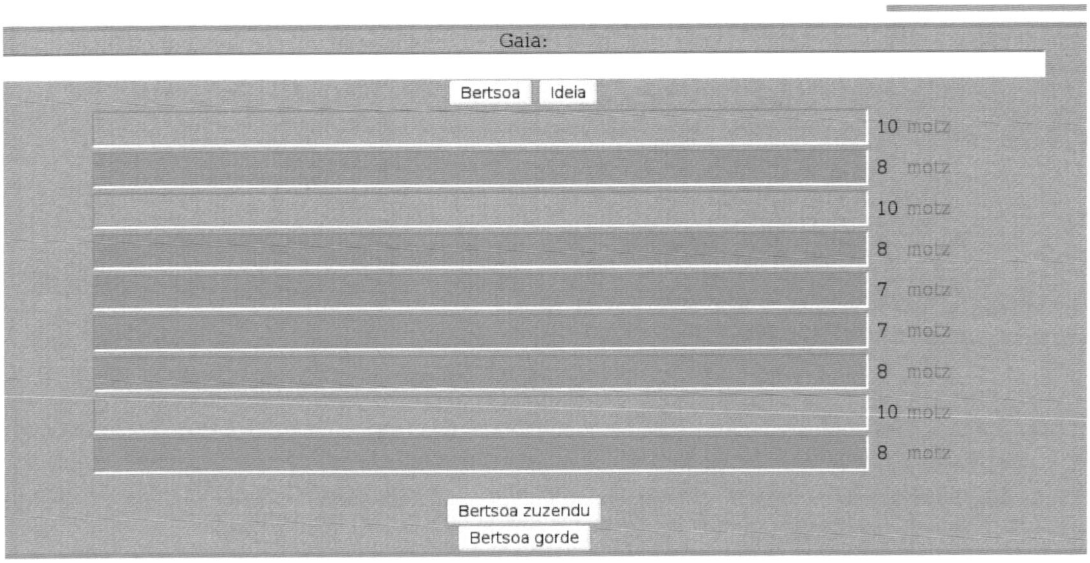


Figure 3: The BAD application before entering a verse, showing two possible rhyme patterns.

## Acknowledgments

This research has been partially funded by the Basque Government (Research Groups, IT344-10).

## References

Iñaki Alegria, Xabier Artola, Kepa Sarasola and Miriam Urkia, "Automatic morphological analysis of Basque", Literary and Linguistic Computing, ALLC, 1996

Xabier Amuriza, "Hiztegi errimatua", Alfabetatze Euskalduntze Koordinakundea, 1981

Bertol Arrieta, Iñaki Alegria, Xabier Arregi, "An assistant tool for Verse-Making in Basque based on Two-Level Morphology", 2001

Daniel Erro, Iñaki Sainz, Ibon Saratxaga, Eva Navas, Inma Hernáez, "MFCC+F0 Extraction and Waveform Reconstruction using HNM: Preliminary Results in an HMM-based Synthesizer", 2010

Joxerra Garzia, Jon Sarasua, and Andoni Egaña, "The art of bertsolaritza: improvised Basque verse singing", Bertsolari liburuak, 2001

John E. Hopcroft, Rajeev Motwani, Jeffrey D. Ullman, "Introducción a la teoría de Autómatas, Lenguajes y Computación", Pearson educación, 2002

Mans Hulden, "Foma: a finite-state compiler and library", Proceedings of the 12th Conference of the European Chapter of the Association for Computational Linguistics: Demonstrations Session, p. 29–32, 2009

Mans Hulden, "Finite-state syllabification", Finite-State Methods and Natural Language Processing, p. 86 – 96, Springer, 2006

Kimmo Koskenniemi. "Two-level morphology: A general computational model for word-form recognition and production". Publication 11, University of Helsinki, Department of General Linguistics, Helsinki, 1983.

Eli Pociello, Eneko Agirre, Izaskun Aldezabal, "Methodology and construction of the Basque WordNet", 2010

Graeme Ritchie, "Current directions in computational humour", Artificial Intelligence Review, Volume 16, Number 2, p. 119 – 135, Springer, 2001

Graeme Ritchie, Ruli Manurung, Helen Pain, Annalu Waller, Dave O'Mara, "The STANDUP interactive riddle builder", Volume 2, Number 2, p. 67 – 69, IEEE Intelligent Systems, 2006

Oliviero Stock and Carlo Strapparava, "Hahacronym: A computational humor system", Proceedings of the ACL 2005 on Interactive poster and demonstration sessions, p. 113 – 116, Association for Computational Linguistics, 2005

Paul Taylor, Alan W. Black and Richard Caley, "The architecture of the Festival speech synthesis system", International Speech Communication Association, 1998

# Toward a Language Independent Methodology for Generating Artwork Descriptions – Exploring Framenet Information

**Dana Dannélls**
Språkbanken
Department of Swedish
University of Gothenburg, Sweden
dana.dannells@svenska.gu.se

**Lars Borin**
Språkbanken
Department of Swedish
University of Gothenburg, Sweden
lars.borin@svenska.gu.se

**Abstract**

Today museums and other cultural heritage institutions are increasingly storing object descriptions using semantic web domain ontologies. To make this content accessible in a multilingual world, it will need to be conveyed in many languages, a language generation task which is domain specific and language dependent. This paper describes how semantic and syntactic information such as that provided in a framenet can contribute to solving this task. It is argued that the kind of information offered by such lexical resources enhances the output quality of a multilingual language generation application, in particular when generating domain specific content.

## 1 Introduction

Today museums and other cultural heritage institutions are increasingly storing object descriptions using structured information representation formats, such as semantic web domain ontologies. To make such cultural heritage content accessible to different groups and individuals in a multilingual world, this information will need to be conveyed in textual or spoken form in many languages, a language generation task which is domain specific and language dependent.

Generating multilingual natural language texts from domain specific semantic representations, such as semantic web domain ontologies, is a task which involves lexicalization and syntactic realization of the discourse relations. This paper deals with the syntactic realization problem, which is best illustrated with an example. Consider the possible formulations of the semantic relation *Create_representation* that has been lexicalized with the English verb *paint*:

1. Leonardo da Vinci *painted* this scene.
2. The lovely Sibyls *were painted* in the last century.
3. The Gerichtsstube *was painted* by Kuhn in 1763.

The syntactic structure of each sentence differs in terms of the semantic roles of the verb arguments and other constituents of the sentence. The first sentence contains the semantic roles *Creator* and *Represented*, the second sentence contains *Represented* and *Time*, and in the third sentence we find *Creator*, *Represented* and *Time*.

As the examples show there are several ways of semantically characterizing the situation expressed by a verb, with implications for the syntactic realization of that verb. When generating natural language from semantic web ontologies it is important to find generic strategies that allow us to identify the semantic elements of a verb and associate them with the appropriate argument realization of that verb. This is particularly relevant in multilingual settings because the semantic and syntactic behavior of verbs will vary depending on the target language, both in the constructions found and in their distribution.

Previous work on natural language generation of cultural heritage information from semantic web ontologies has relied on a large amount of specially tailored manual linguistic information to produce descriptions that are targeted to a specific group of readers (Androutsopoulos et al., 2001; Dannélls, 2008; Konstantopoulos et al., 2009). Although valuable information for generating natural languages is found in computational lexical-semantic resources such as the Berkeley FrameNet (section 3) which exist today in several languages (Erk et al., 2003; Subirats and Petruck, 2003; Ohara et al., 2003; Borin et al., 2010), there has been little emphasis on how to manage digitized data from digital libraries using these open source resources. In this paper we demonstrate how the information available in such electronically available resources can be exploited for generating multilingual artwork descriptions.

In the remainder of this paper we describe a case study on English and Swedish that underscores the importance of using a lexical resource such as a framenet (section 2). We present the kind of information that is offered by two existing framenets (section 3). We demonstrate how a domain specific natural language generator can benefit from the information that is available in both framenets (section 4). We end with a discussion and pointers to future work (section 5).

## 2 Data Collection and Text Analysis

### 2.1 Corpus Data

To identify the semantic and syntactic constructions that characterize object descriptions in the cultural heritage domain, we have collected parallel texts from Wikipedia in two languages: English and Swedish. In total, we analyzed 40 parallel texts that are available under the category *Painting*. Additionally, we selected object descriptions from digital libraries that are available through online museum databases. The majority of the Swedish descriptions were taken from the World Culture Museum,[1] the majority of the English descriptions were collected from the Met Museum.[2]

### 2.2 Semantic Analysis

The strategy we employed to analyze the texts follows the approach presented by McKeown (1985) on how to formalize principles of discourse for use in a computational process. Seven frame elements have been examined, these include: *Location* (L), *Creator* (CR), *Representation* (RE), *Represented* (R), *Descriptor* (D), *Time* (TI), *Type* (T). The text analysis has shown that the following combinations of these major frame elements are the most common:

1. RE, T, CR, TI, L, D, R
2. RE, T, CR, R, TI, L, D
3. RE, TI, T, CR, D, L, R
4. RE, TI, CR, D, R, L

The listed semantic combinations reflect the word order that we have found in the text analysis for the two languages. However, since many of the analyzed sentences that begin with the object in focus (the *Representation*) appear in the passive voice, i.e, *was painted by, was created by*, the word order of these combinations may vary. Furthermore, not all of the listed semantic elements are mandatory in the object descriptions. For example, although corresponding to the first combination of semantic elements, the sentence *De Hooch probably painted this picture in the early 1660s* only contains the frame elements CR, RE and TI.

### 2.3 Syntactic Analysis

The texts have been syntactically annotated using the Maltparser (Nivre et al., 2007). Figure 1 shows two example sentences converted to constituent trees.

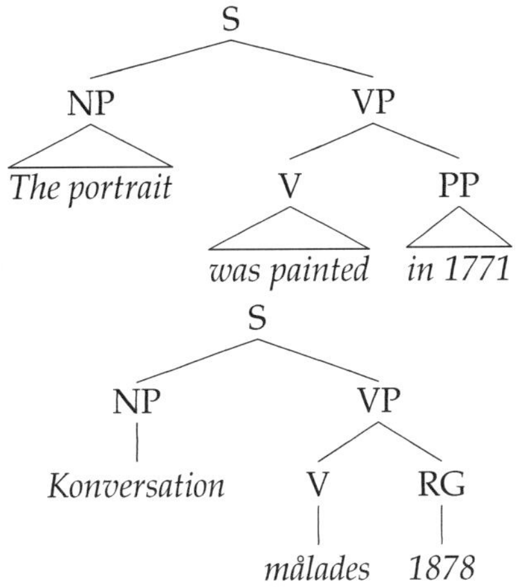


Figure 1: Parse trees for two example sentences.

[1] <http://collections.smvk.se/pls/vkm/rigby.welcome>

[2] <http://www.metmuseum.org>

This small example shows that there is a difference in how syntactic trees are built for each language. While in the English sentence the verb *was painted* is followed by a preposition phrase (PP), the Swedish verb *målades* (the passive form of 'paint') is followed by a cardinal number without a preposition (which could be analyzed as an NP).

## 3 Framenets

### 3.1 The Berkeley FrameNet

The Berkeley FrameNet (BFN)[3] (Fillmore et al., 2003) is an electronic lexical resource based on the notion of Frame Semantics (Fillmore, 1985); we know the meaning of a word through prototypical situations (scenarios) in which the word (called a lexical unit, LU) occurs. A frame can be described with the help of two types of frame elements (FEs) that are classified in terms of how central they are to a particular frame. A *core element* is one that instantiates a conceptually necessary component of a frame while making the frame unique and different from other frames. On the other hand, a *peripheral element* does not uniquely characterize a frame and can be instantiated in any semantically appropriate frame. For example, table 1 describes the lexical units and the frame elements appearing in the frame *Create_representation*, which has the following definition (from the BFN website):

> A *Creator* produces a physical object which is to serve as a *Representation* of an actual or imagined entity or event, the *Represented*.

Each lexical unit appearing in the frame carries information about its related frame elements (semantic valency) and their syntactic realizations (syntactic valency). Examples of the valency patterns that are found for the verb *paint* are listed in table 2.[4]

Examples of sentences that can be formed with these semantic and syntactic representations are:

[3]http://framenet.icsi.berkeley.edu/

[4]The abbreviations in table 2 and table 4 follow the BFN annotation scheme: Dependent (Dep), External Argument (Ext), Object (Obj), Constructional null instantiation (CNI).

| Create_representation | | |
|---|---|---|
| LUs | carve.v, cast.v, draw.v, paint.v, photograph.v, sketch.v | |
| FEs | Core | Creator (C), Represented (R) |
| | Peripheral | Depictive (D), Depictive_of_represented (DR), Means (ME), Instrument (IN), Iteration (I), Material (MA), Manner (M), Place (P), Purpose (PU), Representation (RE), Role (RO), Time (T) |

Table 1: LUs and FEs in the frame *Create_representation* in BFN.

| Creator (CR) | Represented (R) | Time (TI) |
|---|---|---|
| NP.Ext | NP.Obj | PP[at].Dep |
| PP[by].Dep | NP.Ext | PP[in].Dep |

Table 2: FEs and their syntactic realizations found in the *Create representation* frame for the verb *paint*.

1. The Gerichtsstube was painted by Kuhn in 1763.
2. The youngest girl had her portrait painted by him .
3. He painted her at least fourteen times.

### 3.2 The Swedish FrameNet

BFN has formed the basis for the development of computationally oriented freely available framenets for a number of languages (Boas, 2009), among these the Swedish FrameNet (SweFN) (Borin et al., 2010).[5]

SweFN takes its conceptual backbone from BFN, i.e., the core and peripheral elements are exactly the same for frames appearing in both framenets. Each frame also contains semantically annotated example sentences from which we can extract syntactic information. The most notable differences between the frames can be seen from a comparison of table 1 and table 3.

The lexical units in each SweFN frame are linked to the Swedish lexical-semantic resource SALDO (Borin et al., 2008). SweFN is also organized into a domain hierarchy, with a general domain and at present the two spe-

[5]http://spraakbanken.gu.se/swefn/

| Create_representation | |
|---|---|
| LUs | vb: avbilda..1, avporträttera..1, filma..1, fotografera..1, knäppa..5, plåta..1, porträttera..1, skissa..1, skissera..1, skulptera..1;; vbm: måla_av..1;; nn: framställning..1, teckning..1, pennteckning..1, skiss..1, skämtteckning..1, tuschteckning..1, frihandsteckning..1 |
| Domain | Gen/Art |
| Sem Type | Symbolic_creation |
| Compound | Manner+LU, Representation+LU |

Table 3: LUs and FEs in the frame *Create_representation* in SweFN.

cialized domains *Art* and *Medicine*. In addition, each frame in SweFN is associated with a semantic type and a list of compounds instantiating part of a frame configuration.

Syntactic valency information is obtained from the Swedish Simple and Parole lexicons (Lenci et al., 2000). The encoding of this valency information is different from the one provided in BFN. For example, for the verb *avbilda* 'depict' we find the following syntactic valency:

```
S_NP_A/x [vb] DO_NP_B/y
```

*S* denotes the subject of the sentence, *DO* denotes direct object. Both are realized as either animate (*A*, *B*) or inanimate (*x*, *y*) NPs.

In addition, it is possible to extract almost the same information about semantic and syntactic valency from the example sentences for the verb *avbilda* (table 4). It is important to note that the syntactic annotation in SweFN does not follow the BFN model, although we use the same annotation scheme here to facilitate comparison.

Examples of sentences that can be formed using the semantic and syntactic representations listed in table 4 are:

| Creator (CR) | Represented (R) | Time (TI) |
|---|---|---|
| NP.Ext | NP.Obj | AVP.Dep |
| CNI | NP.Ext | |

Table 4: FEs and their syntactic realizations found in the *Create representation* frame for the verb *avbilda* 'depict'.

1. Det förra århundradet hade han avbildat konstnärinnan Anna Maria Ehrenstrahl.
   'The previous century had he depicted the-female-artist Anna Maria Ehrenstrahl.'
2. Här avbildas Gustav Adolf.
   'Here is-depicted Gustav Adolf.'

## 4 Multilingual Language Generation of Museum Object Descriptions

### 4.1 The Language Generator Tool

We have developed a domain specific grammar application to generate multilingual artwork descriptions from domain specific ontologies. The application is developed in the Grammatical Framework (GF) (Ranta, 2004). The key feature of GF is the distinction between an abstract syntax, which acts as a semantic interlingua, and concrete syntaxes, representing linearizations in various target languages, natural or formal. The grammar comes with a resource library which aids the development of new grammars for specific domains by providing syntactic operations for basic grammatical constructions (Ranta, 2009).

The information available in BFN and SweFN on semantic elements and their possible syntactic realizations with specific lexical units has guided the (manual) development of the generation grammars. Below we present the abstract and the concrete grammars of English and Swedish for the semantic elements RE, CR, TI and R.

In the abstract grammar we have a list of discourse patterns (DPs), encoded as functions that specify the semantic roles appearing in the pattern.

```
DP1: representation creator time
DP2: creator represented time
```

In the concrete grammars, patterns are linearized differently for each language. Semantic elements listed in each DP are expressed linguistically with the resource grammar constructors. In the examples below we find six of the GF constructors: `mkPhr` (Phrase), `mkS` (Sentence), `mkCl` (Clause), `mkNP` (Noun Phrase), `mkVP` (Verb Phrase), `mkAdv` (Verb Phrase modifying adverb). The lexicons which we use to lexicalize the verbs and the semantic elements are the OALD for English and SALDO for Swedish.

```
DP1
representation creator time =
str : Phr =  mkPhr
(mkS pastTense
(mkCl (mkNP representation)
(mkVP (mkVP (passiveVP paint_V2)
(mkAdv by8agent_Prep (mkNP creator))
(mkAdv in_Prep (mkNP time))))));
```

```
DP1
representation creator time =
str :  Phr = mkPhr
(mkS pastTense
(mkCl (mkNP representation)
(mkVP (mkVP (passiveVP maala_vb_1)
(mkAdv by8agent_Prep (mkNP creator))
(mkAdv noPrep (mkNP time))))));
```

When used for generating sentences, the above grammatical representations will yield syntactic trees with the structures exemplified in figure 1 above.

### 4.2 Linguistic Realisations from Framenets

The advantage of the implementation strategy presented in section 4.1 is that we can build different syntactic trees for each language to form a description regardless of the order of the semantic elements.

Let us consider the lexical-semantic information provided in tables 2 and 4. This information could be embedded in the application grammar to compute the following linguistic specifications.

```
DP2
creator represented time =
str : Phr = mkPhr (mkS
(mkCl  (mkNP represented)
(mkVP (mkVP (mkVP  paint_V2))
(mkAdv by8agent_Prep (mkNP creator))
(mkAdv in_Prep (mkNP time)))));
```

```
DP2
creator represented time =
 str : Phr = mkPhr (mkS
(mkCl (mkNP creator)
(mkVP (mkVP avbilda_vb_1_1_V)
(mkNP (mkCN represented
(mkAdv noPrep (mkNP time)))))));
```

These specifications can in turn be used to generate sentences like the following:

1. [Captain Frans Banning Cocq]$_R$ painted [by Rembrandt van Rijn]$_{CR}$ [in 1642]$_{TI}$.
2. [Rembrandt van Rijn]$_{CR}$ har avbildat [Kapten Frans Banning Cocq]$_R$ [1642]$_{TI}$.
   'Rembrandt van Rijn has depicted Captain Frans Banning Cocq 1642.'

The discourse patterns can be automatically modified to compute a variety of linguistic specifications that are acquired from lexical-semantic frames.

## 5 Summary

This paper has demonstrated the differences in the syntactic realization of verbs in two languages. We described what kind of semantic and syntactic valency can be obtained from the information given in two framenets to improve syntactic realizations of object descriptions from particular sets of semantic elements.

The cultural heritage domain is a potential application area of a framenet, which we argue is an essential open source resource for generating multilingual object descriptions. We believe it is possible to establish more efficient processing if the framenet is domain-specific and thereby offers linguistic structures that are specific to the domain, in our case the art domain. Even though our generation grammars at the moment have been manually constructed using the framenet information, we hope that we have shown the utility of being able to draw on a framenet in developing such applications. The next logical step will be to attempt to generate (partial) grammars automatically from the framenet information directly. We also intend to increase the grammars to handle a larger set of semantic frames.

## References

Ion Androutsopoulos, Vassiliki Kokkinaki, Aggeliki Dimitromanolaki, Jo Calder, Jon Oberl, and Elena Not. 2001. Generating multilingual personalized descriptions of museum exhibits: the M-PIRO project. In *Proceedings of the International Conference on Computer Applications and Quantitative Methods in Archaeology.*

Hans C. Boas. 2009. *Multilingual FrameNets in Computational Lexicography.* Mouton de Gruyter, Berlin.

Lars Borin, Markus Forsberg, and Lennart Lönngren. 2008. The hunting of the BLARK – SALDO, a freely available lexical database for Swedish language technology. resourceful language technology. In Joakim Nivre, Mats Dahllöf, and Beata Megyesi, editors, *Festschrift in honor of Anna Sågvall Hein*, 7, pages 21–32. Acta Universitatis Upsaliensis: Studia Linguistica Upsaliensia.

Lars Borin, Dana Dannélls, Markus Forsberg, Maria Toporowska Gronostaj, and Dimitrios Kokkinakis. 2010. Swedish FrameNet++. In *The 14th EURALEX International Congress.*

Dana Dannélls. 2008. Generating tailored texts for museum exhibits. In *The 2nd Workshop on Language Technology for Cultural Heritage (LaTeCH 2008)*, pages 17–20, Marrakech, Morocco, May. ELRA - European Language Ressources Association.

Katrin Erk, Andrea Kowalski, Sebastian Padó, and Manfred Pinkal. 2003. Towards a resource for lexical semantics: A large german corpus with extensive semantic annotation. In *Proceedings of the ACL.*

Charles J. Fillmore, Christopher R. Johnson, and Miriam R.L. Petruck. 2003. Background to Framenet. *International Journal of Lexicography*, 16(3):235–250.

Charles J. Fillmore. 1985. Frames and the semantics of understanding. *In Quaderni di Semantica Sign Language Studies*, 6(2):222–254.

Stasinos Konstantopoulos, Vangelis Karkaletsis, and Dimitris Bilidas. 2009. An intelligent authoring environment for abstract semantic representations of cultural object descriptions. In *Proceedings of the ACL-09 Workshop on Language Technology and Resources for Cultural Heritage, Social Sciences, Humanities, and Education*, page 10–17.

Alessandro Lenci, Nuria Bel, Federica Busa, Nicoletta Calzolari, Elisabetta Gola, Monica Monachini, Antoine Ogonowski, Ivonne Peters, Wim Peters, Nilda Ruimy, Marta Villegas, and Antonio Zampolli. 2000. SIMPLE: A general framework for the development of multilingual lexicons. *Lexicography*, 13(4):249–263, December.

Kathleen R. McKeown. 1985. *Text generation : using discourse strategies and focus constraints to generate natural language text.* Cambridge University Press.

Joakim Nivre, Johan Hall, Jens Nilsson, Atanas Chanev, Gülsen Eryigit, Sandra Kübler, Svetoslav Marinov, and Erwin Marsi. 2007. Maltparser: A language-independent system for data-driven dependency parsing. *Natural Language Engineering*, 13(2):95–135.

Kyoko Hirose Ohara, Seiko Fujii, Hiroaki Saito, Shun Ishizaki, Toshio Ohori, and Ryoko Suzuki. 2003. The japanese framenet project: A preliminary report. In *Proceedings of Pacific Association for Computational Linguistics*, pages 249–254.

Aarne Ranta. 2004. Grammatical Framework, a type-theoretical grammar formalism. *Journal of Functional Programming*, 14(2):145–189.

Aarne Ranta. 2009. The GF resource grammar library. *The on-line journal Linguistics in Language Technology (LiLT)*, 2(2). `http://elanguage.net/journals/index.php/lilt/article/viewFile/214/158`.

Carlos Subirats and Miriam R. L. Petruck. 2003. Surprise: Spanish framenet. In *Workshop on Frame Semantics, International Congress of Linguists. Prague, Czech Republic*, Prague, Czech Republic.

# Harvesting Indices to Grow a Controlled Vocabulary: Towards Improved Access to Historical Legal Texts

**Michael Piotrowski**
Law Sources Foundation
of the Swiss Lawyers Society
Zurich, Switzerland
mxp@ssrq-sds-fds.ch

**Cathrin Senn**
sennmantics GmbH
Thalwil, Switzerland
senn@sennmantics.com

**Abstract**

We describe ongoing work aiming at deriving a multilingual controlled vocabulary (German, French, Italian) from the combined subject indices from 22 volumes of a large-scale critical edition of historical documents. The controlled vocabulary is intended to support editors in assigning descriptors to new documents and to support users in retrieving documents of interest regardless of the spelling or language variety used in the documents.

## 1 Introduction

Until quite recently, most critical edition[1] projects produced printed books, even though the *production* of these volumes has been supported by computers since the 1960s, e.g., for concordancing, collation, and statistical analyses, as well as for bibliography management, text editing, and typesetting (see, e.g., Froger (1970)).

Modern edition projects increasingly aim to produce *digital editions* that offer linking, dynamic display of alternative readings, or the integration of related images (in particular facsimiles of original documents), audio, or video. However, the new target medium does not just offer new possibilities, but it also demands sometimes fundamental changes in the editorial process.

One affected area is indexing. In printed books, the manually constructed back-of-the-book index is the only way for readers to access the contents in a non-linear fashion. A good index is not merely a list of words occurring in the text, but it specifies concepts and introduces synonyms and, through cross-references, related terms. The possibility to perform full-text searches on digital texts therefore does not render manually constructed indices obsolete, but complements them (see Savoy (2005) for an evaluation in a comparable scenario). For editions of historical texts, a manually constructed index is indispensable, as spelling variation, meaning shifts, and multilingualism make full-text retrieval difficult for both laypersons and experts.

In book form, collective editions of shorter texts, such as letters, treaties, or charters, form one monolithic entity. The electronic medium allows for direct linking and repurposing of individual parts (or *content objects*) of a collection in new contexts, so the individual edited text is much more independent than it was in a printed volume. This has direct implications for the construction of indices: Traditionally, an index for a book is compiled when it is completed; thus, when selecting keywords, the indexer does not consider individual texts in isolation, but rather within the specific context set by the book. An indexer may thus choose one particular term for describing a concept over another one because it occurs verbatim in the majority of texts; or an indexer may choose to leave out certain possible index terms because they are self-evident in the context of the book, e.g., the index to an edition of letters is unlikely to contain the index term *letter*.

In a digital edition, in contrast, index terms should be rather thought of as metadata assigned to individual content objects to enable retrieval and reuse in different contexts. For example, if an edition of a letter is included in a thematic collection containing various types of documents, it should have the metadata information *letter*, as this may be a distinguishing feature in this collection. It also means that a collection may contain items

[1] In a narrow sense, a critical edition is a scholarly edition that tries to recover the most authentic version of a historical text from extant sources. We use the term loosely to include other types of scholarly editions, in particular diplomatic editions.

annotated by different editors, in contrast to back-of-the-book indices, which are typically created by a single indexer.

In order to ensure interoperability of index terms, a *controlled vocabulary* should be used. We define a controlled vocabulary in accordance with ANSI/NISO Z39.19-2005 (ANSI/NISO, 2005) as a set of canonical terms that are managed by an authority according to certain rules; for multiple terms referring to the same concept, a preferred term (i.e., descriptor) is defined, and a term representing various concepts is made unambiguous. A controlled vocabulary may have defined types of relationships between terms such as in a taxonomy (hierarchy), thesaurus (hierarchy, equivalence, association), or ontology (specific types of relationships like "is produced by").

Construction of controlled vocabularies is a time-consuming and labor-intensive process. Since it requires deep semantic understanding, it cannot be fully automated. However, we noted in our experiments that some stages of building a controlled vocabulary (see Shearer (2004) for a nine-step procedure to build a thesaurus) can be partially automated. In particular, we propose to harvest the information contained in subject indices from earlier or related works.

This paper describes ongoing work along these lines towards a controlled vocabulary for the *Collection of Swiss Law Sources*, a large-scale critical edition of historical texts. The vocabulary is intended to support editors in finding meaningful and agreed-upon descriptors and to facilitate retrieval of documents by both experts and laypersons. We expect that for our purposes a post-coordinate vocabulary[2] will be most useful, but the exact type and structure of the vocabulary will be defined at a later stage.

The main contributions of this paper are (1) to raise awareness for existing manually created information resources, which are potentially valuable for many tasks related to the processing of historical texts, and (2) to describe exploratory work towards using one type of resource, namely indices, for creating a controlled vocabulary.

The paper is structured as follows: Section 2 discusses related work; Section 3 gives an overview of the Collection and its subject indices; Section 4 describes the extraction of index terms and their conflation using base form reduction; Section 5 describes experiments with decompounding; in Section 6 we compare the extracted terms with the headwords of the HRG; Section 7 summarizes our findings and outlines future work.

## 2 Related Work

Vocabularies are inherently domain-specific. For our domain of historical legal texts, there is currently no controlled vocabulary that could be used as a basis. Despite some similarities, modern legal vocabularies such as Jurivoc[3] or the GLIN Subject Term Index[4] are not readily applicable to medieval and early modern jurisdictions (e.g., they lack concepts such as feudal tenure or witchcraft). The *Vocabulaire international de la diplomatique* (Milagros Cárcel Ortí, 1997) is an attempt at a vocabulary for describing types of historical documents, but it is not fine-grained enough and does not consider historical regional differences.

There are various approaches for automatically generating back-of-the-book indices and thus potential descriptors (e.g., Csomai and Mihalcea (2008)), but these are intended for book-length texts in a single language; in the case of historical editions, however, the documents differ widely in length, language, and age.

Romanello et al. (2009) have parsed OCR-processed *indices scriptorum* and extracted information to support the creation of a collection of fragmentary texts. Even though this is a completely different task, the approach is somewhat related to ours, in that it aims to utilize the valuable information contained in manually created indices.

## 3 The Collection of Swiss Law Sources

The *Collection of Swiss Law Sources* is an edition of historical legal texts created on Swiss territory from the early Middle Ages up to 1798. The Collection includes acts, decrees, and ordinances, but also indentures, administrative documents, court transcripts, and other types of documents. Since 1894, the Law Sources Foundation has edited and published more than 60,000 pages of source material and commentary in over 100 volumes.

The primary users of the Collection are historians, but it is also an important source for the Swiss-German Dictionary, which documents the

[2] See ANSI/NISO (2005) for a definition of postcoordination.

[3] `http://bger.ch/jurisdiction-jurivoc-home`

[4] `http://glin.gov/`

German language in Switzerland from the late Middle Ages to the 21st century. See Gschwend (2008) for a more detailed description of the Collection.

The primary sources are manuscripts in various regional historical forms of German, French, Italian, Rhaeto-Romanic, and Latin, which are transcribed, annotated, and commented by the editors. The critical apparatuses are in modern German, French, or Italian. Each volume contains an index of persons and places and a subject index. At the time of this writing, the Collection covers 17 of the 26 Swiss cantons to different extents.

The Collection is an ongoing project; future additions to the Collection will be created as digital editions. Instead of compiling a book, each source considered for addition to the Collection will be stored in a TEI-encoded XML document; virtual volumes, e.g., on a certain topic, place, or period, can then be created by selecting a subset of these documents. To make this possible, each document needs to contain the necessary metadata. Some of the metadata has traditionally been associated with each source text: A modern-language summary, the date, and the place of creation. In addition, each document will need to be assigned a set of descriptors.

The basis for the work described in this paper are the 22 latest volumes of the Collection, for which digital typesetting data is available; this subset is referred to as *DS21* (Höfler and Piotrowski, 2011). We have converted the typesetting files of the indices into an XML format that makes the logical structure of the indices explicit, i.e., headwords, glosses, spelling variants, page and line references, etc. The conversion process is described in detail by Piotrowski (2010).

DS21 contains volumes from ten cantons representing most linguistic and geographic regions of Switzerland and spans 1078 years. We therefore believe DS21 to be a good sample of the types of documents contained in the Collection, and we therefore expect high-frequency index terms to be good candidates for inclusion in the controlled vocabulary. The subject indices of the DS21 volumes contain a total of 70,531 entries (plus 43,264 entries in the indices of persons and places). In the work described below we have focused on the German-language volumes; the volumes in French and Italian will be considered at a later stage. The subject indices of the German-language volumes comprise a total of 47,469 entries.

weinschänckh, weinschenk, wi/ynschenck; schenckleüth *m Weinschenk* $329^{12}$, $384^{10}$–$386^{7}$, $547^{32}$–$551^{9}$, $600^{6}$, $601^{37}$, $628^{28}$, $645^{21}$, $706^{30}$, $740^{15}$–$741^{29}$, $752^{8}$, $821^{13}$–$824^{43}$, $890^{8}$–$891^{13}$
weinschenckhhaüßere *pl. Schenkhäuser, s.* schenckheüsser
weinstockh *m Rebstock* $665^{13-18}$
weinstraffen *pl. Weinbussen* $605^{41}$
weinter *m, s.* winter
*Weintrinkverbot* $313^{33}$–$314^{42}$, $397^{21}$, $399^{27}$–$400^{36}$, $405^{30}$
wein umgeltner *m Umgeldverwalter* $812^{10}$, *s.* umgelter
*Weinzehnt* $693^{27}$
*Weinzins* $18^{16-21}$, $51^{1}$; win gůlt $396^{17-22}$
werber, wärber *m Söldneranwerber* $834^{4-7}$
werbung *f Brautwerbung* $375^{2}$; *Söldneranwerbung* $833^{33}$–$834^{16}$
werch, wärch, werckh *n Hanf, Garn* $327^{35}$–$328^{16}$, $332^{3}$, $594^{35}$, $681^{31}$, $825^{22}$, $842^{4}$; alt w. $328^{20}$
werch *pl. Taten, s.* werken
werchen, wårchen, werckhen *v. arbeiten* $329^{47}$, $350^{35}$, $424^{21}$, $439^{27}$, $541^{37-40}$, $700^{7}$
werchlûtten *pl. Handwerker* $178^{16}$
werch rybe *f Hanfreibe* $579^{24}$–$580^{21}$
werd *n* $98^{18}$
weren, wåran, währen, wehren *v. ausrichten* $37^{23}$, $158^{6-9}$, $199^{33}$, $247^{13}$–$248^{7}$, $350^{36}$–$351^{31}$, $525^{23}$, $529^{8}$, $664^{7}$; in der statt w. $99^{8}$, $103^{28\,f.}$, $720^{27}$; *wehren, verwehren*

Figure 1: Extract from a subject index as it appears in a printed volume of the *Collection of Swiss Law Sources* (Rechtsquellenstiftung, 2007).

```
<p xml:id="GL06142" class="index">
  <dfn class="hist">weinschänckh</dfn>,
  weinschenk, wi/ynschenck; schenckleüth
  <i>m Weinschenk</i> 329:12, 384:10-386:7,
  547:32-551:9, 600:6, 601:37, 628:28,
  645:21, 706:30, 740:15-741:29, 752:8,
  821:13-824:43, 890:8-891:13</p>
<p xml:id="GL06143" class="index">
  <dfn class="hist">weinschenckhhaüßere</dfn>
  <i>pl. Schenkhäuser, s.</i>
  schenckheüsser</p>
```

Figure 2: XML version (automatically created from typesetting data) of the first two entries from Figure 1.

Figure 1 shows an excerpt of a subject index as it appears in print; Figure 2 shows two of the entries in the XML format we used as basis for the experiments described here. Since the subject indices also serve as glossaries, a particular feature is that they contain both historical and modern headwords; words in italics are modern terms, all other are historical words.

## 4 Extracting and Conflating Index Terms

Due to high variability of the historical index terms we decided to first concentrate on the modern index terms. Since different historians have worked on the subject indices, our first question was whether the extracted terms would overlap at all, and, if they do, to what extent and in which areas. In total, 6370 subject index word forms were extracted using a Perl script from the 16 German-language volumes. In a first step towards merging the extracted keywords, we manually removed irrelevant terms from the list of unique keywords (e.g., historical terms mistagged as modern terms), resulting in 5138 terms. We normalized the remaining entries by removing punctuation and grammatical information given with some entries. About 85% of the unique terms occur only once. Thus, the vast majority of terms are associated with a specific volume.

Of the 15% of keywords that occur more than once the most frequent one is *Erbrecht* 'inheritance law' with 10 appearances. Although specific legal terms like *Erbrecht* are, as would be expected, relatively frequent, a similar number of keywords is linked to people's social, religious, and professional roles (reflected in terms like vagrant, baptist, pope, baker, tanner, etc.) together with terminology related to trades (for example livestock trade, animal market, sawmill). This indicates that a controlled vocabulary for the Collection should not only take into account legal terminology but also focus on roles and trades, which could potentially be covered by a separate controlled vocabulary facet (for a list of potential law subject facets see also Broughton (2010, p. 38)).

We were surprised by the small intersection between the volumes' subject indices. Looking for ways to further conflate the terms, we noted a number of mismatches due to morphological variation (such as singular and plural forms), even though subject indices are not as inflectionally rich as normal German text.

Since many index terms are highly domain-specific or specific to Swiss German (e.g., compounds of the term *Anke* 'butter' like *Ankenballen* or *Ankenhaus*), we did not use a rule-based morphological analyzer (such as GERTWOL, Stripy Zebra, or Morphisto; for an overview see Mahlow and Piotrowski (2009)) but the Baseforms tool from the ASV Toolbox (Biemann et al., 2008), which is based on pretree classifiers. The Baseforms tool does not perform morphological analysis, but is more akin to a stemmer, so that its output is not necessarily linguistically correct; however, since we are primarily interested in term conflation, this is not a major problem. When the output of the system was empty or malformed we used the original term to ensure maximum overlap. We manually reviewed and, where necessary, corrected the base forms, also to get a better understanding of the kind of potential conflations. This cut down the list of keywords from 5138 to 4881 terms, i.e., 490 terms were morphological variants that could be conflated to 233 "concepts."

The majority of term conflations concern variation in number (*Kapelle* 'chapel' and *Kapellen* 'chapels'), derivations (*Heirat* 'marriage' and *heiraten* 'to marry'), and variant compound forms (*Lehenherr* and *Lehensherr* 'liege').

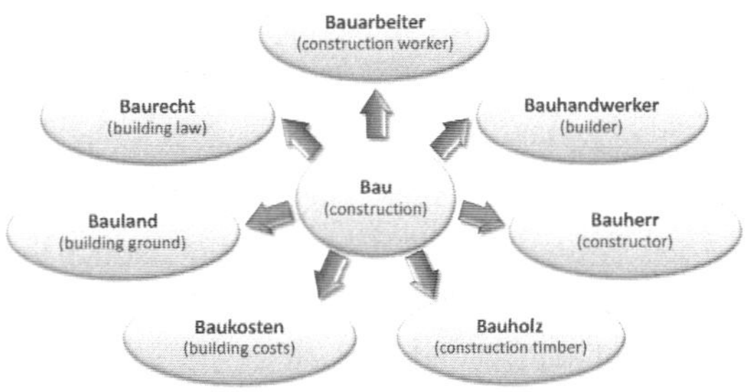


Figure 3: Map of terms based on *Bau* 'construction' with matching first compound elements.

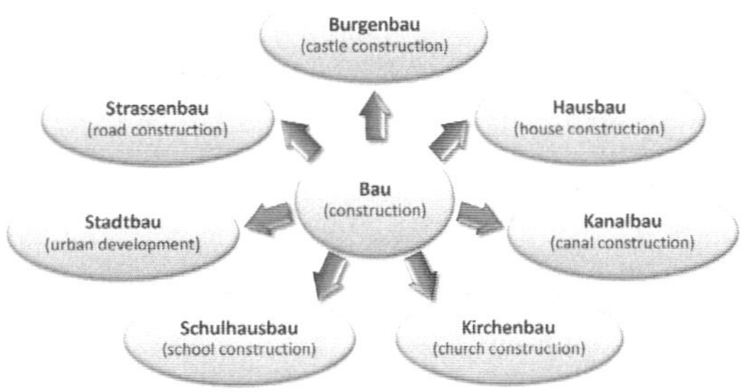


Figure 4: Map of terms based on *Bau* 'construction' with matching last compound elements.

## 5 Experiments with Compounds

German is well-known for its tendency to form compound nouns to express complex concepts. For vocabulary construction, compounds are interesting because related terms often share constituent parts. Our idea was therefore to use decompounding to identify potential related terms. The relationships between these terms are usually weaker than between equivalent terms (like plural and singular variants), but will still be valuable in building a controlled vocabulary. For the following experiments we used the decompounding as produced by the ASV Baseforms tool with manual corrections.

In a first experiment, we extracted groups of compound-word terms that share the same *first* element. This gives us, for example, *Bau* 'construction', *Bauarbeiter* 'construction worker', and *Bauherr* 'constructor'. The terms found in this way could, for example, be used to build a map on the topic "construction" as shown in Figure 3. In total, we found 2555 matches by first compound elements. Note that partial matching without compound splitting would lead to unwanted hits like *Bauer* 'farmer' and *Baumgarten* 'tree garden'.

In a second experiment, we identified terms sharing the same *last* compound element. Overall this resulted in 2477 matches. Due to the structure of German compounds, terms sharing the final compound element are usually more closely related than those sharing the first element. Examples along the lines of *Bau* 'construction' are *Hausbau* 'house construction' and *Kirchenbau* 'church construction'; see Figure 4. Although not all of the matches will be equally relevant (for example *Erbfall* 'case of succession' and *Wasserfall* 'waterfall' are not semantically related), matches tend to point to terms on the same hierarchical level, meaning that the base form consisting of one element only (if it exists) acts as the broader term (*Bau*) of the compound matches which are the narrower terms (*Hausbau* and *Kirchenbau*).

At the moment our approach does not take into account homonyms and polysemes[5] such as *Gericht* 'court' vs. *Gericht* 'dish' or *Kirche* 'church as a building' vs. *Kirche* 'church as an institution'. Such semantic unknowns would need to be analyzed in the context of the text passages that the back-of-the-book subject indices refer to. Such a semantic review will be conducted at a later stage when the terms are prepared to be grouped in a controlled vocabulary.

## 6 Comparison to HRG Headwords

As noted in Section 4, the majority of index terms occur only once, i.e., in a single volume. In order to answer the question of how many of our terms are just locally useful and how many may be of more general utility, we compared our list to the list of headwords of the *Handwörterbuch zur deutschen Rechtsgeschichte* (HRG) (Cordes et al., 2008 ), the standard reference work on German history of law. The rationale is that the intersection of both lists contains those index terms that are highly likely to be useful as descriptors in a controlled vocabulary.

The comparison of the 3395 headwords taken from the online version of the HRG[6] (excluding entries for persons) with the 4881 stemmed index terms of our list yielded an intersection of 447 matches, i.e., 9% of our index terms also appear as headwords in the HRG.

A closer inspection shows that the rather small intersection of terms is due to the broader scope of the *Collection of Swiss Law Sources* and the fact that the HRG focuses on German rather than Swiss history. The former is illustrated by the fact that the second most frequent term in our list of index terms after *Erbrecht* is *Bäcker* 'baker', which does not appear in the list of HRG keywords. While professional roles related to legal duties like *Notar* 'notary' or *Landvogt* 'bailiff', as well as religious roles like *Papst* 'pope' or *Kleriker* 'clergyman' are also HRG headwords, terminology related to crafts and trades—like *Gerber* 'tanner' or *Schuhmacher* 'shoemaker'—is rare.

However, from a legal perspective, the terms in the intersection between the Collection and the HRG are indeed highly relevant. We also noted that high-frequency index terms from the Collection are in fact more likely to appear in the list of HRG headwords than low-frequency terms. As expected, *Erbrecht* 'inheritance law', the most frequent term in our list of index terms also occurs in the list of HRG headwords. A third of the terms appearing three times or more (306 terms) are also covered by the HRG (102 headwords), in contrast to an overlap of less than 7% for the terms occurring only once in the indices of the Collection. The index terms that occur more than once in our indices (i.e., 18% of our 4881 base form terms) account for over 46% of the terms in the intersection with the HRG headwords.

## 7 Conclusion and Future Work

In this paper, we have described ongoing work on the extraction of index terms from back-of-the-book subject indices in order to build a controlled vocabulary for the *Collection of Swiss Law Sources*. We have used base form reduction for term conflation and decompounding for discovering potential hierarchical relations.

We have found that index terms that are also HRG headwords are likely to be highly relevant; the terms in the intersection between our index terms and the HRG headwords will therefore be reviewed by the editors of the Collection to verify whether they are a good foundation for a controlled vocabulary.

[5] In the linguistic sense; ANSI/NISO (2005) defines homonyms and polysemes differently and would refer to homographs in this context without distinguishing whether one or more lexemes are involved.

[6] `http://www.hrgdigital.de/`

At this point, we have only examined index terms in modern language. However, the majority (85%) of modern word forms appears only once; this means that the bulk of the concepts contained in the indices must be represented by historical-language index terms. For the construction of a controlled vocabulary it is thus necessary to also consider these terms.

While there are only 6370 modern word forms (5160 unique terms) in the subject indices, we have extracted 41,099 historical word forms (28,860 unique terms). The reduction of about 30% for historical versus about 20% for modern terms indicates that historical index terms are more evenly spread across the analyzed volumes.

The percentage of historical index terms occurring only once is only slightly lower than for modern terms (80% vs. 85%); however, the historical terms exhibit a high degree of spelling variation. We therefore expect that many terms are spelling variants that can be conflated. We are currently working on methods for clustering different historical spellings of related terms.

## Acknowledgements

We would like to thank Pascale Sutter for fruitful discussions and for her historical expertise.

## References

ANSI/NISO. 2005. Z39.19-2005. Guidelines for the Construction, Format, and Management of Monolingual Controlled Vocabularies.

Chris Biemann, Uwe Quasthoff, Gerhard Heyer, and Florian Holz. 2008. ASV Toolbox: a modular collection of language exploration tools. In Nicoletta Calzolari, Khalid Choukri, Bente Maegaard, Joseph Mariani, Jan Odjik, Stelios Piperidis, and Daniel Tapias, editors, *Proceedings of the Sixth International Conference on Language Resources and Evaluation (LREC'08)*, pages 1760–1767, Paris. European Language Resources Association (ELRA).

Vanda Broughton. 2010. The use and construction of thesauri for legal documentation. *Legal Information Management*, 10(01):35–42.

Albrecht Cordes, Heiner Lück, Dieter Werkmüller, and Ruth Schmidt-Wiegand, editors. 2008–. *Handwörterbuch zur deutschen Rechtsgeschichte*. Erich Schmidt, Berlin, Germany, 2nd edition.

Andras Csomai and Rada Mihalcea. 2008. Linguistically motivated features for enhanced Back-of-the-Book indexing. In *Proceedings of ACL-08: HLT*, pages 932–940, Morristown, NJ. ACL.

Jacques Froger. 1970. La critique des textes et l'ordinateur. *Vigiliae Christianae*, 24(3):210–217.

Lukas Gschwend. 2008. Rechtshistorische Grundlagenforschung: Die Sammlung Schweizerischer Rechtsquellen. *Schweizerische Zeitschrift für Geschichte*, 58(1):4–19.

Stefan Höfler and Michael Piotrowski. 2011. Building corpora for the philological study of Swiss legal texts. *Journal for Language Technology and Computational Linguistics*, 26(2):77–88.

Cerstin Mahlow and Michael Piotrowski. 2009. A target-driven evaluation of morphological components for German. In Simon Clematide, Manfred Klenner, and Martin Volk, editors, *Searching Answers – Festschrift in Honour of Michael Hess on the Occasion of his 60th Birthday*, pages 85–99. MV-Verlag, Münster, Germany.

Maria Milagros Cárcel Ortí, editor. 1997. *Vocabulaire international de la diplomatique*. Universitat de València, Valencia, Spain, second edition.

Michael Piotrowski. 2010. Document conversion for cultural heritage texts: FrameMaker to HTML revisited. In Apostolos Antonacopoulos, Michael Gormish, and Rolf Ingold, editors, *DocEng 2010: Proceedings of the 10th ACM Symposium on Document Engineering*, pages 223–226, New York, NY. ACM.

Rechtsquellenstiftung, editor. 2007. *Rechtsquellen der Stadt und Herrschaft Rapperswil*, volume SSRQ SG II/2/1: Die Rechtsquellen der Stadt und Herrschaft Rapperswil) of *Sammlung Schweizerischer Rechtsquellen*. Schwabe, Basel, Switzerland. Prepared by Pascale Sutter.

Matteo Romanello, Monica Berti, Alison Babeu, and Gregory Crane. 2009. When printed hypertexts go digital: information extraction from the parsing of indices. In *Proceedings of the 20th ACM conference on Hypertext and hypermedia (HT '09)*, pages 357–358, New York, NY. ACM.

Jacques Savoy. 2005. Bibliographic database access using free-text and controlled vocabulary: an evaluation. *Information Processing & Management*, 41(4):873–890.

James R. Shearer. 2004. A practical exercise in building a thesaurus. *Cataloging & Classification Quarterly*, 37(3-4):35–56.

# Ontology-Based Incremental Annotation of Characters in Folktales

**Thierry Declerck**
DFKI GmbH
Stuhlsatzenhausweg, 3
66123 Saarbrücken, Germany
declerck@dfki.de

**Nikolina Koleva**
DFKI GmbH
Stuhlsatzenhausweg, 3
66123 Saarbrücken, Germany
Nikolina.Koleva@dfki.de

**Hans-Ulrich Krieger**
DFKI GmbH
Stuhlsatzenhausweg, 3
66123 Saarbrücken, Germany
krieger@dfki.de

**Abstract**

We present on-going work on the automated ontology-based detection and recognition of characters in folktales, restricting ourselves for the time being to the analysis of referential nominal phrases occurring in such texts. Focus of the presently reported work was to investigate the interaction between an ontology and linguistic analysis of indefinite and indefinite nominal phrase for both the incremental annotation of characters in folktales text, including some inference based co-reference resolution, and the incremental population of the ontology. This in depth study was done at this early stage using only a very small textual base, but the demonstrated feasibility and the promising results of our small-scale experiment are encouraging us to deploy the strategy on a larger text base, covering more linguistic phenomena in a multilingual fashion.

## 1 Introduction

In this submission we present on-going work dealing with the automatic annotation of characters in folktales. Focus of the investigation lies in using an iterative approach that combines an incremental ontology population and an incremental linguistic annotation. Our starting point is given by an in-house developed ontology, which is having as its core the description of family relations, but also some typical elements of folktales, like supernatural entities, etc.

The use of ontologies in the field of folktales is not new, but to our knowledge no attempt has been done so far to use ontologies in combination with natural language processing for automatizing the annotation of folktales, or for automatically populating a knowledge base of characters of folktales. The work by (Peinado et al., 2004) is dealing in first line with the Proppian functions that character can play and is also geared towards generation of interactive stories. (Zoelllner-Weber, 2008) is much closer to our aim, and in fact the author is proposing lines of research we want to implement in the near future, but her work is explicitly not dealing with the automation of annotation, and she is also not concerned with linguistic annotation in particular, but with general TEI annotation[1] of text structures.

At the present stage of development, we restricted ourselves to investigate the role indefinite and definite nominal phrases (NPs) can play for the detection of characters and their storage as instances of ontology classes. This decision is echoing well-established investigations on one possible function of indefinite NPs, namely to introduce a new referent in a discourse (see among others (von Heusinger, 2000)), whereas indefinite NPs can be used in the subsequent text to refer back to the introduced referential entities. This fact has also been acknowledged in the field of folktales and narratives and (Herman, 2000), for example, stressed the importance of analyzing sequences of referring expressions for achieving a more complete and accurate view on the role of participants in narratives.

Discourse models resulting from the sequence of referring expressions can thus support the comprehension of narratives (see (Herman, 2000),p. 962). Agreeing with this study, we further think that the automated analysis of referential expres-

[1] TEI stands for "Text Encoding Initiative, see www.tei-c.org

sions in folktales, delivering essential elements for the character models used in the interpretation of narratives, can be of help in the automated analysis of the whole folktale, and more generally for the automated analysis of narratives.

While (Herman, 2000) treats the role of anaphora used in transcripts of ghost stories, we deal (for the time being) only with the relation between characters introduced by indefinite NPs and their subsequent enunciation by definite NPs.

In the next sections we present the main components of the current version of our system. We discuss also the results of a first evaluation study, and conclude with indication on future work.

## 2 The Ontology

As mentioned above, our starting point is an ontology, developed at our lab. This ontology will be made publicly available, after merging it with further ontological elements relevant to the field of narratives, as those are for example described in (Zoelllner-Weber, 2008), and associating its classes and relations with elements relevant for the linguistic and semantic annotation of folktales, as described for example in (Scheidel and Declerck, 2010).

The class hierarchy and the associated relations (or properties) are equipped with natural language labels and comments. The labels are available in four languages: Bulgarian, English, German and Russian. But our work is dealing for the time being only with English.

An example of class of the ontology, with its labels is given just below:

```
<owl:Class rdf:about="#BiolDaughter">
  <owl:equivalentClass>
    <owl:Class>
      <owl:intersectionOf rdf:parseType="Collection">
        <owl:Restriction>
          <owl:onProperty rdf:resource="#hasBiolParent"/>
          <owl:onClass rdf:resource="#BiolParent"/>
          <owl:minQualifiedCardinality
          rdf:datatype="&xsd;nonNegativeInteger">
            1</owl:minQualifiedCardinality>
        </owl:Restriction>
        <owl:Restriction>
          <owl:onProperty rdf:resource="#hasGender"/>
          <owl:hasValue>f</owl:hasValue>
        </owl:Restriction>
      </owl:intersectionOf>
    </owl:Class>
  </owl:equivalentClass>
  <rdfs:subClassOf rdf:resource="#BiolChild"/>
  <rdfs:subClassOf rdf:resource="#Daughter"/>
  <rdfs:comment>The class of biological daughther is
    a subclass of biological child and of daughter.
    This class designates all biological daughters.
    Each member of this class has gender female
    and at least one biological parent.
  </rdfs:comment>
  <dc:language xml:lang="bg">
    &#1073;&#1080;&#1086;&#1083;&#1086;&#1075;&#1080;&#1095;
    &#1085;&#1072; &#1044;&#1098;&#1097;&#1077;&#1088;&#1103;
  </dc:language>
  <dc:language xml:lang="de">
    biologische Tochter
  </dc:language>
  <dc:language xml:lang="en">
    biological Daughter
  </dc:language>
  <dc:language xml:lang="ru">
    &#1073;&#1080;&#1086;&#1083;&#1086;&#1075;&#1080;
    &#1095;&#1077;&#1089;&#1082;&#1072;&#1103; &#1044;
    &#1086;&#1095;&#1100;
  </dc:language>
</owl:Class>
```

The ontology also encodes inference rules that allow establishing automatically family relations between entities (characters) that have been stored at the instance level, which is the process of ontology population resulting from detection in the text.

1. hasParent(?x, ?x1), hasParent(?x, ?x2), hasParent(?y, ?x1), hasParent(?y, ?x2), hasGender(?x, "f"), notEqual(?x, ?y) → Sister(?x)
2. Daughter(?d) , Father(?f) , Son(?s) → hasBrother(?d, ?s), hasChild(?f, ?s), hasChild(?f, ?d), hasSister(?s, ?d)

The first rule is about class inference. It states that if two different individuals in the ontology (represented by the variables `x` and `y`) share the same parents (represented by the variables `x1` and `x2`) and if the gender of one of the two individuals is female, then this individual can be considered as an instance of the ontology class *Sister*.

According to the second rule, various relations (or properties) can be inferred from the fact that we have three individuals (represented by the variables `d`, `f` and `s`) that are instances of the classes

*Daughter*, *Father* and *Son* respectively. The first inferred relations state that the *Daughter* has the *Son* as her *Brother* and the *Son* reciprocally has the *Daughter* as his *Sister*. In addition, the *Father* is being assigned twice the HASCHILD property, once for the *Daughter* and second for the *Son*.

## 3 Processing Steps

We submit first a folktale, here the "Magic Swan Geese"[2], to a linguistic processing engine (the NooJ platform, see (Silberztein, 2003)), applying to the text nominal phrases recognition rules (including coordination), which are differentiated in being either indefinite or definite (we do not consider pronouns for the time being). All annotated NPs are indexed with ID numbers.

In the following step, our algorithm extracts from the whole annotated text the nominal heads of the indefinite NPs and compares them with the labels present in the ontology. In case a match can be established, the nominal head of this phrase is used for populating the corresponding ontology class as an individual and the text is annotated with the nominal head being a (potential) character, as can be seen in the annotation example below, where the reader can observe that the (potential) characters are also enumerated, this time on the base of the (unique) ID they get during the ontology population phase. In this step thus, all candidate characters in text are automatically marked-up with both linguistic and character information derived from the ontology.

```
<text>
There lived
<NPCOORD id="z_coord_ph1" Nb="p" HEAD1="man"
  HEAD2="woman" Type="and">
  <NP id="indef_ph1" SPEC="a" HEAD="man"
      Gender="m" Num="s">
  <CHAR id="ch1" TYPE="man" Gender="m"
   Num="s">
  an old man</CHAR>
  </NP>
  and
  <NP id="indef_ph2" SPEC="a" HEAD="woman"
      Gender="f" Num="s">
  <CHAR id="ch2" TYPE="woman" Gender="f"
   Num="s">
  an old woman</CHAR>
  </NP>
</NPCOORD>
;
they had
<NPCOORD id="z_coord_ph2" Nb="p" HEAD1=
"daughter" HEAD2="son" Type="and">
<NP id="indef_ph3" SPEC="a"
HEAD="daughter" Gender="f" Num="s">
<CHAR id="ch3" TYPE="daughter"
Gender="f" Num="s">
a daughter</CHAR>
</NP>
  and
  <NP id="indef_ph4" SPEC="a" HEAD="son"
   Gender="m" Num="s">
<CHAR id="ch4" TYPE="son" Gender="m"
 Num="s">
a little son</CHAR>
</NP>
</NPCOORD>
```

In the next step, the inference rules of the ontology are applied to the candidate characters (the individuals stored so far in the knowledge base). In the particular tale we are analysing the class associated with the potential character `ch2` (*Woman*) can be equated with the class *Mother* and its associated string in the label (`mother`), so that all occurrences of the two strings in the text can be marked as referring to the same character.

Also some relations are established between the individuals by the application of the inference rules described in the ontology section above: Wife_of, Mother_Of, etc. (together with the strings listed in the labels). If the related strings are found in definite NPs in the text, the corresponding segment can then be annotated by

[2]http://en.wikipedia.org/wiki/The_Magic_Swan_Geese

our linguistic processing engine with the original character identifier. In the example below, the reader can see that on the base of the inference rules, the string `mother` in the definite NP (with ID DEF_PH6) is referred to `ch2` (see the first annotation example above for the first occurrence of `ch2`).

```
<NP id="def_ph6" SPEC="the" HEAD="mother"
 Gender="f" Num="s">
 the mother</NP>
said: "Daughter, daughter, we are going
 to work; we shall bring you back
<NP id="indef_ph7" SPEC="a" HEAD="bun"
 Gender="n" Num="s">
<CHAR id="ch6" TYPE="bun" Gender="n"
 Num="s">a little bun</CHAR>
</NP>
, sew you <NP id="indef_ph8" SPEC="a"
HEAD="dress" Gender="n" Num="s">
<CHAR id="ch7" TYPE="dress"
 Gender="n" Num="s">
a little dress</CHAR>
</NP>
```

The same remark is valid for the `ch3` ("a daughter" introduced in the first sentence of the tale). In the definite NP with ID 12, the string (`daughter`) is occurring in the context of a definite NP, and thus marked as referring to `ch3`. The string (`girl`) is occurring four times in the context of definite NPs (with IDs 18, 25, 56 and 60) and for all those 4 occurrences the inference driven mark-up of the nominal head with `ch3` turns out to be correct.

In this annotation example, the reader can also see that the heads of all indefinite NPs are first considered as potential characters. A preliminary filtering of such expression like `dress` is not possible, since in folktales, every object can be an actant. So for example in this tale, an `oven`, an `apple tree` or a `river of milk` are playing an important role, and are characters involved in specific actions. Our filtering is rather taking place in a post-processing phase: strings that get only once related to a potential character ID and which are not involved in an action are at the end discarded.

The next steps are dealing with finding other occurrences of the potential characters (within definite NPs), or to exclude candidates from the set.

## 4 Evaluation of the approach

In order to be able to evaluate our approach, even considering that we are working on a very small text base, we designed a first basic test data and annotated manually the folktale "The magic swan geese" with linguistic and character annotation. The linguistic annotation is including co-referential information. In the longer term, we plan to compare our work applied to more folktales with a real gold standard, the UMIREC corpus (http://dspace.mit.edu/handle/1721.1/57507)

Our evaluation study shows results in terms of correct detection of tale characters in comparison with the manually annotated data. Eight of the real characters were correctly classified by the tool. Three of the instances are actually characters but they were not detected. One candidate is not a character according to the manually annotated data, but the system classified it as character. Seven entities were correctly detected as non characters. On this small basis, we calculated the accuracy of the tool, which is 79%. We also computed the precision, the recall and the F-measure. The precision amounts to 88%; the recall to 73%; and the value of the balanced F-measure is 80%. So these metrics confirm what the accuracy has been already expressing: the results are encouraging.

Looking at the errors made by the tool, we know that it does not consider the characters that are mentioned only one time. In our text, *a hedgehog* occurs only once. However, the human intuition is that it is a character and differs from the phrases *a bun* and *a dress*, which have just descriptive function. In a next version of the tool, it will be checked if the head of an indefinite NP, which is present only once in the text, is having an active semantic role, like Agent. In this case, it can be considered as a character.

Another problem of our actual approach is that we do not consider yet the possessive phrases and pronominal expressions. Precise analysis of these anaphoric expressions will improve the approach in augmenting the number of occurrences of candidate characters. We also expect the availability of related instances in the knowledge base to help in resolving pronominal co-reference phenomena.

The applied method does not detect one of the main characters in the sample text namely the *swan-geese*. The *swan-geese* are introduced in the discourse only via a definite noun phrase. If there are some equivalent phrases, for example occurring in the title of the tale, they can be annotated as character by the tool. An additional problem we have, is the fact that our NP grammar has analyzed the words *swan* and *geese* as separate nouns and not as a compound noun. So that the linguistic analysis for English compounds has to be improved.

## 5 Conclusion and future work

Our in depth investigation of the interaction of an ontology and language processing tools for the detection of folktale characters and their use for incrementally populating an ontology seems to be promising, and it has allowed for example to associate a unique character ID to occurrences of different nominal heads, on the base of their inferred semantic identity. A possible result of our work would lie in the constitution of larger database containing characters of narratives extracted automatically from text.

We plan to tackle the processing of pronominal and possessive expressions for completing the coreference task. We plan also to extend our work to other languages, and we already started to do this for anaother folktale in German, in which much more complex family relationships are involved (the German version of the tale "Father Frost"). But more challenging will be to deal with languages, which do not know have the difference between indefinite and definite NPs.

## Acknowledgments

The work presented in this paper has been partly supported by the R&D project. "Monnet", which is co-funded by the European Union under Grant No. 248458.

## References

Marc Cavazza and David Pizzi. 2006. Narratology for interactive storytelling: A critical introduction. In *TIDSE*, pages 72–83.

Maja Hadzic, Pornpit Wongthongtham, Tharam Dillon, Elizabeth Chang, Maja Hadzic, Pornpit Wongthongtham, Tharam Dillon, and Elizabeth Chang. 2009. Introduction to ontology. In *Ontology-Based Multi-Agent Systems*, volume 219 of *Studies in Computational Intelligence*, pages 37–60. Springer Berlin / Heidelberg.

Knut Hartmann, Sandra Hartmann, and Matthias Feustel. 2005. Motif definition and classification to structure non-linear plots and to control the narrative flow in interactive dramas. In *International Conference on Virtual Storytelling*, pages 158–167.

David Herman. 2000. Pragmatic constraints on narrative processing: Actants and anaphora resolution in a corpus of north carolina ghost stories. *Journal of Pragmatics*, 32(7):959 – 1001.

Harry R. Lewis and Christos H. Papadimitriou. 1998. *Elements of the theory of computation*. Prentice-Hall.

Deborah L. McGuinness and Frank van Harmelen. 10 February 2004. OWL Web Ontology Language Overview. W3C Recommendation.

Federico Peinado, Pablo Gervás, and Belén Díaz-Agudo. 2004. A description logic ontology for fairy tale generation. In *Language Resources for Linguistic Creativity Workshop, 4th LREC Conference*, pages 56–61.

Vladimir IA. Propp, American Folklore Society., and Indiana University. 1968. *Morphology of the folktale / by V. Propp ; first edition translated by Laurence Scott ; with an introduction by Svatava Pirkova-Jakobson*. University of Texas Press, Austin :, 2nd ed. / revised and edited with a preface by louis a. wagner ; new introduction by alan dundes. edition.

Antonia Scheidel and Thierry Declerck. 2010. Apftml - augmented proppian fairy tale markup language. In Sándor Darányi and Piroska Lendvai, editors, *First International AMICUS Workshop on Automated Motif Discovery in Cultural Heritage and Scientific Communication Texts: Poster session. International Workshop on Automated Motif Discovery in Cultural Heritage and Scientific Communication Texts (AMICUS-10), located at Supporting the Digital Humanities conference 2010 (SDH-2010), October 21, Vienna, Austria*. Szeged University, Szeged, Hungary, 10.

Max Silberztein. 2003. Nooj manual. available for download at: www.nooj4nlp.net.

Klaus von Heusinger. 2000. The reference of indefinites. In K. von Heusinger and U. Egli, editors, *Reference and Anaphoric Relations*, pages 247–265. Kluwer.

Amelie Zoelllner-Weber. 2008. *Noctua literaria - A Computer-Aided Approach for the Formal Description of Literary Characters Using an Ontology*. Ph.D. thesis, University of Bielefeld, Bielefeld, Germany, may.

# Advanced Visual Analytics Methods for Literature Analysis

**Daniela Oelke**
University of Konstanz
Data Analysis and Visualization
Konstanz, Germany
oelke@inf.uni-konstanz.de

**Dimitrios Kokkinakis**
Språkbanken
Department of Swedish
University of Gothenburg
Gothenburg, Sweden
dimitrios.kokkinakis@gu.se

**Mats Malm**
Department of Literature,
History of Ideas and Religion
University of Gothenburg
Gothenburg, Sweden
mats.malm@lit.gu.se

## Abstract

The volumes of digitized literary collections in various languages increase at a rapid pace, which results also in a growing demand for computational support to analyze such linguistic data. This paper combines robust text analysis with advanced visual analytics and brings a new set of tools to literature analysis. Visual analytics techniques can offer new and unexpected insights and knowledge to the literary scholar. We analyzed a small subset of a large literary collection, the Swedish Literature Bank, by focusing on the extraction of persons' names, their gender and their normalized, linked form, including mentions of theistic beings (e.g., Gods' names and mythological figures), and examined their appearance over the course of the novel. A case study based on 13 novels, from the aforementioned collection, shows a number of interesting applications of visual analytics methods to literature problems, where named entities can play a prominent role, demonstrating the advantage of visual literature analysis. Our work is inspired by the notion of *distant reading* or *macroanalysis* for the analyses of large literature collections.

## 1 Introduction

Literature can be studied in a number of different ways and from many different perspectives, but text analysis - in a wide sense - will surely always make up a central component of literature studies. If such analysis can be integrated with advanced visual methods and fed back to the daily work of the literature researcher, then it is likely to reveal the presence of useful and nuanced insights into the complex daily lives, ideas and beliefs of the main characters found in many of the literary works. Therefore, the names of all characters appearing in literary texts can be one such line of enquiry, which is both an important subfield of literature studies (*literary onomastics*) and at the same time the result obtained by a mature language technology (*named entity recognition*) which can be turned into a tool in aid of text analysis in this field. (Flanders et al., 1998) discuss that references to one type of names, namely that of people, are of intrinsic interest because they reveal networks of friendship, enmity, and collaboration; familial relationships; and political alliances. People's names can be an appropriate starting point for research on biographical, historical, or literary issues, as well as being a key linguistic and textual feature in its permutations and usage.

We argue that the integration of text analysis and visualization techniques, which have turned out to be useful in other scientific fields such as bioinformatics (Nature Methods, 2010), could be put to effective use also in literature studies. We also see an opportunity to devise new ways of exploring the large volumes of literary texts being made available through national cultural heritage digitization projects.

Digitized information and the task of storing, generating and mining an ever greater volume of (textual) data becomes simpler and more efficient with every passing day. Along with this opportunity, however, comes a further challenge: to create the means whereby one can tap this great potentiality and engage it for the advancement of (scientific) understanding and knowledge mining.

We apply a *supra-textual* perspective to the analysis of literary texts by encompassing a rather global visualization of a document. As a case study, we have analyzed a subset, 13 novels, of the Swedish Literature Bank[1] collection through two levels of inquiry by focusing on person names, their gender and their normalized, linked form, including mentions of theistic beings (e.g. Gods' names and mythological characters), and examining their appearance in sentences, paragraphs and chapters.

Our aim is to explore the usage of alternative visualization means that provide additional insight by showing the data at higher resolution levels or that permit an analysis of the development of the story in the course of the text. The employed visualization techniques are scalable enough to display several novels at once and therefore allow a literature scholar to compare different literary texts to each other. By combining advanced natural language processing techniques with visualization techniques, we aim to allow the user to rapidly focus on key areas of interest (based on name mentions) and provide the ability to discover e.g. semantic patterns in large collections of text. Therefore, our work is based on individual texts, by looking for certain patterns of variation based on a particular named entity type. Our work is also inspired by the notions of *distant reading* or *macroanalysis* applied to the analyses of literature collections which we find appealing for the research we describe. However, we do not consider such techniques to be used as a substitution for reading a book sequentially but as a useful supplement.

[1]The Swedish Literature Bank (*Litteraturbanken*, `http://litteraturbanken.se`) is a co-operation between the Swedish Academy, the Royal Library of Sweden, the Royal Swedish Academy of Letters, History and Antiquities, the Language Bank of the University of Gothenburg, the Swedish Society for Belles Lettres, and the Society of Swedish Literature in Finland. The Swedish Literature Bank also focuses on neglected authors and genres, effectively establishing a set of 'minor classics' alongside the canonical works. So far, mainly texts in Swedish are available, but over time, selected works will be offered in translation as well. Currently, the Swedish Literature Bank offers literary works either as searchable e-text, as facsimiles of the original edition, as PDF files or as EPUB files - often in more than one format. The texts are available free of charge and the software is developed as open source. The website is directed towards the general public and students and teachers at every level, as well as towards scholars. The digital texts are based on printed first editions or on later scholarly editions. They are carefully proof-read, thus establishing a basis for scholarly work. For the common reader, introductions and essays provide fresh perspectives on the classics.

## 2 Background

Computer-assisted literary criticism is a rather young field in literature analysis (Juola, 2008). Typically, researchers in literary studies use computers only to collect data that is afterwards analyzed conventionally. Yet, there are some cases in which the computer has already proven useful, e.g., for the analysis of prosody and poetic phonology or for comparing an author's revisions (from version to version). Computer-assisted studies have also been performed in the context of sequence analysis in the past, such as assigning quoted passages to speakers and locating them in the sequence of the text (Butler, 1992).

### 2.1 Distant Reading and Macroanalysis

(Moretti, 2005) coined the term "distant reading" in which "the reality of the text undergoes a process of deliberate reduction and abstraction". According to this view, understanding literature is not accomplished by studying individual texts, but by aggregating and analyzing massive amounts of data. This way it becomes possible to detect possible hidden aspects in plots, the structure and interactions of characters becomes easier to follow enabling experimentation and exploration of new uses and development that otherwise would be impossible to conduct, e.g., quantifying the difference between prose styles.

Distant reading or its near synonym *macroanalysis* is a technique to analyze literature, as opposed to "close reading" of a text that is the careful, sustained interpretation of a brief passage of text where great emphasis is placed on the particular over the general, paying close attention to individual words, syntax, and the order in which sentences and ideas unfold as they are read. The most fundamental and important difference in the two approaches/terms is that the macroanalytic approach reveals details about texts that are for all intents and purposes unavailable to close-readers of the texts. Distant reading is in *no* way meant to be a replacement for close readings and in traditional humanities, as Moretti puts it (Schulz, 2011), "distant reading should supplant, not supplement, close reading".

### 2.2 Visual Analytics for Literature Analysis

Visual Analytics is "the science of analytical reasoning facilitated by visual interactive interfaces" (Thomas et al., 2005). The central idea of visual analytics is that by tightly integrating the human expert and the machine, the strengths of both can be leveraged in the analysis process. Visual Analytics has been applied successfully to many application domains in the past such as text analysis, geographical data analysis, security applications, (computational) biology or multimedia data.[2]

However, visual analytics is not often used in the context of literature analysis. Commonly, a text is read sequentially and then analyzed by the researcher bit by bit. Only during recent years some literary scholars have started to employ visualization techniques in their studies.

One of them is Franco Moretti, who advocated the usage of visual representations such as graphs, maps, and trees for literature analysis (Moretti, 2005). (Vuillemot et al., 2009) suggested the usage of word clouds and self-organizing graphs and presented a tool that allows to analyze a novel interactively with respect to several properties. In (Plaisant et al., 2006) a tabular representation that is enriched with visual symbols was used to present the results of an automatic algorithm for detecting erotic statements. (Rydberg-Cox, 2011) generated social network graphs of characters in Greek tragedies, based on information taken from linguistic dependency treebanks, which permit to visualize the interactions between characters in the plays. Furthermore, scatterplot views allowed the user to search for correlations between several variables of the meta data that comes with the novels. Rohrer et al. (1998) experimented with using implicit surfaces to compare single documents with respect to the most frequent terms and to visualize a document collection.

Pixel-based visualizations come with the advantage that the documents can be analyzed at a higher resolution level. The Compus system (Fekete and Dufournaud, 2000) used dense pixel displays to visualize the structure of richly annotated XML documents of books of the $16^{th}$ century. Keim and Oelke (2007) focused more on the analysis of documents with respect to certain text properties to compare authors with respect to their writing style or to learn more about the characteristics of a literary book. The two techniques also differ from each other in terms of how structural information is encoded and how they deal with the problem of overplotting that occurs if a pixel encodes several feature values.

[2] *Cf.* proceedings of the IEEE Conference on Visual Analytics Science and Technology (IEEE VAST), http://visweek.org/.

## 3 Named Entity Recognition

*Named entity recognition* (NER) is an important supporting technology with many applications in various human language technologies. It has emerged in the context of *information extraction* (IE) and *text mining* (TM). The automatic recognition and marking-up of names (in a wide sense) and some other related kinds of information - e.g., time and measure expressions and/or terminology - has turned out to be a recurring basic requirement. Hence, NER has become core language technology of great significance to numerous applications and a wide range of techniques (Jackson and Moulinier, 2007).

In our study involving 19th century fiction, we use a slightly adapted NER system to the language used in fiction around the turn of the twentieth century (Borin and Kokkinakis, 2010). Moreover, the nature and type of named entities vary, depending on the task under investigation or the target application. In any case, *person*, *location* and *organization names* are considered 'generic'. The system we applied implements a rather fine-grained named entity taxonomy with several main named entity types and subtypes but for our case study we chose to only use the type *person* which usually incorporates people's names (forenames, surnames), groups of people, animal/pet names, mythological names, theonyms and the like. Note that we haven't performed any formal evaluation of the entity or the gender annotation in this work. In previous studies, based on data from the same source and applying the same NER-tools (Borin et al., 2007), we have shown high figures on precision and recall (96-98%) on, particularly, person recognition.

### 3.1 Gender Attribution

Current NER systems are limited to the recognition of a small set of entity types without attempting to make finer distinctions between them. The system we use goes beyond this in the sense that it attempts to also automatically determine the referential gender of all person entities. Referential gender relates linguistic expressions, both persons and groups of individuals, to "female", "male" or "gender-indefinite". This is an important constraint which contributes to better performance in subsequent language processing applications based on NER, such as anaphora resolution, by filtering-out of gender-incompatible candidates (Evans and Orasan, 2000). The approach to gender discrimination is based on applying a combination of the following heuristics:

- NER has a high accuracy in identifying person names, a large number of which are assigned gender. A pre-classified list of 16,000 common first names assigns gender to commonly used first names. This way a first distinction is already being made between entities that carry gender. The list has been acquired from various internet sites.

- Use of gender-marked pronouns in the vicinity of person entities (a simplistic form of pronoun resolution where simple decisions are made by matching a genderless person entity with a gender bearing personal pronouns, *han* 'he', *hans* 'his', *hon* 'she' and *hennes* 'her'). Also, various types of honorifics and designators, manually pre-categorized into gender groups, provide the evidence that is explored for the annotation of both animate instances but also their gender. Inherent characteristics for a large group of these designators (e.g., morphological cues), indicate biological gender. Examples of gender-bearing male designators are e.g. the nouns *baron* and *herr* 'Mr', and adjectives with suffix bearing gender, namely *-e*, such as *starke* 'strong', *hygglige* 'kind' and *gamle* 'old'; while female-bearing designators are e.g. *tant* 'aunt' and *fru* 'wife'. Gender is also captured using a simplified set of suffix matching rules, such as *-inna/innan*, *-erska/erskan* (typical suffixes for female) and *-man/mannen*, *-iker/ikern* (typical suffixes for male).

- Labeling consistency is a technique that operates over the whole annotated text. This module reviews the annotations made so far, in order to support gender attribution of unassigned cases based on unambiguous previous gender assignments. This is a simple but robust approach that does not rely on pre-compiled statistics of any kind. In order to capture such consistency we employ a two stage labeling approach. During the first stage, we note the instances of person entities with unknown gender, and search for a context where the same entity has been assigned gender (male, female) due to a gender-indicating context and for which no other occurrences of the same entity are found in the document with a different gender. If this is the case, then all occurrences of that entity are assigned the same gender throughout the document. During the second stage, the system investigates if there are any conflicting, ambiguous annotations for gender for which the local context and the supporting resources (e.g., first names' gazetteer) cannot decide the gender attribution. If this is the case and more than one possible annotation for gender is recorded, we choose the most frequently assigned gender label for the entity in question, in case of a tie we mark the gender as *unknown*.

### 3.2 Name Linking

Since the same name can be referred to in various ways, extracting named entities alone is not sufficient for many tasks. Therefore, mapping and linking multiple linguistic variations to a single referent is necessary. We apply a simplified form of co-reference resolution based on salient features and pattern matching that links (hopefully) all mentions that refer to a single person entity. Consider the aggregated occurrences for the name *O'Henny* appearing in the novel "Clownen Jac" [lb904603] (1930). All 92 occurrences of the figure *O'Henny* will be linked to the same individual since there is sufficient and reliable evidence which is based on gender match, no annotation conflicts (i.e. other individual named *Denny* or *Henny* with the same gender) and orthographic characteristics: *O'Henny* (58); *Denny* (19); *Denny O'Henny* (7); *Henny-Denny* (4); *Denny-Henny* (3); *Henny* (1).

## 4 Material

Prose fiction is just one type of textual material that has been brought into the electronic "life" using large scale digitized efforts. But it must be considered an essential source within many disciplines of humanities (history, religion, sociology, linguistics etc.) and social studies and an invaluable source for understanding the movements of society by its ability to demonstrate what forces and ideas are at work in the society of its time. Prose fiction is complex and difficult to use not only because of interpretational complexity but also because of its limited availability.

The Swedish Literature Bank, and its sister project "the 19th Century Sweden in the Mirror of Prose Fiction", aims to change this by developing a large representative corpus which mirrors society at given points in time, chronologically selected in such a way that historical comparisons can be made. A substantial part of the material is all fiction, written in the original and published separately for the first time, that appeared in Swedish starting from the year 1800 and collected during consecutive twenty year intervals. The material provides a whole century of evolution and social, aesthetic, scientific, technical, cultural, religious and philosophical change. Out of this data we selected the literary production, 13 novels, of a single author, namely Hjalmar Bergman (1883-1931). The selected novels (followed by their id) are:

- Savonarola (1909); id=lb443177
- Amourer (1910); id=lb1611717
- Hans nåds testamente (1910); id=lb1611719
- Vi Bookar, Krokar och Rothar (1912); id=lb494265
- Loewenhistorier (1913); id=lb1631349
- Falska papper (1916); id=lb1525006
- Herr von Hancken (1920); id=lb1524996
- Farmor och Vår Herre (1921); id=lb1187656
- Eros' begravning (1922); id=lb1470072
- Chefen fru Ingeborg (1924); id=lb1524995
- Flickan i frack (1925); id=lb1470073
- Kerrmans i paradiset (1927); id=lb1317426
- Clownen Jac (1930); id=lb904603

## 5 Visual Exploration of the Data

In this chapter we report on our experiences with different visualization techniques that can be employed for analyzing novels with respect to the characters involved in the plot. Besides network representations two alternative, not as well known, visualization techniques are tested. Our goal is to learn about their strengths and weaknesses with respect to the task and identify challenges that are specific for the field. We show how visualization can be used to gain insight into literary work that otherwise would be much more laborious to get.

### 5.1 Network representation

Traditionally, persons in a novel are analyzed in terms of the relations that exist between them. Obviously, graph visualizations are well suited for representing this kind of information. Figure 1 shows a person network for the novel "Eros' begravning" ('Eros' funeral') (1922). Nodes represent characters of the plot and an edge is inserted between two persons if they co-occur in at least one sentence of the novel.[3] In such a representation it is easy to identify protagonists that are connected to many other characters (e.g., *Ludwig von Battwyhl* or *Olga Willman-Janselius*). Furthermore, it is possible to see clusters of characters. Figure 1 also shows that *Casimir Brut* is the person that connects the two main groups of characters of the novel, in the sense that he introduces one group of characters to another. The thickness of an edge encodes the number of times that two names co-occur which could be regarded as the strength of the relationship. A strong connection seems to exist between *Brita Djurling* and *Ludwig von Battwyhl* but also between *Hans Hinz Faber* and *Gruber*. It is interesting to see that *Gruber* is only weakly connected with other characters of the plot but almost exclusively occurs together with *Hans Hinz Faber*. Presumably, because *Hans Hinz Faber* was the faithful servant of *Gruber*.

The example shows that network representations can provide interesting insight with respect to the relationship between different persons in the plot. However, one question that this plot cannot answer is how these relationships evolve over the course of the novel.

### 5.2 Summary Plots

Summary plots are tabular representations in which each column represents a text unit (here:

[3]Note that using co-occurrence can be just considered an approximation. More advanced methods would be needed to ensure that all and only well-established relationships between characters are extracted.

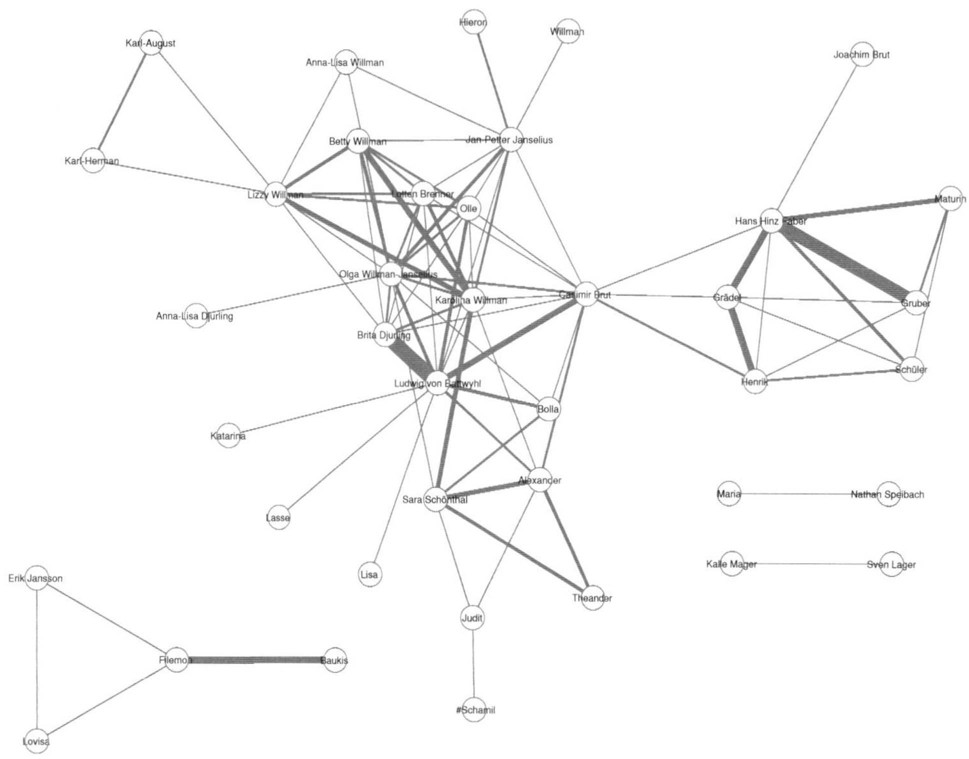


Figure 1: Network representation based on the co-occurrences of the person names in "Eros' begravning"

a chapter) and each line corresponds to a person of the novel. Table cells are colored according to the frequency of the character in the specific text unit (normalized with respect to the number of words in the chapter). The person names are sorted in descending order according to the overall frequency of the person name in the novel.

In such a heatmap-like representation it is easy to see which characters co-occur in a chapter but also how this develops in the course of the document. *Do always the same persons meet? Is there one main protagonist in the book that is almost always present or is the story line more complex in terms of characters?* Being able to answer this kind of questions provides the analyst with insight about the development of the story that would not be visible in a person network.

Figure 2 shows the summary plot for the novel "Eros' begravning" in which some interesting characteristics become apparent. For example, some person names are only mentioned in a specific chapter (see lines of *Hans Hinz Faber*, *Grädel*, *Schmil*, *Lisbeth* etc.). Besides, the chapters differ significantly with respect to the number of unique person names that are mentioned. The first and the last chapter are the ones in which most characters are mentioned whereas in the third chapter only four characters play a role.

A closer look into the text reveals that the novel consists of a "frame text", where different people meet and tell each other stories. The stories constitute chapters in the novel, and thus become a bit like short stories. The first chapter, which does not have a title, introduces a large number of people. This number of participating people then decreases during the course of the following stories (chapters), but towards the end of each chapter the discussion is returned to the overall story once again, where people are talking with each other about various things before the next story starts. Also, in the individual chapters there exist people who do not participate outside of a single chapter.

### 5.3 Literature Fingerprints

Summary plots allow literature scholars to see which characters co-occur in one chapter. However, they do not permit to analyze the usage of the person names within one chapter. In contrast to this, pixel-based visualizations avoid such ag-

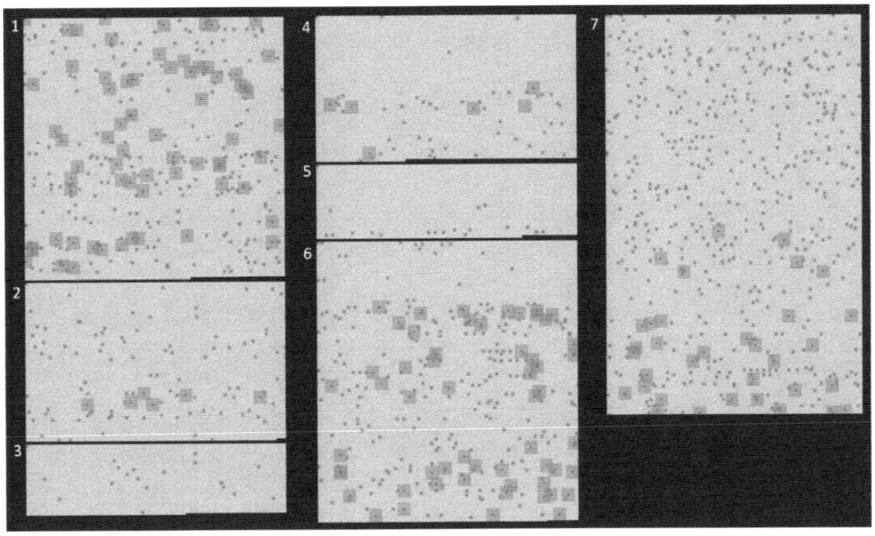


Figure 3: Literature Fingerprint for the novel "Eros' begravning". Red pixels mark mentions of the protagonist "Olga Willman-Janselius, green pixels highlight the position of other names.

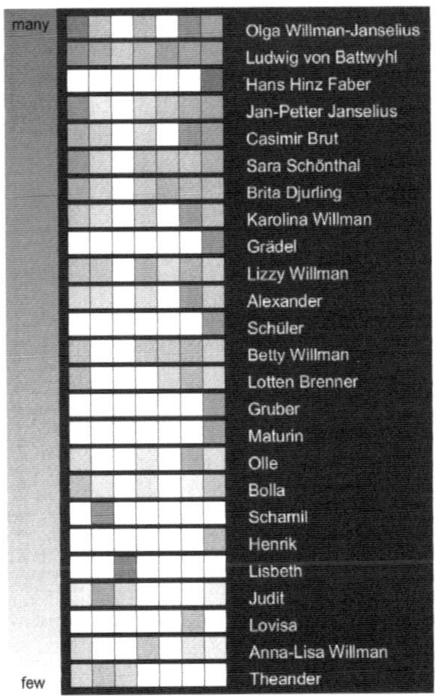


Figure 2: Summary plot for novel "Eros' begravning" ('Eros' funeral').

gregation and enable an inspection of the data on a much higher resolution level.

We use the literature fingerprinting technique (Keim and Oelke, 2007) to inspect the novel "Eros' begravning" in more detail. Each pixel represents one word. Pixels are arranged from left to right and top to bottom and are grouped according to chapters. The color of a pixel can be used to encode a value. In this case pixels were colored in red if they represent the name of the most frequent protagonist, *Olga Willman-Janselius*, and in green if another name was mentioned. The technique is scalable enough to display the whole book at this high resolution level. However, the colored pixels are sparse and would likely be lost in the sea of uncolored pixels. We therefore use semi-transparent halos around the colored pixels to increase their visual saliency. (For more visual boosting techniques for pixel-based visualizations see (Oelke et al., 2011)). In this visualization it is now possible to see where in the course of the novel the main protagonist, *Olga Willman-Janselius*, plays a role. Furthermore, it becomes obvious that there are parts in which almost no person name at all is mentioned. This is in line with the fact that the book tells several separate stories that are integrated at the end of each chapter into the overall story (see also explanation in section 5.2).

Alternatively, we also could have highlighted the positions of several names using one color per protagonist to compare their distribution. This way an analyst can learn about the relations between different characters. However, the number of different names that can be highlighted at the same time is restricted by the human ability to distinguish different colors easily (*cf.* (Ware, 2008)).

Figure 4 shows fingerprints for all 13 novels. Again each pixel represents a word but this time all words that neither are a name of a person nor of a theistic being are disregarded. This way a

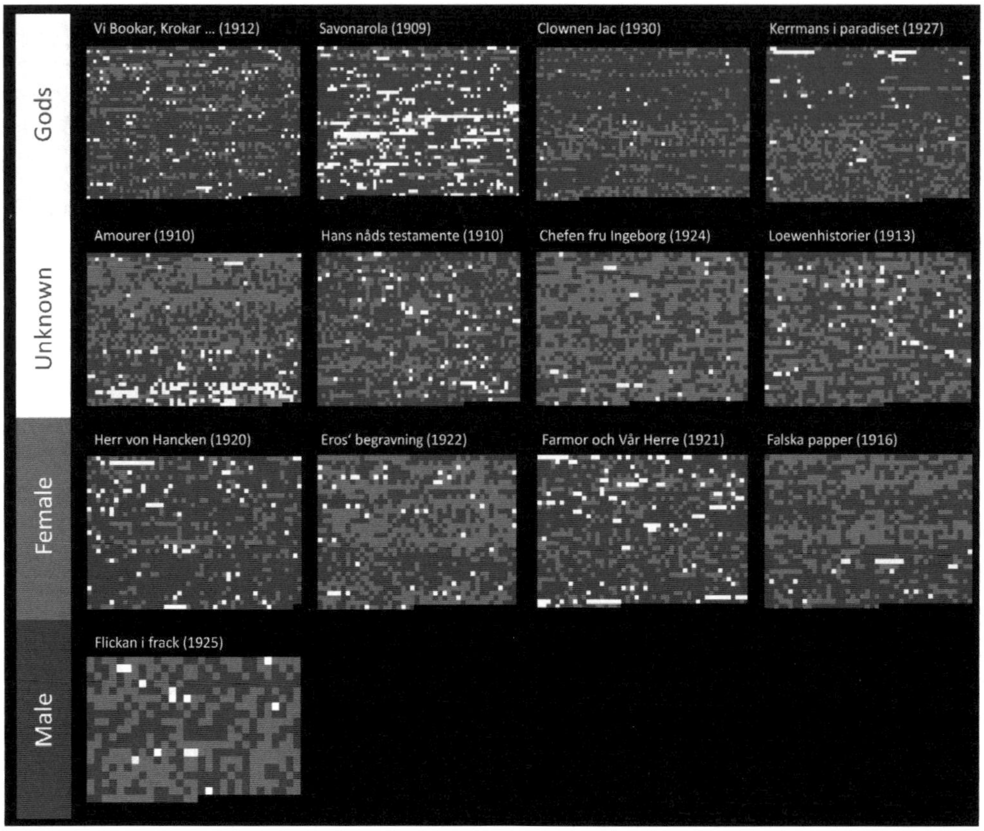


Figure 4: Fingerprints for the 13 novels. Color is used to encode the three categories male, female, gods.

focus is put on the order in which the mentions of the three categories (male, female, gods) appear. Words that the algorithm recognized as a name but could not assign to one of the categories are marked as unknown and are colored in white.

Some interesting patterns become visible in the visualization. One book (first one in the second row) sticks out because of its high number of mentions of theistic beings. "Amourer" [lb1611717] (1910) is a collection of short stories. The last story, "The False Cristoforo", varies the theme of *Christopher*, who carried Jesus Christ across the river which results in the peak of names of theistic beings that can be observed at the end of the book.

Another interesting observation is that in the beginning of the book "Kerrmans i paradiset" [lb1317426] (1927) (last one in first row), male characters are clearly dominant which is almost reversed in the book's second part. A closer look into the book reveals that this is because the book is divided into two main parts. The first part is more about prestige and position in society, i.e., social games with other men, while the second part is more personal and relates clearly to women. The summary plot of the book (Figure 5) reveals that there are not fewer male characters involved in the second part of the book but overall they are less frequently mentioned. At the same time, female characters that had in the first part of the book only a minor role become more dominant in the plot.

### 5.4 Discussion

Each of the visualization techniques that we experimented with has its strengths and weaknesses if used for the analysis of a novel with respect to its characters. Person networks come with the advantage that they can show relationships between characters. This way clusters of persons that form a group within the story become visible. In contrast to this, summary plots can only show co-occurrence within a chapter (or smaller text unit). But their strength is to show the development of the set of persons involved in the plot. In such a tabular representation it is easy to compare the in-

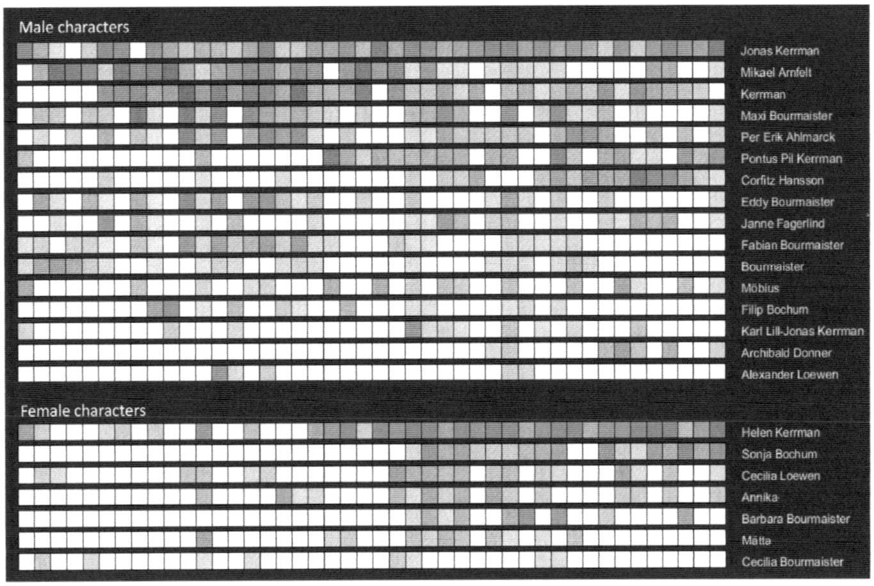


Figure 5: Summary plot for the novel "Kerrmans i paradiset". Lines are grouped according to the two categories male / female and are sorted within each category according to the overall frequency of the characters.

volvement of different characters across the document. Even more details are provided by the literature fingerprinting technique. Because the technique is very scalable, every single word can be visualized. Coloring is used to encode text properties of interest. Again, the development of the characters across a document is visible, this time even within single chapters. However, compared to the summary plot technique, fewer person names can be distinguished.

Obviously, a combination of the three techniques is advisable for analyzing novels with respect to the persons involved. But our comparison of the three techniques also allows us to identify a missing type of visualization: One that is able to show the development of the story in terms of the characters involved and at the same time is able to display their relationships.
Furthermore, the techniques lead to interesting insight but these newly generated hypotheses need to be checked in the text. A tighter integration of the actual text source into the visualization tools could therefore be a valuable extension.

## 6 Conclusions

The combination of robust text analysis with visual analytics brings a new set of tools to literature analysis, provides powerful insights on document collections, and advances our understanding of the evolution of human behavior, society, technological advancement and cultural trends. As a matter of fact, (Michel, 2010), introduced the term "Culturomics", i.e. the application of high-throughput data collection, digital book archives and the like, and analysis to the study of human culture and we believe that novel insights towards this direction can be gained by combining such technologies. In this paper we have shown that quantifiable data such as (person) names can be identified, extracted, and visualized in novel ways.

In the future we intend to further extend the capabilities for visual literature analysis. One research goal is the development of a visualization technique that allows to investigate the development of a story across a novel but at the same time shows the relationships between the characters. Furthermore, we believe that interactive visual analysis tools (instead of static visualizations) open up additional possibilities for literature scholars to explore the large volumes of digitized literary collections that are nowadays available.

## Acknowledgments

This work was supported by the Zukunftskolleg of the University of Konstanz and the Centre of Language Technology in Gothenburg.

## References


Yevgeni Berzak, Michal Richter, Carsten Ehrler and Todd Shore. 2011. Information Retrieval and Visualization for the Historical Domain. *Language Technology for Cultural Heritage - Theory and Applications of Natural Language Processing.* Pp. 197–212. Springer.

Lars Borin and Dimitrios Kokkinakis. 2010. Literary Onomastics and Language Technology. *Literary Education and Digital Learning. Methods and Technologies for Humanities Studies.* Pp. 53–78. IGI Global.

Lars Borin, Dimitrios Kokkinakis and Leif-Jran Olsson. 2007. Naming the past: Named entity and animacy recognition in 19th century Swedish literature. *Proceedings of the ACL Workshop: Language Technology for Cultural Heritage Data (LaTeCh).* Prague. Pp. 1–8.

Christopher S. Butler. 1992. *Computers and Written Texts.* Basil Blackwell.

Richard Evans and Constantin Orasan. 2000. Improving anaphora resolution by identifying animate entities in texts. *Proceedings of the Discourse Anaphora and Anaphor Resolution Colloquium (DAARC) 2000.* Lancaster, UK. Pp. 154–162.

Jean-Daniel Fekete and Nicole Dufournaud. 2000. Compus: visualization and analysis of structured documents for understanding social life in the 16th century. *Proceedings of the fifth ACM conference on Digital libraries.* San Antonio, Texas, United States. Pp. 47–55, ACM.

Julia Flanders, Syd Bauman, Paul Caton and Mavis Cournane. 1998. Names proper and improper: Applying the TEI to the classification of proper nouns. *Computers and the Humanities.* 31(4), pp. 285–300.

Peter Jackson and Isabelle Moulinier. 2007. *Natural language processing for online applications: Text retrieval, extraction and categorization.* Amsterdam: John Benjamins.

Patrick Juola. 2008. Killer applications in digital humanities. *Literary and Linguistic Computing.* 23(1): 73–83.

Daniel A. Keim and Daniela Oelke. 2007. Literature Fingerprinting: A New Method for Visual Literary Analysis. *Proceedings of the IEEE Symposium on Visual Analytics Science and Technology (VAST).* Pp. 115–122.

Jean-Baptiste Michel *et al.* 2010. Quantitative Analysis of Culture Using Millions of Digitized Books. *Science* 331 (6014): 176. "http://www.sciencemag.org/content/early/2010/12/15/science.1199644".

Franco Moretti. 2005. *Graphs, maps, trees: abstract models for a literary history.* R. R. Donnelley & Sons.

Nature Methods. 2010. Visualizing biological data. *Supplement to Nature Publishing Group journals.* 7 (3s): S1-S68.

Daniela Oelke, Halldor Janetzko, Svenja Simon, Klaus Neuhaus and Daniel A. Keim. 2011. Visual Boosting in Pixel-based Visualizations. *Computer Graphics Forum.* 30 (3): 871-880.

Catherine Plaisant, James Rose, Bei Yu, Loretta Auvil, Matthew G. Kirschenbaum, Martha Nell Smith, Tanya Clement and Greg Lord. 2006. Exploring erotics in Emily Dickinson's correspondence with text mining and visual interfaces. *Proceedings of the 6th ACM/IEEE-CS joint conference on Digital libraries.* Pp. 141-150, ACM.

Randall M. Rohrer, David S. Ebert, and John L. Sibert. 1998. The Shape of Shakespeare: Visualizing Text using Implicit Surfaces. *Proceedings of the 1998 IEEE Symposium on Information Visualization.* Pp. 121-129.

Jeff Rydberg-Cox. 2011. Social Networks and the Language of Greek Tragedy. *Journal of the Chicago Colloquium on Digital Humanities and Computer Science.* 1(3): 1-11.

Kathryn Schulz. 2011. The Mechanic Muse - What Is Distant Reading? The New York Times - Sunday Book Review. Page BR14. "http://www.nytimes.com/2011/06/26/books/review/the-mechanic-muse-what-is-distant-reading.html".

James J. Thomas and Kristin A. Cook. 2005. *Illuminating the Path: The Research and Development Agenda for Visual Analytics.* National Visualization and Analytics Center.

Romain Vuillemot, Tanya Clement, Catherine Plaisant and Amit Kumar. 2009. What's Being Said Near "Martha"? Exploring Name Entities in Literary Text Collections. *Proceedings of the IEEE Symposium on Visual Analytics Science and Technology (VAST).* Atlantic City, New Jersey, USA. Pp. 107–114.

Colin Ware. 2008. *Visual Thinking for Design.* Morgan Kaufmann.

# Distributional techniques for philosophical enquiry


**Aurélie Herbelot**
Institut für Linguistik
Universität Potsdam
Karl-Liebknecht-Str. 24-25
14476 Golm, Germany
aurelie.herbelot@cantab.net

**Eva von Redecker**
Institut für Philosophie
Humboldt Universität
Unter den Linden 6
10099 Berlin, Germany
redeckee@hu-berlin.de

**Johanna Müller**
Institut für Philosophie
Humboldt Universität
Unter den Linden 6
10099 Berlin, Germany
johannammueller@gmail.com



## Abstract

This paper illustrates the use of distributional techniques, as investigated in computational semantics, for supplying data from large-scale corpora to areas of the humanities which focus on the analysis of concepts. We suggest that the distributional notion of 'characteristic context' can be seen as evidence for some representative tendencies of general discourse. We present a case study where distributional data is used by philosophers working in the areas of gender studies and intersectionality as confirmation of certain trends described in previous work. Further, we highlight that different models of phrasal distributions can be compared to support the claim of intersectionality theory that 'there is more to a phrase than the intersection of its parts'.


## 1 Introduction

Research in the social sciences rely heavily on linguistic analysis. Since what came to be called the 'linguistic turn' (Rorty, 1967) researchers across all humanities subjects have been highly aware of the fact that our access to the world, let alone cultural artefacts, is mediated by language and cast in our conceptual scheme.

Guided by the theory originating in Wittgenstein's *Philosophical Investigations* (1953), one of the basic assumptions in contemporary analytic philosophy is now that the meaning of words is given by their usage in ordinary language. Conceptual analysis, i.e. the process of making explicit the rules that guide the applicability of a certain term, consequently forms a major occupation of the philosophical profession. The method exemplified by the French philosopher Michel Foucault – discourse analysis – has become paradigmatic in the social sciences and cultural studies and constitutes a diachronic, historical version of the linguistic turn. One of the fundamental assumptions of this approach is that different eras produce different frameworks (or 'episteme' in Foucault's terminology; see Foucault 1970) for understanding reality. Such frameworks manifest themselves as discursive patterns or specific formulations. According to Foucault, social power and the silencing of deviating utterances guarantee the temporary stability of a particular social regime. A similar methodology was pursued by the 'Cambridge School' of political theorists and historians, who tried to trace back the emergence of concepts like 'state' or 'liberty' not only to the ideas of a few canonical thinkers but to the ordinary use of those terms at the time (hence this approach is called 'contextualism', see Pocock 1975; Skinner 1998).

So far, such research has relied both on extensive manual work and on linguistic introspection. Manual methods, however, have clear drawbacks: they are time-consuming, expensive and likely to introduce bias in the data. This paper suggests that distributional techniques, as used in computational lexical semantics, may hold the key to automating the process of discourse analysis just described. We present a case study in philosophy, where two standard problems (the analysis of power in gender structures and the issue of so-called *intersectionality*) are reviewed in the light of distributional data. Not only do the produced distributions offer a rational way to highlight characteristic relationships between concepts, using an amount of data far greater than what could be annotated manually, but we show that building on the relatively recent and novel research in composing distributions (Clark and Pulman, 2007), we can computationally illustrate the main thesis advocated by researchers on intersectionality.

This paper has a slightly unconventional format. We hope to exemplify a certain type of possible collaboration between computational linguistics and the humanities, which is less about providing an application to solve a particular problem than about drawing parallels between certain linguistic representations, known to have certain properties, and humanities-based theories. We felt that a fair amount of philosophical background was needed to show the relevance of our system's data to the particular type of investigation presented here. Therefore, a comprehensive philosophical introduction is given in §2. We then describe the system and corpus underpinning our research (§3 and 4) and discuss the theoretical aspects of lexical composition from a computational point of view, drawing parallels with the philosophical theory of intersectionality. Sections 5 and 6 discuss the worth of the data from a philosophical point of view.

## 2 Two philosophical problems

### 2.1 Gender and power

For a feminist philosopher, as for many people working in critical theory, the aim of research is twofold. First, to understand a given social structure, as for example the dynamics of gender relations and identities; second, to transform that structure towards greater freedom and equality. From its formation as an academic discipline in the second half of the 20th century onwards, one of the main concerns of feminist theory has been to show how social and institutional (man-made) factors have shaped what we are sometimes inclined to see as 'normal' or 'natural' gender identities. This approach is called social constructivism, because it ascribes the causal role for how gender identities emerge to processes of social construction. A prototypical example of this viewpoint, Simone de Beauvoir's famous claim that *one is not born a woman but becomes one* (Beauvoir, 1949) led to the distinction between biological 'sex' and social 'gender'. Such work has created an interest in the historical contingencies which decide what counts as a properly masculine or feminine identity. But while competing biologistic explanations of gender differences naturally have something they can point to (neurones, genes, or anatomy) social constructivist theories have sometimes lacked hard evidence for their claims. As a result, there has been a constant recurrence of theories claiming one natural cause for all aspects of gendered behaviour – and this, despite the fact that every single one has been proved wrong by the scientific community (Fine, 2010).

This state of affairs delineates a desideratum for feminist philosophy: giving more evidence of the cultural factors which instill gendered behaviour and associations in humans. While a lot of the cultural information concerning gender is visual (cinema, magazine covers, advertisement, etc), and the ways to initiating people into specific codes of gendered behavior can be non-verbal, the content of our notions of gender are vastly represented in text. Following this insight, Simone de Beauvoir reviewed a corpus of five modern novels to extract the characteristic aspects of what she coined the 'condition feminine' (Beauvoir, 1949). More recently, Judith Butler (1990) tried to explain how the use of certain concepts – gender, sex, desire, sexual practice – and associated notions were consolidating the dominant, binary distinction between masculinity and femininity.

The studies just mentioned, though central to their field, can always be met with suspicion. Objections such as *This is not how I use the word* or *You simply looked at books that distorted the understanding of the phenomenon in question* can only be met on the grounds of large-scale data. As a result, there have been attempts in historical research to produce statistical databases on gendered distributions. Hausen (1976), for example, focused on the turn of the 18th century in Germany, when a particular modern bourgeois understanding of gender roles is said to have emerged together with a new organisation of labour. However, the manual tasks involved in preparing such data are time-consuming and tedious and consequently, this type of work still has a limited coverage. We want to argue in this paper that entrusting the production of such resources to computational corpus linguistics would a) provide the ongoing philosophical investigation with an appropriate amount of data and b) help overcome the issues linked to the selective nature of the sources a human reader might choose as relevant.

### 2.2 Intersectionality

Coined by the legal scientist Kimberlé Crenshaw (1991), the term **intersectionality** has spread into the humanites and social sciences as a perspective which has widened the scope of research on inequality and oppression within social contexts.

Scientists working with the intersectional perspective claim that the combination (intersection) of various forms of inequality (for example being black in a white dominated environment or being a women in an environment dominated by men) makes a qualitative difference not only to the self-perception/identity of social actors, but also to the way they are addressed through politics, legislation and other instiutions (Ngan-Ling Chow, 2011).

The founding case out of which Kimberlé Crenshaw developed the concept of intersectionality was a law suit that black women filed against the hiring policy of General Motors. Within the traditionally race and gender segregated automobile industry, women were only allowed to work in customer service or other office jobs while African-Americans were confined to factory work. As a consequence, African-American women faced the problem of being denied both office jobs and factory work. The women filed a lawsuit for discrimination. But the case was dismissed on the grounds that the plaintiffs hadn't been able to proof that they had been discriminated for either racial or sexist reasons. This case demonstrated our general additive understanding of discrimination: we act against sexism and we act against racism but we fail to address cases where they interact. The court was unable to take this interaction into account and Crenshaw made the case for a reform of the US anti-discrimination-law, which was based on the situation of white women in gender-dependent cases and of men in race-dependent cases.

So the aim of intersectionality is to localise and make visible discrimination that traditional thought cannot conceive of, in particular where various forms of oppression or inequality overlap. The claim is that social categories can only be explained in relation to other categories that define us as social beings within a society. For instance, what it means to be in the situation of a black woman can only be gauged in relation to the political, cultural, socio-economic, religious, etc. background of that woman, and not with respect to being a woman or being a person of colour in isolation. Indeed, these different factors can override, exacerbate, conflict with each other, or simply run in parallel when they come to interact. Additionally, intersectionality also reminds us that the meaning of social categories also depends on historical eras. This proliferation of factors increases the complexity a researcher is confronted with to a point where it is doubtful whether the intersectional perspective can be transformed into a manageable methodology at all. Dealing with this level of complexity using automatically produced data might be of help on two levels:

1. the synchronic level, at which the intersectionality researcher seeks to grasp the qualitative differences between the concepts of, say, woman and black woman.

2. the diachronic level, at which historians working with intersectionality research conceptual change over texts from various eras.

In this work, we concentrate on the conceptual aspects of the synchronic level. In what follows, we will attempt to show that the intersectional approach can indeed be illustrated by the linguistic data obtained from a large contemporary corpus.

## 3 A distributional semantics system

### 3.1 Distributional semantics

Presented as a complement to model-theoretic semantics, distributional semantics aims to represent lexical meaning as a function of the contexts in which a given word appears (Wittgenstein, 1953; see also Harris, 1954, credited with the 'distributional hypothesis' which states that words which are similar in meaning occur in similar contexts).

Following this idea, some work in computational linguistics (starting with Harper, 1965) has been devoted to building and evaluating models which represent words as **distributions**, i.e., vectors in a multidimensional space where each dimension corresponds to a potential context for a lexical item (Curran, 2003). The notion of context itself has been studied to try and determine which representations work best for various tasks.

Word windows (Lund and Burgess, 1996), dependencies (Padó and Lapata, 2007) and syntactic relations (Grefenstette, 1994) have been proposed.

In our work, we use as context the words appearing in the same sentence as the query. This simple model is attractive from the point of view of using distributional techniques across the wide range of texts considered by humanities researchers. It ensures that a corpus is processable as long as it is digitalised – regardless of the language it is written in and the era it belongs to. Given that resources for parsing rare languages and older states of modern languages are still scarce, the word-based model has the advantage of flexibility.

Another issue in producing distributions relates to weighing the various dimensions. A number of possibilities have been suggested. Binary models attribute a weight of 1 to a context if it cooccurs at least once with the term that the distribution must represent, and 0 otherwise. Frequency-based models use as weights the number of cooccurrences of a particular context with the term under consideration. More complex models use functions like mutual information, which attempt to represent how 'characteristic' a particular context is for the term rather than how 'frequent' it is in conjunction with that term. The notion of a characteristic context is particularly important to us, as we wish to provide conceptual representations (distributions) which mirror what a 'standard' individual would associate with a given word. To achieve this, frequency models are not sufficient. Words like *do, also, new*, etc co-occur with many terms but are in no meaningful relation with those terms. Instead, we want to choose a function which gives high weights to contexts that appear frequently with the term to be modelled and not very frequently with other terms. By doing this, we will have a way to describe salient associations for a particular concept. In §3.3, we will spell out such a function, borrowed from Mitchell and Lapata (2010).

### 3.2 Intersectionality in linguistic terms

It has been suggested that in order to integrate distributional semantics with model theoretic formalisms, methods should be found to compose the distributions of single words (Clark and Pulman, 2007). It is clear that the representation of *carnivorous mammal* in formal semantics can be written as $\text{carnivorous}'(x) \wedge \text{mammal}'(x)$ but it is less clear how the lexical semantics of the phrase should be described in distributional terms.

The work done so far on distributional compositionality has focused on finding equivalents for the well-known formal semantics notion of intersection. All models assume that the intersective composition of two elements should return a distribution, i.e. a lexical meaning, which is made of the individual distributions, or meanings, of those elements. But there are differences in how those models are evaluated. Two categories can be drawn: models designed to emulate the distribution of the resulting phrase itself, as it would be observed given a large enough corpus (Guevara, 2010 and 2011; Baroni and Zamparelli, 2010), and those which only focus on the composition operation and try to produce an adequate representation of the semantic intersection of the phrase's components, independently from the phrasal distribution (Mitchell and Lapata, 2010; Grefenstette and Sadrzadeh, 2011). The former, which we will refer to as **phrasal models** are trained and evaluated against phrases' distributions while the latter, **intersective models**, call for task-based evaluations (for instance, similarity ratings: see Mitchell and Lapata, 2010).

We argue that phrasal and intersective models are bound to produce different aspects of meaning. Consider, for instance, the phrase *big city*. Principles of semantic intersection tell us that a big city is a city which is big. This is a correct statement and one which should come out of the composition of the *big* distribution and the *city* distribution[1]. But arguably, there is more to the meaning of the phrase (see Partee, 1994, for a discussion of non-intersective adjectival phrases). We expect people to readily associate concepts like *loud, underground, light, show, crowd* to the idea of a big city. Our hypothesis is that this 'extra' (non-intersective) meaning can be clearly observed in **phrasal distributions** while it is, in some sense, 'hidden' in distributions which are the result of a purely intersective operation (because the entire distributions of the two components are used, and not just the contexts relevant to the particular association of *big* and *city*).

This observation, made at the linguistic level,

[1]For the sake of this argument, we will ignore the suggestion that the gradable adjective might affect the intersective status of the phrase

is also the foundation of intersectionality theory. The argument, presented in Section 2, is that the prejudices attached to black women, for instance, (that is, the way that the concept *black woman* is understood and used) are different from the simple combination of the prejudices attached to black people and women separately. So although it is correct to say that a black woman is a woman who is black (in the relevant sense of *black*), the concept reaches further.

If the basic tenet of intersectionality theory holds, and if we accept that distributions are a valuable approximation of lexical meaning, we would expect that the **phrasal distribution** of, say, *black woman* would significantly differ from its **compositional distribution**. Further, such a significant difference would also have linguistic relevance, as it would indicate the need to take phrasal distributions into account when 'computing meaning' via distributional techniques. Both phrasal models and intersective models could be said to contribute to a complete and accurate representation.

In Section 6, we will make a first step in investigating this issue by thoroughly analysing the phrasal and compositional distributions of *black woman*.

### 3.3 System description

The two systems we use in this paper have the same basis. They produce a distribution for a phrase based on a raw Wikipedia[2] snapshot, preprocessed to remove the wiki markup (Flickinger et al, 2010). Distributions are vectors in a space $S$ made of 10000 dimensions which correspond to the 10000 most frequent words in the corpus. The distribution of a word or phrase in the corpus is taken to be the collection of all words that co-occur with that word or phrase within a single sentence (we use a list of stop words to discard function words, etc). The weight of each co-occurring term in the distribution is given by a function borrowed from Mitchell and Lapata (2010):

$$w_i(t) = \frac{p(c_i|t)}{p(c_i)} = \frac{freq_{c_i,t} * freq_{all}}{freq_t * freq_{c_i}} \quad (1)$$

where $w_i(t)$ is the weight of word $t$ for dimension $i$, $freq_{c_i,t}$ is the count of the co-occurrences of a context word $c_i$ with $t$, $freq_{all}$ is the total number of words in the corpus, $freq_t$ and $freq_{c_i}$ are respectively $t$ and $c_i$'s frequencies in the corpus.

We choose an intersective model based on multiplication, as this operation has been shown to give excellent results in previous experiments (Erk and Padó, 2008; Mitchell and Lapata, 2010): the distributions of the two components of the phrase are multiplied in a point-wise fashion to give the final distribution. This corresponds to the model $\mathbf{p}=\mathbf{u}\odot\mathbf{v}$ of Mitchell and Lapata.

As for the phrasal model, the final distribution is simply the distribution obtained from looking at the co-occurrences for the phrase itself.

The data passed on to the philosophers for further consideration takes the form of a list of the 100 most 'characteristic' contexts for the query, that is, the 100 words with heighest weights in the distribution, filtered as described in §3.3.1.

#### 3.3.1 Filtering the results

One potential issue with our implementation is that words belonging to frequent named entities end up in the top characteristic contexts for the query. So for instance, *wonder* is one of the most characteristic contexts for *woman* because of the comic character *Wonder Woman*. Arguably, such contexts should only be retrieved if they are as significant in their 'non-name' form as in their named entity form (e.g. if the string *wonder woman* was significantly more frequent than *Wonder Woman*, there would be a case for retaining it in the results). We filter the relevant named entities out using the following heuristic:

1. We call the query $q$ and its capitalised version $Q$. Let $c_1...c_n$ be the top characteristic contexts for $q$ and $C_1...C_n$ their capitalised equivalent.

2. For each context $c_k$ in $c_1...c_n$:

   (a) We compute the corpus frequencies of the patterns $qc_k$, $c_kq$, $qwc_k$ and $c_kwq$, where $w$ is an intervening word. $s_k$ is the sum of those frequencies.

   (b) Similarly, we compute the corpus frequencies of the patterns $QC_k$, $C_kQ$, $QwC_k$ and $C_kwQ$, where $w$ is an intervening word. $S_k$ is the sum of those frequencies.

[2]http://www.wikipedia.org/

(c) $r$ is the ratio $S_k/s_k$. If $r$ is over a certain threshold $t$, we remove $c_k$ from the characteristic contexts list.

In our experiments, we use $t = 0.6$. This threshold allows us to successfully remove many spurious contexts. For example, *wonder* and *spider* are deleted from the results for *woman* (among others) and *isle*[3], *elephant* and *iron* from the results for *man*.

## 4 The corpus

The number of experiments that can be devised using distributional techniques is only limited by the number of digitalised corpora available to researchers in the humanities. It is easy to imagine a range of comparative studies showing the conceptual differences highlighted by the use of a word or phrase at various times, in various countries, or in various communities. The aim of this study is to analyse the discursive use of some concepts over a fairly large sample. We chose the English Wikipedia[4] as our corpus because of its size and because of its large contributor base (around 34,000 'active editors' in December 2011[5]). Wikipedia's encyclopedic content also makes it less explicitly biased than raw Internet text, although we have to be aware of implicit bias: most of Wikipedia's contributors are male and the encyclopedia's content is heavily skewed towards items of popular culture (Cohen, 2011). The latter point is unproblematic as long as it is acknowledged in the discussion of the results.

In the next two sections, we analyse the distributions obtained for the phrases *man*, *woman*, *black woman* and *Asian woman*. It is worth mentioning that more data was extracted from our corpus, which, due to space constraints, we will not discuss here. The broad claims made with respect to the above four noun phrases, however, are consistent with the rest of our observations.

## 5 Discussing gender

This section discusses the produced distributions from the perspective of gender theory. The aim of the discussion is to illustrate the type of information that may be relevant for discourse analysis. Note that it follows the philosophical methodology highlighted in Haslanger (2005) for conceptual analysis.

Table 1 shows the most characteristic contexts for *woman* and *man*, after filtering. There are three levels on which the data discussed here could be usefully interpreted within feminist research – the conceptual, the constructivist and the deconstructivist. We will concentrate on the first two.

In recent years a strong trend in Gender Studies has emphasised that our investigations shouldn't repeat the historical bias which regards men as 'universal' (or default) and women as 'particular', as a specific 'other' to be investigated (Honegger, 1991). An advantage of our automatically produced data is that it returns just as much material to focus on the cultural fabrication of masculinity as on that of femininity. The male position proves to indeed carry a broader variety of seemingly non-gendered contexts, for instance, *wise, innocent, sin, fat, courage, salvation, genius, worthy* and *rescued* – none of which is characteristic of *woman*. But what is most striking is the strong occurrence of military contexts. We find *enlisted* at the top of the list, followed by *wounded, IRA, officers, militia, regiments, garrison, platoons, casualties, recruits* and diverse military ranks. It is sometimes unclear what counts as 'military-related' (see *killing*, *brave*). We would have to go back to the original text to investigate this. But we see here very clearly how attributes that rank high when it comes to defining stereotypical masculinity and might be thought as 'general' characteristics clearly owe their prominence to the military cluster. The characteristic contexts list seems to give distilled evidence to what has as yet still only been partly analyzed in socio-historical research, namely how the norms of masculinity are to a large extent of military descent (for the German context see Frevert, 2001). *Brave, angry, courage, cruel* are all things that Wikipedia – just like popular imagination – won't associate with women.

The meaning of *woman* seems to revolve around the three interrelated clusters of reproduction, sex and love. *Pregnant* and *pregnancy* rank very high, as well as reproduction-related terms such as *abortion, children* and *mothers*. There are more sexual terms (*sexually, sexual, sexual-*

[3]As in *Isle of Man*

[4]http://en.wikipedia.org/wiki/Main_Page

[5]http://stats.wikimedia.org/EN/SummaryEN.htm

| Woman | Man |
|---|---|
| women, woman, pregnant, feminist, abortion, womens, men, husbands, elderly, pregnancy, sexually, rape, breast, gender, equality, minorities, lesbian, wives, beautiful, attractive, pornography, dressed, sexual, marry, sexuality, dress, est., wear, young, sex, african-american, naked, comfort, homosexual, discrimination, priesthood, womens, violence, loved, children, clothes, man, male, marriages, hair, mysterious, wearing, homeless, loves, boyfriend, wore, her., ladies, mistress, lover, attitudes, hiv, advancement, relationships, homosexuality, wealthy, mothers, worn, murdered, ordained, mortal, unnamed, girls, depicts, slavery, lonely, female, equal, cancer, goddess, roles, abuse, kidnapped, priests, portrayal, witch, divorce, screening, clothing, murders, husband, romantic, forbidden, loose, excluded | men, man, enlisted, women, wise, homosexual, wounded, gay, woman, dressed, young, elderly, ira, homeless, wives, brave, angry, officers, marry, marched, sexually, wealthy, killed, wounds, innocent, militia, homosexuality, mans, mysterious, god, tin, elves, mortal, ladies, wearing, priesthood, sin, con, courage, fat, equality, numbering, regiments, garrison, numbered, brotherhood, murdered, rape, lonely, platoon, casualties, knew, recruits, reinforcements, recruited, blind, loved, sexual, sex, thousand, mask, clothes, salvation, commanded, loves, lover, sick, detachment, genius, cruel, gender, killing, col., lt., drunk, worthy, tall, flank, convicted, surrendered, contingent, rescued, naked |

Table 1: Most characteristic contexts for *woman* and *man*, after filtering

*ity, sex*) in the characteristic list for *woman* and mentions of *loved, loves, lover* are higher up than in the results obtained for *man*. Further, a variety of terms, mostly absent from the *man* list, create a close link between femininity and relationality: *husband(s), marriage* (though, further down, *divorce* comes up too), *boyfriend* and *relationships*. While *beautiful, attractive, comfort* and *romantic* might at least suggest that positive sentiments are attached to the inbuilt feminine relationality, another set of female contexts highlights the very vulnerability inscribed in the cluster around intimacy: *rape, pornography, violence, slavery, abuse, kidnapped* quantitatively capture a correlation between relationality, sexuality and violence which characterises the use of the lexeme *woman*.

Another set of exclusively feminine concepts which at first sight seem to create interesting singular contexts – *breast, comfort, hair, HIV, cancer* – are united by reference to a physicality that seems, apart from the wounds apparently contracted in war, peculiarly absent in man. Such clustering sheds light on the fact that certain associations 'stick' to women and not to men. Though it takes two to marry or divorce and have children, those exclusively form contexts for woman. Most dramatically, this can be observed when it comes to rape. Though the majority of cases imply a male perpetrator, *rape* is very high up, in 12th position, in the female list (that is before any mention of love), while it is returned as characteristic of men only to the extent that *loneliness* or *brotherhood* are, at rank 49.

These observations highlight the kind of associations implicitly present in discursive data – whether retrieved by machines or humans. We do not learn how matters are 'in fact' but simply integrate the linguistic patterns most characteristic for a certain phenomenon. This, again, does have tremendous effects on reality – so-called 'constructive' effects. Indeed, when it comes to phenomena that touch on human self-understanding, discourse implies more than a mirror of meaning. It partakes in the making of real identities. It provides the material people craft their self-understanding from and model their behavior after. It is this very effect of our characteristic usage of language which prompts social philosophers to ascribe 'power' to language.

## 6 Discussing intersectionality

Table 2 shows the most characteristic contexts for the phrase *black woman* after filtering, as given by the intersective and phrasal models. We should point out that the phrase *black*

| Multiplicative model | Phrasal model |
|---|---|
| stripes, makeup, pepper, hole, racial, white, woman, spots, races, women, whites, holes, colours, belt, shirt, african-american, pale, yellow, wears, powder, coloured, wear, wore, colour, dressed, racism, leather, colors, hair, colored, trim, shorts, silk, throat, patch, jacket, dress, metal, scarlet, worn, grey, wearing, shoes, purple, native, gray, breast, slaves, color, vein, tail, hat, painted, uniforms, collar, dark, coat, fur, olive, bear, boots, paint, red, lined, canadiens, predominantly, slavery | racism, feminist, women's, slavery, negro, ideology, tyler, filmmaker, african-american, ain't, elderly, whites, nursing, patricia, abbott, gloria, freeman, terrestrial, shirley, profession, julia, abortion, diane, possibilities, argues, reunion, hiv, blacks, inability, indies, sexually, giuseppe, perry, vince, portraits, prevention, beacon, gender, attractive, tucker, fountain, riley, beck, comfortable, stern, paradise, twist, anthology, brave, protective, lesbian, domestic, feared, breast, collective, barbara, liberation, racial, rosa, riot, aunt, equality, rape, lawyers, playwright, white, argued, documentary, carol, isn't, experiences, witch, men, spoke, slaves, depicted, teenage, photos, resident, lifestyle, aids, commons, slave, freedom, exploitation, clerk, tired, romantic, harlem, celebrate, quran, interred, stargate, alvin, ada, katherine, immense |

Table 2: Most characteristic contexts for *black woman*. Multiplicative and phrasal model, after filtering

*woman/women* only occurs 384 times in our corpus, so the vector obtained through the phrasal model suffers from some data sparsity problems.[6] In particular, overall infrequent events are given high weights by our algorithm, resulting in a relatively high number of surnames being present in the produced vector. Despite this issue, a number of observations can be made, which agree with both our linguistic and philosophical expectations.

We first considered to what extent the phrasal and multiplicative models emphasised the characteristics already present in their components'distributions. We found that the top contexts for the phrasal distribution of *black woman* only overlap 17 times with the top contexts of *woman* and 9 times with the top contexts for *black*. The multiplicative model produces an overlap of only 12 items with *woman* but 64 with *black*.[7] This highlights a large conceptual difference between the phrase seen as a single entity and its components. In contrast, the composition of the constituents via the multiplicative model returns a distribution fairly close to the distribution of those constituents.

We looked next at the characteristic contexts that were particular to each representation. We found that the phrasal model vector presents 73 terms which are absent from the top contexts for *black* and *woman*. In contrast, none of the terms in the top contexts of the multiplied vector is specific to the composed phrase: all of them are either highly characteristic of *black* or *woman* (e.g. *racial, African-American* and *breast, dress*).[8] This indicates that the salient contexts for the phrase are very different from the associations commonly made with its constituents.

Finally, we observed that the vector obtained through the phrasal model only overlaps 8 times with the composed one. The shared words are *racial, white, whites, African-American, racism, breast, slaves* and *slavery*. Again, we can conclude from this that the two representations capture very different aspect of meaning, although they both retrieve some high-level associations with the concept of race and race-related history.

[6]We should add that this small number of occurrences is in itself significant, and mirrors problems of social marginalisation. We note that the phrase *African-American woman/women* is even sparser, with 236 occurrences in our corpus.

[7]The weights in the *black* vector clearly override those from the *woman* vector. Mitchell and Lapata (2010) discuss possible improvements to the multiplicative model which involve putting a positive weight on the noun component when performing the composition.

[8]Because our system does not perform any sense disambiguation, we return contexts such as *pepper* for *black pepper*, *hole* for *black hole*, etc.

From the point of view of intersectionality, our results confirm the basic claim of the theory: there are cases where the discourse on individuals belonging to two different social groups is radically different than the discourse pertaining to those social groups taken separately.

In addition, the data supports further arguments made by intersectionality researchers. In particular, comparing the distributions for *woman*, *black woman* and *Asian woman*[9] shows that colour or ethnicity has a crucial impact on how women are represented. Looking at *woman*, the word *rape* appears at position 12, but it appears much further down the list in *black woman* and not at all in *Asian woman*. At the same time the word *nursing* is only associated with black women while *pornography* hits position number 3, shortly followed by *exotic* and *passive* when we look at *Asian woman*. These three words do not occur in the top contexts for *woman* or *black woman*. This indicates that we are getting results concerning sexuality which depend on 'ethnical' connotation: white women are shown as victims of abuse (*rape*), black women as responsible for *nursing*, and Asian women represented as *passive* and objects of *pornography*.

Just looking at this data (and there would be a lot more to analyse) we can find a connection with what the latest historical research working with intersectionality has brought to light: historians have shown that the historical discourse on prostitution has increased and reinforced racist stereotypes and prejudices. Whyte (2012) shows, (looking at the 'white slavery' panic of the early twentieth century which is a key point in the history of prostitution) that the construction of the white, innocent victim of prostitution is central to the creation of the myth of the 'white slavery' in many ways and that it has shaped the construction and understanding of contemporary human trafficking. The broader history of slavery (particularly in the North American context) forms the backdrop for 'writing out' women of colour as victims of sexual violence. This is appropriately illustrated by our data.

[9]Due to space constraints, we are not showing the distribution of *Asian woman*.

## 7 Conclusion

This paper sought to demonstrate that linguistic representations of the type used in distributional semantics may provide useful data to humanities researchers who analyse discursive trends. We presented a case study involving two subfields of philosophy: gender theory and intersectionality.

We hope to have shown that a) distributional data is a useful representation of social phenomena which have been described by theorists and social scientists but never linguistically observed on a large scale b) this data lends itself to a fine-grained analysis of such phenomena, as exemplified by the discussions in §5 and §6. Further, we have highlighted that the philosophical theory of intersectionality can be illustrated, at least for some concepts, via a quantitative analysis of the output of different distributional models. We suggest that this observation should be investigated further from the point of view of computational linguistics: there may be some aspect of meaning which is not expressed by those distributional compositional models that do not take phrasal distributions into account (i.e. additive, multiplicative, circular convolution models).

A natural extension of this work would be to design experiments focusing on particular types of discourse and corpora, and pursue conceptual analysis at the diachronic level. This presupposes the existence of digitalised corpora which may not be available at this point in time. Efforts should therefore be made to acquire the needed data. We leave this as future work.

## Acknowledgments

This work was in part enabled by an Alexander von Humboldt Fellowship for Postdoctoral Researchers awarded to the first author. We would like to thank the Alexander von Humboldt Foundation for their financial support.

## References

Marco Baroni and Roberto Zamparelli. 2010. Nouns are vectors, adjectives are matrices: Representing adjective-noun constructions in semantic space. Proceedings of the 2010 Conference on Empirical Methods in Natural Language Processing (EMNLP10).

Simone de Beauvoir. 1949. *Le deuxième sexe*. Gallimard, Paris.

Judith Butler. 1990. *Gender Trouble. Feminism and the Subversion of Identity.* Routledge, New York.

Stephen Clark and Stephen Pulman. 2007. Combining Symbolic and Distributional Models of Meaning. *Proceedings of the AAAI Spring Symposium on Quantum Interaction*, pp.52–55. Stanford, CA.

Noam Cohen. 2011. Define Gender Gap? Look Up Wikipedias Contributor List. *The New York Times*, 31 January 2011, pp.A1 New York edition.

Kimberlé Crenshaw. 1991. Mapping the Margins: Intersectionality, Identity Politics, and Violence against Women of Color. *Stanford Law Review*, 43:6, pp. 1241–1299.

James Curran. 2003. *From Distributional to Semantic Similarity*. PhD dissertation. Institute for Communicating and Collaborative Systems. School of Informatics. University of Edinburgh, Scotland, UK.

Katrin Erk and Sebastian Padó. 2008. A Structured Vector Space Model for Word Meaning in Context. *Proceedings of the 2008 Conference on Empirical Methods in Natural Language Processing*. Honolulu, HI.

Cordelia Fine. 2008. *Delusions of Gender. The Real Science Behind Sex Differences.* Icon Books. London.

Dan Flickinger and Stephan Oepen and Gisle Ytrestol 2010. WikiWoods: Syntacto-Semantic Annotation for English Wikipedia. *Proceedings of the Seventh International Conference on Language Resources and Evaluation (LREC10).*

Michel Foucault. 1966. *Les mots et les choses.* Gallimard, Paris.

Ute Frevert. 2001. *Die kasernierte Nation. Militrdienst und Zivilgesellschaft in Deutschland.* Beck, Munich.

Edward Grefenstette and Mehrnoosh Sadrzadeh. 2011. Experimental Support for a Categorical Compositional Distributional Model of Meaning. *Proceedings of the 2011 Conference on Empirical Methods in Natural Language Processing*, pp. 1394–1404. Edinburgh, Scotland, UK.

Gregory Grefenstette. 1994. *Explorations in Automatic Thesaurus Discovery*. Kluwer Academic Publishers.

Emiliano Guevara. 2010. A Regression Model of Adjective-Noun Compositionality in Distributional Semantics. *Proceedings of the 2010 Workshop on Geometrical Models of Natural Language Semantics, ACL 2010*, pp. 33–37. Uppsala, Sweden.

Emiliano Guevara. 2011. Computing Semantic Compositionality in Distributional Semantics. *Proceedings of the Ninth International Conference on Computational Semantics (IWCS 2011)*, pp. 135–144. Oxford, England, UK.

Kenneth E. Harper. 1965. Measurement of similarity between nouns. *Proceedings of the 1965 conference on Computational linguistics (COLING 65)*, pp. 1–23. Bonn, Germany.

Zelig Harris. 1954. Distributional Structure. *Word*, 10(2-3):146–162.

Sally Haslanger. 2005. What Are We Talking About? The Semantics and Politics of Social Kinds *Hypatia*, 20:10–26.

Karin Hausen. 1976. Die Polarisierung der "Geschlechtscharaktere". Eine Spiegelung der Dissoziation von Erwerbs- und Familienleben. *Sozialgeschichte der Familie in der Neuzeit Europas.* Conze and Werner, Editors, pp. 363–393 Klett-Cotta, Stuttgart.

Claudia Honegger. 1991. *Die Ordnung der Geschlechter: Die Wissenschaften vom Menschen und das Weib, 17501850.* Campus, Frankfurt am Main and New York.

Kevin Lund and Curt Burgess. 1996. Producing high-dimensional semantic spaces from lexical cooccurrence. *Behavior Research Methods, Instrumentation, and Computers*, 28, pp. 203–208.

Jeff Mitchell and Mirella Lapata. 2010. Composition in Distributional Models of Semantics. *Cognitive Science*, 34(2010):1388–1429.

Esther Ngan-Ling Chow. 2011. *Analyzing Gender, Intersectionality, and multiple inequalities: global, transnational and local contexts*. Esther Ngan-Ling Chow, Marcia Texler Segal and Tan Lin, Editors. Emerald Group Publishing.

Sebastian Padó and Mirella Lapata. 2007. Dependency-based construction of semantic space models. *Computational Linguistics*, 33(2), 161–199.

Barbara Partee. 1994. Lexical Semantics and Compositionality *Invitation to Cognitive Science, second edition. Part I: Language*. Daniel Osherson, General Editor. Lila Gleitman and Mark Liberman, Editors. MIT Press.

John G.A. Pocock. 1975. *The Machiavellian moment. Florentine political thought and the Atlantic republican tradition.* Princeton University Press, Princeton, NJ.

Richard Rorty. 1967. *The Linguistic Turn: Recent Essays in Philosophical Method.* Richard Rorty, Editor. University of Chicago Press, Chicago.

Quentin Skinner. 1998. *Liberty before liberalism.* Cambridge University Press, Cambridge, UK.

Dominic Widdows. 2008. Semantic Vector Products: Some Initial Investigations. *Second AAAI Symposium on Quantum Interaction*. Oxford, UK.

Christine Whyte. 2012. Praise be, prostitutes as the women we are not – Using intersectionality to analyse race, class and gender in history. *Intersektionalität und Kritik.* Vera Kallenberg, Jennifer Meyer, Johanna M. Müller, Editors. Wiesdaben. Forthcoming.

Ludwig Wittgenstein. 1953. *Philosophische Untersuchungen.* Blackwell, Oxford, UK.

# Linguistically-Adapted Structural Query Annotation for Digital Libraries in the Social Sciences

**Caroline Brun** **Vassilina Nikoulina** **Nikolaos Lagos**

Xerox Research Centre Europe
6, chemin de Maupertuis
38240, Meylan France
{firstname.lastname}@xrce.xerox.com

**Abstract**

Query processing is an essential part of a range of applications in the social sciences and cultural heritage domain. However, out-of-the-box natural language processing tools originally developed for full phrase analysis are inappropriate for query analysis. In this paper, we propose an approach to solving this problem by adapting a complete and integrated chain of NLP tools, to make it suitable for queries analysis. Using as a case study the automatic translation of queries posed to the Europeana library, we demonstrate that adapted linguistic processing can lead to improvements in translation quality.

## 1 Introduction

Query processing tools are essential components of digital libraries and content aggregators. Their operation varies from simple stop word removal and stemming to advanced parsing, that treats queries as a collection of phrases rather than single terms (Mothe and Tanguy, 2007). They are used in a range of applications, from information retrieval (via search engines that provide access to the digital collections) to query analysis.

Current query processing solutions tend to use out-of-the-box Natural Language Processing (NLP) tools that were originally developed for full phrase analysis, being inappropriate for query analysis.

Correct query annotation and interpretation is even more important in the cultural heritage or social sciences domain, as a lot of the content can be in multimedia form and only metadata (most of the times in the form of tags) is exploitable by traditional text-oriented information retrieval and analysis techniques.

Furthermore, as recent studies of user querying behavior mention, queries in these domains are not only very short but are also quite specific in terms of content: they refer to artist names, titles, dates, and objects (Koolen and Kamps, 2010; Ireson and Oomen, 2007). Take the example of a query like *"coupe apollon"* ("bowl apollon"). While in standard analysis *"coupe"* would be identified as a verb ("couper", i.e. "to cut"), in the context of a query it should be actually tagged as a noun, which refers to an object. Such a difference may lead to different preprocessing and worse retrieval.

In this paper, we propose an approach to solving this problem by adapting a complete and integrated chain of NLP tools, based on the Xerox Incremental Parser (XIP), to make it suitable for queries' analysis. The adaptation includes recapitalization, adapted Part of Speech (PoS) tagging, adapted chunking and Named Entities (NE) recognition. We claim that several heuristics especially important for queries' analysis, such as favoring nominal interpretations, result in improved linguistic structures, which can have an impact in a wide range of further applications (e.g. information retrieval, query translation, information extraction, query reformulation etc.).

## 2 Prior art

The problem of adapted query processing, often referred to as structural query annotation, includes capitalization, NEs detection, PoS tagging and query segmentation. Most of the existing works treat each of these steps independently and address only one of the above issues.

Many works address the problem of query segmentation. According to Tan and Peng (2008), query segmentation is a problem which is close to the chunking problem, but the chunking problem is directly linked to the PoS tagging results, which are often noisy for the queries. Thus, most of the works on query segmentation are based on the statistical interaction between a pair of query words to identify the border between the segments in the query (Jones et al., 2006; Guo et al., 2008). Tan and Peng (2008) propose a generative language model enriched with Wikipedia to identify "concepts" rather than simply "frequency-based" patterns. The segmentation proposed by Bergsma and Wang (2007) is closer to the notion of NP chunking. They propose a machine-learned query segmentation system trained on manually annotated set of 500 AOL queries. However, in this work PoS tagging is used as one of the features in query segmentation and is done with a generic PoS tagger, non adapted for queries.

PoS tagging is an important part of query processing and used in many information analytics tasks (query reformulation, query segmentation, etc.). However very few works address query-oriented PoS tagging. Allan and Raghavan (2002) consider that PoS tagging might be ambiguous for short queries and propose to interact with the user for disambiguation. Barr et al. (2008) produce a set of manually annotated queries, and then train a Brill tagger on this set in order to create an adapted PoS tagger for search queries.

A notable work is the one by Bendersky et al. (2010), which addresses the capitalization, PoS tagging and query segmentation in the same paper. However, this approach proposes for each of the above steps a probabilistic model that relies on the document corpus rather on the query itself. Such an approach is not applicable for most digital content providers who would reluctantly give access to their document collection. Moreover, the query expansion, which is the central idea of the described approach, is not possible for most of digital libraries that are organized in a database. Secondly, Bendersky et al. (2010) proposes adapting each processing step independently. Although this is not mentioned in the paper, these three steps can be applied in a sequence, where PoS tagging can profit from the recapitalization, and chunking from the PoS tagging step. However, once the recapitalization is done, it can not be changed in the following steps. This work doesn't address the adaptation of the NE recognition component, as we do, and which might change the final chunking and PoS tagging in certain cases.

In our approach, part of the recapitalization is done during the PoS tagging, in interaction with the NE recognition, which allows us to consider these two steps as interleaved. Moreover, the linguistic processing we propose is generic: corpus-independent (at least most of its parts except for NE recognition) and doesn't require access to the document collection.

## 3 Data

This work is based on search logs from Europeana[1]. These are real users' queries, where Named Entities are often lowercased and the structures are very different from normal phrase structure. Thus, this data is well adapted to demonstrate the impact of adapted linguistic processing.

## 4 Motivation

We show the importance of the adapted linguistic query processing using as example the task of query translation, a real need for today's digital content providers operating in a multilingual environment. We took a sample of Europeana queries and translated them with different MT systems: in-house (purely statistical) or available online (rule-based). Some examples of problematic translations are shown in the Table 1.

| | **Input query** | **Automatic Translation** | **Human translation** |
|---|---|---|---|
| | French-English | | |
| 1 | journal panorama paris | newspaper panorama bets | newspaper panorama paris |
| 2 | saint jean de luz | saint jean of luz | saint jean de luz |
| 3 | vie et mort de l'image | life and died of the image | life and death of image |
| 4 | langue et réalité | and the reality of language | language and reality |
| | English-French | | |
| 5 | maps europe | trace l'Europe | cartes de l'Europe |
| 6 | 17th century saw | Du 17ème siècle a vu | scie du 17ème siècle |
| 7 | chopin george sand | george sable chopin soit | chopin george sand |

Table 1: Examples of the problematic query translations

[1] A portal that acts as an interface to millions of digitized records, allowing users to explore Europe's cultural heritage. For more information please visit http://www.europeana.eu/portal/

Although in general, the errors done by statistical and rule-based models are pretty different, there are some common errors done in the case of the query translation. Both models, being designed for full-sentence translation, find the query structure very unnatural and tend to reproduce the full sentence in the output (ex. 1, 3, 4, 5, 6). The errors may come either from a wrong PoS tagging (for rule-based systems), or from the wrong word order (statistical-based systems), or from the choice of the wrong translation (both types of systems).

One might think that the word order problem is not crucial for queries, because most of the IR models use the bag of words models, which ignore the order of words. However, it might matter in some cases: for example, if *and/or* are interpreted as a logical operator, it is important to place them correctly in the sentence (examples3, 4).

Errors also may happen when translating NEs (ex.1, 2, 7). The case information, which is often missing in the real-life queries, helps to deal with the NEs translation.

The examples mentioned above illustrate that adapted query processing is important for a task such as query translation, both in the case of rule-based and empirical models. Although the empirical models can be adapted if an appropriately sized corpus exists, such a corpus is not always available.

Thus we propose adapting the linguistic processing prior to query translation (which is further integrated in the SMT model). We demonstrate the feasibility and impact of our approach based on the difference in translation quality but the adaptations can be useful in a number of other tasks involving query processing (e.g. question answering, query logs analysis, etc.).

## 5 Linguistic Processing Adaptation

As said before, queries have specific linguistic properties that make their analysis difficult for standard NLP tools. This section describes the approach we have designed to improve query chunking. Following a study of the corpus of query logs, we rely on the specific linguistic properties of the queries to adapt different steps of linguistic analysis, from preprocessing to chunking.

These adaptations consist in the following very general processes, for both English and French:

Recapitalization: we recapitalize, in a preprocessing step, some uncapitalized words in queries that can be proper nouns when they start with a capital letter.

Part of Speech disambiguation:

- the part of speech tagging favors nominal interpretation (whereas standard part of speech taggers are designed to find a verb in the input, as PoS tagging generally applies on complete sentences);
- the recapitalization information transmitted from the previous step is used to change the PoS interpretation in some contexts.

Chunking: the chunking is improved by:

- considering that a full NE is a chunk, which is not the case in standard text processing, where a NE can perfectly be just a part of a chunk;
- grouping coordinated NEs of the same type;
- performing PP and AP attachment with the closest antecedent that is morphologically compatible

These processes are very general and may apply to queries in different application domains, with maybe some domain-dependent adaptations (for example, NEs may change across domains).

These adaptations have been implemented within the XIP engine, for the French and English grammars. The XIP framework allows integrating the adaptations of different steps of query processing into a unified framework, where the changes from one step can influence the result of the next step: the information performed at a given step is transmitted to the next step by XIP through linguistic features.

### 5.1 Preprocessing

Queries are often written with misspelling errors, in particular for accents and capital letters of NEs. See the following query examples extracted from our query log corpus:

```
lafont Robert (French query)
henry de forge et jean mauclère
(French query)
muse prado madrid (French query)
carpaccio queen cornaro (English
query)
man ray (English query)
```

This might be quite a problem for linguistic treatments, like PoS tagging and of course NE recognition, which often use capital letter information as a triggering feature.

Recapitalizing these words at the preprocessing step of a linguistic analysis, i.e. during the morphological analysis, is technically relatively easy, however it would be an important generator of spurious ambiguities in the context of full sentence parsing (standard context of linguistic parsing). Indeed, considering that all lower case words that can be proper nouns with a capital letter should also have capitalized interpretation, such as *price, jean, read, us, bush, lay*, etc., in English or *pierre, médecin*, … in French) would be problematic for a PoS tagger as well as for a NE recognizer. That's why it is not performed in a standard analysis context, considering also that misspelling errors are not frequent in "standard" texts. In the case of queries however, they are frequent, and since queries are far shorter in average than full sentences the tagging can be adapted to this context (see next section), we can afford to perform recapitalization using the following methodology, combining lexical information and contextual rules:

1. The preprocessing lexicon integrates all words starting with a lower case letter which can be first name (*henry, jean, isaac* …), family and celebrity name (*chirac, picasso*...) and place names (*paris, saint pétersbourg*, …) when capitalized.

2. When an unknown word starting with a lower case letter is preceded by a first name and eventually by a particle (*de, van, von* …), it is analyzed as a last name, in order to be able to trigger standard NE recognition. This is one example of interleaving of the processes: here part-of-speech interpretation is conditioned by the recapitalization steps which transmits information about recapitalization (via features within XIP) that triggers query-specific pos disambiguation rules.

The recapitalization (1) has been implemented within the preprocessing components of XIP within finite state transducers (see (Karttunen, 2000)). The second point (2) is done directly within XIP in the part-of-speech tagging process, with a contextual rule. For example, the analysis of the input query "*jean mauclère*" gets the following structure and dependency output with the standard French grammar.

```
Query: jean mauclère
NMOD(jean, mauclère)
0>GROUP[NP[jean] AP[mauclère]]
```

Because *jean* is a common noun and mauclère is an unknown word which has been guessed as an adjective by the lexical guesser.

It gets the following analysis with the preprocessing adaptations described above:

```
NMOD(jean,mauclère)
PERSON_HUM(jean mauclère)
FIRSTNAME(jean,jean mauclère)
LASTNAME(mauclère,jean mauclère)
0>GROUP[NP[NOUN[jean mauclère]]]
```

Because *jean* has been recognized as a first name and consequently the unknown word after has been inferred has a proper noun (last name) by the pos tagging contextual rule; the recapitalization process and part-of-speech interpretation are therefore interleaved.

### 5.2 Part of speech disambiguation

In the context of query analysis, part-of-speech tagging has to be adapted also, since standard part-of-speech disambiguation strategies aim generally at disambiguating in the context of full sentences. But queries are very different from full sentences: they are mostly nominal with sometimes infinitive, past participial, or gerundive insertions, e.g.:

```
statuettes hommes jouant avec un
chien (French query)
coupe apollon (French query)
architecture musique (French
query)
statue haut relief grecque du 5
siecle (French query)
david playing harp fpr saul (Eng-
lish query)
stained glass angel (English
query)
```

Standard techniques for part-of-speech tagging include rule based methods and statistical methods, mainly based on hidden Markov models (see for example (Chanod and Tapanainen, 1995)). In this case, it would be possible to recompute the probabilities on a corpus of queries manually annotated. However, the correction of part-of-speech tags in the context of queries is easy to develop with a small set of rules. We focus on English and French, and in queries, the main problems come from the ambiguity between noun and verbs, which has to be solved differently than in the context of a standard sentence.

The approach we adopt to correct the tagging with the main following contextual rules:

- If there is a noun/verb ambiguity:
  - If the ambiguity is on the first word of the query (e.g. "*coupe apollon*", "*oil flask*"), select the noun interpretation;
  - If the ambiguity is on the second word of the query, prefer the noun interpretation if the query starts with an adjective or a noun (e.g. in "*young people social competences*", select the noun interpretation for *people*, instead of verb)
  - Select noun interpretation if there is no person agreement with one of the previous nouns (e.g. "*les frères bissons*", *frères* belongs to the 3rd person but *bissons* to the 1st one of the verb "*bisser*")
  - For a verb which is neither at the past participle form nor the infinitive form, select the noun interpretation if it is not followed by a determiner (e.g. "*tremblement terre lisbonne*", *terre* is disambiguated as a noun"))
  - Choose the noun interpretation if the word is followed by a conjunction and a noun or preceded by a noun and a conjunction (e.g. in "*gauguin moon and earth*", choose the noun interpretation for *moon*, instead of verb[2]).
- In case of ambiguity between adjective and past participle verb, select the adjective interpretation if the word is followed by a noun (e.g. "*stained glass angel*", *stained* is disambiguated as an adjective instead of a past participle verb)

### 5.3 Chunking

The goal of chunking is to assign a partial structure to a sentence and focuses on easy to parse pieces in order to avoid ambiguity and recursion. In the very specific context of query analysis, and once again since queries have specific linguistic properties (they are not sentences but mostly nominal sequences), chunking can be improved along several heuristics. We propose here some adaptations to improve query chunking to deal with AP and PP attachment, and coordination, using also NE information to guide the chunking strategy.

**AP and PP attachment**

In standard cases of chunking, AP and PP attachment is not considered, because of attachment ambiguity problems that cannot be solved at this stage of linguistic analysis.

Considering the shortness of queries and the fact that they are mostly nominal, some of these attachments can be solved however in this context.

For the adjectival attachment in French, we attach the post modifier adjectival phrases to the first previous noun with which there is agreement in number and gender. For example, the chunking structure for the query "*Bibliothèque europeenne numerique*" is:

```
NP[ [Bibliothèque AP[europeenne]
AP[numerique] ]
```

while it is

```
NP[Bibliothèque] AP[europeenne]
AP[numerique]
```

with our standard French grammar.

For PP attachment, we simply consider that the PP attaches systematically to the previous noun. For example, the chunking structure for "*The history of the University of Oxford*" is:

```
NP[the history PP[of the University
PP[of Oxford] ] ]
```

instead of:

```
NP[The history] PP[of the Univer-
sity] PP[of Oxford ]
```

**Coordination**

Some cases of coordination, usually very complex, can be solved in the query context, in particular when NEs are involved. For both English and French, we attach coordinates when they belong to the same entity type (person conj person, date conj date, place conj place, etc.), for example, "*vase achilles et priam*" :

```
NP[vase] NP[Achille et Priam]
```

instead of:

```
NP[vase] NP[Achille] et NP[Priam]
```

[2] *To moon about*

We also attach coordinates when the second is introduced by a reflexive pronoun, such as in: "[*Le laboureur et ses enfants] La Fontaine*" and attach coordinates within a PP when they are introduced by the preposition "*entre*" in French and "*between*" in English.

**Use of NE information to guide the chunking strategy**

We also use information about NEs present in the queries to guide the query chunking strategy. In standard analysis, NEs are generally part of larger chunking units. In queries, however, because of their strong semantic, they can be isolated as separate chunking units. We have adapted our chunking strategy using this information: when the parser detects a NE (including a date), it chunks it as a separate NP. The following examples show the chunking results for this adapted strategy versus the analysis of standard grammar:

- "*Anglo Saxon 11th century*" (English)
Adapted chunking:
`NP[Anglo Saxon] NP[ 11th century]`

Standard chunking:
`NP[Anglo Saxon 11th century ]`

- "*Alexandre le Grand Persepolis*" (French)
Adapted chunking:
`NP[Alexandre le Grand] NP[Perspolis]`

Standard chunking:
`NP[Alexandre le Grand Perspolis]`

The whole process is illustrated in Figure 1.

When applying the full chain on an example query like "*gauguin moon and earth*", we have the following steps and result:
Preprocessing: *gauguin* is recognized as *Gauguin* (proper noun of celebrity);
Part of speech tagging: *moon* is disambiguated as a noun instead of a verb);
Chunking: *moon and earth* are grouped together in a coordination chunk, *gauguin* is a NE chunked separately.
So we get the following structure:

`NP[Gauguin] NP[moon and earth]`

and *gauguin* is recognized as a person name, instead of

`SC [3] [NP[gauguin] FV [4] [moon]] and NP[earth],`

*gauguin* remaining unknown, with the standard English grammar.

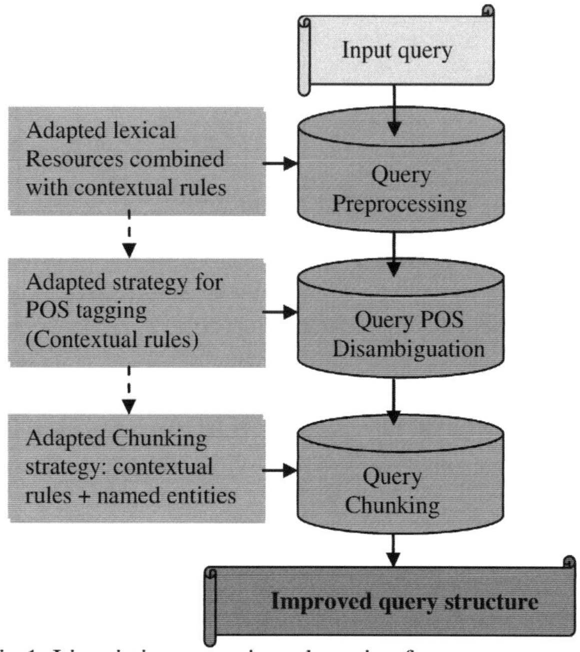


Fig 1: Linguistic processing adaptation for queries

### 5.4 Examples of query structures

The following table shows the differences of query structures obtained with the standard linguistic processing and with the adapted linguistic processing.

| | |
|---|---|
| 1. | Albert Camus la peste |
| | Standard LP: NP {albert} AP {camus} NP {la peste} |
| | Adapted LP: NP {albert camus} NP {la peste} |
| 2. | dieux ou héros grec |
| | Standard LP: NP {dieux} COORD {ou} NP {héros} AP {grec} |

[3] SC: chunk tag for sentential clause
[4] FV: finite verb chunk

| | |
|---|---|
| | Adapted LP: NP {dieux} COORD {ou} NP {héros grec} |
| 3. | pierre bergé |
| | Standard LP: NP {pierre} VERB {bergé} |
| | Adapted LP: NP {pierre bergé} |

Table 2: Some examples of query structure produced by standard and adapted linguistic processing.

The evaluation of this customization is done indirectly through query translation, and is described in the next section

# 6 Experiments

## 6.1 Experimental settings

In our experiments we tried to enrich our baseline SMT system with an adapted linguistic processing in order to improve the query translation. These experiments have double goal. First, to show that the adapted linguistic processing allows to improve query translation compared to a standard linguistic processing, and second, to show that enriching an SMT model with a linguistic processing (adapted) is helpful for the translation.

We use an open source toolkit Moses (trained on Europarl) as a baseline model for query translations. Based on the examples from the section 5, we choose to integrate the chunking and NE information in the translation. We integrate this knowledge in the following way:

- **Chunking:** We check whether the query matches one of the following patterns: "NP1 and NP2", "NP1 or NP2", "NP1 NP2", "NP1, NP2", etc. If it is the case, the NPs are translated independently. Thus, we make sure that the output query will preserve the logical structure, if "and/or" are treated as logical operators. Also, translating NPs independently might result at different (hopefully better) lexical choices.
- **Named entities:** We introduce XML tags for person names where we propose a possible translation. During the translation process the proposed translation competes with the possible translations from a bi-phrase library. The translation maximizing internal translation score is chosen. In these experiments we propose not to translate an NE at all, however in more general case we could imagine having an adapted NE dictionary.

## 6.2 Evaluation

We have translated the totality of available Europeana French logs to English (8870 distinct queries), with the following translation models:

- Moses trained on Europarl (Baseline MT)
- Baseline MT model enriched with linguistic processing (as defined in 6.1) based on *basic* grammar (Baseline MT + basic grammar)
- Baseline MT enriched with linguistic processing based on *adapted* grammar (Baseline MT + adapted grammar)

Our approach brings two new aspects compared to simple SMT system. First, an SMT system is enriched with linguistic processing as opposed to system without linguistic processing (baseline system), second: usage of an adapted linguistic processing as opposed to standard linguistic processing. Thus, we evaluate:

1. The impact of linguistic processing on the final query translations;
2. The impact of grammar adaptation (adapted linguistic processing) in the context of query translation.

First, we measure the overall impact of each of the two aspects mentioned above. Table 3 reflects the general impact of linguistic enrichment and grammar adaptation on query structure and translation.

First, we note that the linguistic processing as defined in 6.1 won't be applied to all queries. Thus, we count an amount of queries out of our test set to which this processing can actually be applied. This corresponds to the first line of the Table 3 (26% of all queries).

Second, we compare the queries translation with and without linguistic processing. This is shown in the second line of the Table 3: the amount of queries for which the linguistic processing lead to different translation (25% of queries for which the linguistic processing was applied).

The second part of the table shows the difference between the standard linguistic processing and an adapted linguistic processing. First, we check how many queries get different structure after grammar adaptation (Section 5) (~42%) and second, we check how many of these queries actually get different translation (~16% queries with new structure obtained after adaptation get different translations).

These numbers show that the linguistic knowledge that we integrated into the SMT framework may impact a limited portion of queries' translations. However, we believe that this is due, to some extent, to the way the linguistic knowledge was integrated in SMT, which explores only a small portion of the actual linguistic information that is available. We carried out these experiments as a proof of concept for the adapted linguistic processing, but we believe that a deeper integration of the linguistic knowledge into the SMT framework will lead to more significant results. For example, integrating such an adapted linguistic processing in a rule-based MT system will be straightforward and beneficial, since the linguistic information is explored directly by a translation model (e.g. in the example 6 in Table 1 tagging "saw" as a noun will definitely lead to a better translation).

Next, we define 2 evaluation tasks, where the goal of each task is to compare 2 translation models. We compare:

1. Baseline MT versus linguistically enriched translation model (Baseline MT+adapted adapted linguistic processing). This task evaluates the impact of linguistic enrichment in the query translation task with SMT.
2. Translation model using *standard linguistic processing* versus translation model using *adapted linguistic processing*. This task evaluates the impact of the adapted linguistic processing in the query translation task.

For each evaluation task we have randomly selected a sample of 200 translations (excluding previously the identical translations for the 2 models compared) and we perform a pairwise evaluation for each evaluation task. Thus, for the first evaluation task, a baseline translation (performed by standard Moses without linguistic processing) is compared to the translation done by Moses + adapted linguistic processing. In the second evaluation task, the translation performed by Moses + standard linguistic processing is compared to the translation performed by Moses + adapted linguistic processing.

The evaluation has been performed by 3 evaluators. However, no overlapping evaluations have been performed to calculate intra-evaluators agreement. We could observe, however, the similar tendency for improvement in each on the evaluated sample (similar to the one shown in the Table 2).

We evaluate the overall translation performance, independently of the task in which the translations are going to be used afterwards (text understanding, text analytics, cross-lingual information retrieval etc.)

| | |
|---|---|
| *Linguistic enrichment* | |
| Nb of *queries* to which the adapted linguistic processing was applied before translation. | 2311 (26% of 8870) |
| Nb of *translations* which differ between baseline Moses and Moses with adapted linguistic processing. | 582 (25% of 2311) |
| *Grammar adaptation* | |
| Nb of *queries* which get different *structures* between *standard linguistic processing* and *adapted linguistic processing*. | 3756 (42% of 8870) |
| Nb of *translations* which differ between *Moses+standard linguistic processing* and *Moses+adapted linguistic processing* | 638 (16 % of 3756) |

Table 3: Impact of linguistic processing and grammar adaptation for query translation

The difference between slight improvements and important improvements as in the examples below has been done during the evaluation.

```
src1: max weber
t1:max mr weber
t2:max weber (slight improvement)

src2: albert camus la peste
t1:albert camus fever
t2:albert camus the plague (impor-
tant improvement)
```

Thus, each pair of translations (t1, t2) receives a score from the scale [-2, 2] which can be:

- 2, if t2 is much better than t1,
- 1, if t2 is better than t1,
- 0, if t2 is equivalent to t1,
- -1, if t1 is better than t2,
- -2, if t1 is much better than t2,

Table 4 presents the results of translation evaluation.

Note, that a part of slight decreases can be corrected by introducing an adapted named entities dictionary to the translation system. For example, for the source query "*romeo et juliette*", keeping NEs untranslated results at the following translation: "*romeo and juliette*", which is considered as a slight decrease in comparison to a baseline translation: "*romeo and juliet*". Creating an adapted NEs dictionary, either by crawling Wikipedia, or other parallel resources, might be helpful for such cases.

Often, the cases of significantly better translations could potentially lead to the better retrieval. For example, a better lexical choice (*don juan moliere* vs. *donation juan moliere*, *the plague* vs. *fever*) often judged as significant improvement may lead to a better retrieval.

Based on this observation one may hope that the adapted linguistic processing can indeed be useful in the query translation task in CLIR context, but also in general query analysis context.

## 7 Conclusion

Queries posed to digital library search engines in the cultural heritage and social sciences domain tend to be very short, referring mostly to artist names, objects, titles, and dates. As we have illustrated with several examples, taken from the logs of the Europeana portal, standard NLP analysis is not well adapted to treat that domain. In this work we have proposed adapting a complete chain of linguistic processing tools for query processing, instead of using out-of-the-box tools designed to analyze full sentences.

Focusing on the cultural heritage domain, we translated queries from the Europeana portal using a state-of-the-art machine translation system and evaluated translation quality before and after applying the adaptations. The impact of the linguistic adaptations is quite significant, as in 42% of the queries the resulting structure changes. Subsequently, 16% of the query translations are also different. The positive impact of the adapted linguistic processing on the translation quality is evident, as for 99 queries the translation (out of 200 sample evaluated) is improved when compared to having no linguistic processing. We observe also that 78 queries are better translated after adapting the linguistic processing components.

Our results show that customizing the linguistic processing of queries can lead to important

| | Important ++ | Total nb+ | Important - - | Total nb - | Overall impact |
|---|---|---|---|---|---|
| **Moses< Moses+ adapted** | 35 | 87 | 4 | 19 | 99 |
| **Moses+ basic< Moses+ adapted** | 28 | 66 | 2 | 12 | 80 |

Table 4: Translation evaluation. Total nb+ (-): total number of improvements (decreases), not distinguishing whether it is slight or important; important ++ (--): the number of important improvements (decreases). Overall impact = (Total nb+) + (Importan++ ) – (Total nb-) – (Important --)

improvements in translation (and eventually to multilingual information retrieval and data mining). A lot of the differences are related to the ability of properly identifying and treating domain-specific named entities. We plan to further research this aspect in future works.


### Acknowledgements

This research was supported by the European Union's ICT Policy Support Programme as part of the Competitiveness and Innovation Framework Programme, CIP ICT-PSP under grant agreement nr 250430 (Project GALATEAS).


## References


Bin Tan and Fuchun Peng. 2008. Unsupervised query segmentation using generative language models and wikipedia. In Proceedings of the 17th international conference on World Wide Web (WWW '08). ACM, New York, NY, USA, 347-356.

Cory Barr, Rosie Jones, Moira Regelson. 2008. The Linguistic Structure of EnglishWeb-Search Queries, Proceedings of ENMLP'08, pp 1021–1030, Octobre 2008, Honolulu.

James Allan and Hema Raghavan. 2002. Using part-of-speech patterns to reduce query ambiguity. In Proceedings of the 25th annual international ACM SIGIR conference on Research and development in information retrieval (SIGIR '02). ACM, New York, NY, USA, 307-314.

Jeann-Pierre Chanod, Pasi Tapanainen. 1995. Tagging French - comparing a statistical and a constraint-based method. Proc. From Texts To Tags:

Issues In Multilingual Language Analysis, EACL SIGDAT workshop. Dublin, 1995.

Jiafeng Guo, Gu Xu, Hang Li, Xueqi Cheng. 2008. A Unified and Discriminative Model for Query Refinement. Proc. SIGIR'08, July 20–24, 2008, Singapore.

Josiane Mothe and Ludovic Tanguy. 2007. Linguistic Analysis of Users' Queries: towards an adaptive Information Retrieval System. International Conference on Signal-Image Technology & Internet–Based Systems, Shangai, China, 2007. http://halshs.archives-ouvertes.fr/halshs-00287776/fr/ [Last accessed March 3, 2011]

Lauri Karttunen. 2000. Applications of Finite-State Transducers in Natural Language Processing. Proceedings of CIAA-2000. Lecture Notes in Computer Science. Springer Verlag.

Marijn Koolen and Jaap Kamps. 2010. Searching cultural heritage data: does structure help expert searchers?. In Adaptivity, Personalization and Fusion of Heterogeneous Information (RIAO '10). Le centre des hautes etudes internationals d'informatique documentaire, Paris, France, 152-155.

Michael Bendersky, W. Bruce Croft and David A. Smith. 2010. Structural Annotation of Search Queries Using Pseudo-Relevance Feedback. Proceedings of CIKM'10, October 26-29, 2010, Toronto, Ontario, Canada

Neil Ireson and Johan Oomen. 2007. Capturing e-Culture: Metadata in MultiMatch., J. In Proc. DELOS-MultiMatch workshop, February 2007, Tirrenia, Italy.

Rosie Jones, Benjamin Rey, Omid Madani, and Wiley Greiner. 2006. Generating query substitutions. In Proceedings of the 15th international conference on World Wide Web (WWW '06). ACM, New York, NY, USA, 387-396.

Shane Bergsma and Qin Iris Wang. 2007. Learning Noun Phrase Query Segmentation, Proceedings of the 2007 Joint Conference on Empirical Methods in Natural Language Processing and Computational Natural Language Learning, pp. 819–826, Prague, June 2007.

# Parsing the Past – Identification of Verb Constructions in Historical Text

**Eva Pettersson**[†]**, Beáta Megyesi and Joakim Nivre**
Department of Linguistics and Philology
Uppsala University
[†]Swedish National Graduate School
of Language Technology
firstname.lastname@lingfil.uu.se

## Abstract

Even though NLP tools are widely used for contemporary text today, there is a lack of tools that can handle historical documents. Such tools could greatly facilitate the work of researchers dealing with large volumes of historical texts. In this paper we propose a method for extracting verbs and their complements from historical Swedish text, using NLP tools and dictionaries developed for contemporary Swedish and a set of normalisation rules that are applied before tagging and parsing the text. When evaluated on a sample of texts from the period 1550–1880, this method identifies verbs with an F-score of 77.2% and finds a partially or completely correct set of complements for 55.6% of the verbs. Although these results are in general lower than for contemporary Swedish, they are strong enough to make the approach useful for information extraction in historical research. Moreover, the exact match rate for complete verb constructions is in fact higher for historical texts than for contemporary texts (38.7% vs. 30.8%).

## 1 Introduction

Today there is an abundance of NLP tools that can analyse contemporary language and extract information relevant to a particular user need, but there is a real lack of tools that can handle historical documents. Historians and other researchers working with older texts are still mostly forced to manually search large amounts of text in order to find the passages of interest to their research. Developing tools to facilitate this process is a great challenge, however, as historical texts vary greatly in both spelling and grammar between different authors, genres and time periods, and even within the same text, due to the lack of spelling conventions. In addition to this, there is a shortage of annotated resources that can be used for the development and evaluation of new tools.

The work presented in this paper has been carried out in cooperation with historians, who are studying what men and women did for a living in the Early Modern Swedish society. Currently, the historians are manually extracting segments describing work activities from a number of historical texts, and entering them into a database, the Gender and Work Database. Their work so far has shown that the typical segment describing an activity of work is a verb construction, that is, a verb together with its complements (Ågren et al., 2011). (Examples of such segments can be found below in Table 1.) It is very likely that the manual effort and the time needed by the historians to find these segments and enter them into the database could be substantially reduced if verbs and their complements were automatically extracted and presented to the historian. This would give a general overview of the content of a text, and the task of the historian would be to select those segments that are actually describing work activities. By linking extracted segments back to larger passages of text, historians would also be able to find additional segments that were missed by the first automatic extraction. The core of such a system would be a component for identifying verb constructions in running text.

We propose a method for automatically identifying verbs and their complements in various types of historical documents, produced in the Early Modern Swedish period (1550–1800). The method is based on using existing NLP tools for contemporary Swedish, in particular a part-of-speech tagger and a syntactic parser, and automatically normalising the input text into a more modern orthography before running it through the tagger and parser. In order to increase the precision of complement extraction, we use valency dictionaries to filter out unlikely complements in the output of the syntactic parser. Using this method, we are able to identify verbs with an F-score of 77.2% and find a partially or completely correct set of complements for 55.6% of the verbs. To our knowledge, extracting verb constructions from historical texts is a task that has not been directly addressed in previous research, which means that these results are also important in setting benchmarks for future research.

The paper is structured as follows. Section 2 reviews related work. Section 3 describes the method for identification of verbs and complements in more detail. Section 4 presents the data and evaluation metrics used in our experiments, and Section 5 discusses the results of the evaluation. Finally, Section 6 concludes the paper.

## 2 Related Work

Using NLP tools for analysing historical texts is still to a large extent unexplored. There is however a growing interest in this area, and there have been attempts to analyse historical texts (1) by using contemporary NLP tools as they are, (2) by using such tools in combination with normalisation rules and/or dictionaries covering historical language variation, and (3) by training new tools on annotated historical corpora.

Pennacchiotti and Zanzotto (2008) concluded that contemporary NLP tools are not suitable as they are for analysing historical text. They tried to use a contemporary dictionary, morphological analyser and part-of-speech tagger to analyse Italian texts from the period 1200–1881. In their experiments, the dictionary only covered approximately 27% of the words in the oldest text, as compared to 62.5% of the words in a contemporary Italian newspaper text. Consequently, the morphological analyser based on the dictionary reached an accuracy of only 48%, as compared to 91% for contemporary text. Similarly, the part-of-speech tagger used reached an accuracy of only 54%, as compared to 97% for contemporary text.

Oravecz et al. (2010) included a standardisation/normalisation step in their work on semi-automatically annotating a corpus of Old Hungarian. Normalisation was performed using a noisy channel model combined with morphological analysis filtering and decision tree reranking. Combining these methods, they reached a normalisation precision of 73.3%.

Rocio et al. (1999) used a grammar of contemporary Portuguese to syntactically annotate medieval Portuguese texts. A dictionary and inflectional rules for medieval Portuguese were added to the parser, to make it suitable for handling these texts. This approach proved to be successful for partial parsing of medieval Portuguese texts, even though there were some problems remaining concerning grammar limitations, dictionary incompleteness and insufficient part-of-speech tagging.

Sánchez-Marco et al. (2011) adapted an existing NLP tool to deal with Old Spanish. The adapted tool had an accuracy of 94.5% in finding the right part of speech, and 89.9% accuracy in finding the complete morphological tag. The adaptation was performed on the basis of a 20 million token corpus of texts from the 12th to the 16th century, and included expansion of the dictionary, modification of tokenisation and affixation rules, and retraining of the tagger. The retraining was based on a gold standard of 30,000 tokens, where the tokens were first pre-annotated with the contemporary tagger, and then manually corrected. Adding new words to the dictionary had the highest impact on the results. This was done by automatically generating word forms through mapping old spelling variants to their contemporary counterparts.

Pettersson and Nivre (2011) presented a study on automatically extracting verbs from Swedish 17th century texts, using contemporary language technology tools combined with normalisation of the input text. The verb extraction process included an iterative process of normalisation and morphological analysis, followed by part-of-speech tagging for disambiguation of competing interpretations and for analysing words still unknown to the morphological analyser after all normalisation rules had been applied. Using this method, verbs were extracted with 82% precision and 88% recall. The study also included the results of using only the part-of-speech tagger for verb recognition, i.e., dropping the morphological analyser. This resulted in a small decrease in precision to 81% and in recall to 86%.

## 3 Extraction of Verb Constructions

In this paper, we will focus on adapting existing NLP tools by adding normalisation rules prior to processing. We will mainly follow the methodology for verb extraction described in Pettersson and Nivre (2011), but adding the extraction of not only the verbs themselves, but also their adherent complements. It would perhaps have been desirable to use tools specifically trained for analysing historical texts. This would however be a resource-demanding task, considering the lack of annotated data and the language variation, and is currently not a realistic scenario.

The goal is to automatically extract verbs and relevant complements from historical texts, in order to give an overview of the contents and present segments that are possibly describing work activities. In this context, we use the term *complement* in a broad sense and do not impose a sharp distinction between complements and adjuncts, especially not for prepositional phrases. This is motivated by the fact that in the Gender and Work Database, both segments that would traditionally be seen as complements and phrases that would rather be categorised as adjuncts have been considered relevant.

A closer look at the database shows that 67% of the entered segments consist of a verb with a direct object. Other common constructions are verbs with a prepositional complement (11%), verbs with both a direct object and a prepositional complement (10%), and (intransitive) verbs without complements (7%). Table 1 illustrates the most common construction types found in the database, which have been used to define the rules for extracting complements from parsed sentences. There were also a small number of segments (8 in total), that we were not able to categorise.

| Freq | Comp | Source Text Example |
|---|---|---|
| 273 | dobj | *dhe bärgadhe [Höö]*<br>they harvested [Hay] |
| 47 | pcomp | *[med een häst] kiörtt*<br>driven [with a horse] |
| 43 | dobj<br>+<br>pcomp | *[det kiöpet] Han*<br>*[med hänness man] giort*<br>[the bargain] He<br>made [with her husband] |
| 30 | intrans | *mala*<br>to grind |
| 5 | dobj<br>+<br>infc | *hulpit [Muremest:]*<br>*[inläggia Trappestenar]*<br>helped [the Bricklayer]<br>[to make a Stone Stair] |
| 3 | indobj<br>+<br>dobj | *[honom] [Järnet] sålltt*<br>sold [him] [the Iron] |
| 1 | subc | *tillsee [att icke barnen*<br>*skulle göra skada]*<br>see to it [that the children<br>do not do any harm] |

Table 1: Segments describing work activities in the Gender and Work Database; verbs underlined; complements in brackets. Grammatical functions: dobj = direct object, pcomp = prepositional complement, intrans = intransitive, indobj = indirect object, infc = infinitive clause, subc = subordinate clause.

### 3.1 System Overview

The extraction of verbs and their complements is basically performed in five steps:

1. Tokenisation
2. Normalisation
3. Part-of-speech tagging
4. Parsing
5. Extraction of verb constructions

Tokenisation is performed with a simple tokeniser for Swedish that has not been adapted for historical texts.

### 3.2 Normalisation

After tokenisation, each word is normalised to a more modern spelling using a set of 29 handcrafted rules. The rules were developed using a text sample from *Per Larssons dombok*, a selection of court records from 1638 (Edling, 1937), a sample that has not been used in subsequent evaluation. An example of a normalisation rule is the transformation of the letter combination *sch* into *sk*, as in the old spelling *schall* that is normalised to the contemporary spelling *skall* ("shall/should"). Some additional rules were also formulated based on the reformed Swedish spelling introduced in 1906 (Bergman, 1995). This set of rules includes the transformation of double vowels into a single vowel, as in *sööka*, which is normalised into *söka* ("search").

### 3.3 Part-of-speech Tagging

The purpose of part-of-speech tagging in our experiments is both to find the verbs in the text and to prepare for the parsing step, in which the complements are identified. Part-of-speech tagging is performed using HunPOS (Halácsy et al., 2007), a free and open source reimplementation of the HMM-based TnT-tagger by Brants (2000). The tagger is used with a pre-trained language model based on the Stockholm-Umeå Corpus (SUC), a balanced, manually annotated corpus of different text types representative of the Swedish language in the 1990s, comprising approximately one million tokens (Gustafson-Capková and Hartmann, 2006). Megyesi (2009) showed that the HunPOS tagger trained on SUC, is one of the best performing taggers for (contemporary) Swedish texts.

### 3.4 Parsing

The normalised and tagged input text is parsed using MaltParser version 1.6, a data-driven dependency parser developed by Nivre et al. (2006a). In our experiments, the parser is run with a pre-trained model[1] for parsing contemporary Swedish text, based on the Talbanken section of the Swedish Treebank (Nivre et al., 2006b). The parser produces dependency trees labeled with grammatical functions, which can be used to identify different types of complements.

### 3.5 Extraction of Verb Constructions

The extraction of verb constructions from the tagged and parsed text is performed in two steps:

1. Every word form analysed as a verb by the tagger is treated as the head of a verb construction.

2. Every phrase analysed as a dependent of the verb by the parser is treated as a complement provided that it has a relevant grammatical function.

The following grammatical functions are defined to be relevant:

1. Subject (SS)

2. Direct object (OO)

3. Indirect object (IO)

4. Predicative complement (SP)

5. Prepositional complement (OA)

6. Infinitive complement of object (VO)

7. Verb particle (PL)

Subjects are included only if the verb has been analysed as a passive verb by the tagger, in which case the subject is likely to correspond to the direct object in the active voice.

In an attempt to improve precision in the complement extraction phase, we also use valency dictionaries for filtering the suggested complements. The valency frame of a verb tells us what complements the verb is likely to occur with. The assumption is that this information could be useful for removing unlikely complements, i.e., complements that are not part of the valency frame for the verb in question. The following example illustrates the potential usefulness of this method:

*J midler tijd* <u>*kom*</u> ***greffuinnans gotze*** *fougte thijtt*
However, **the Countess' estate** bailiff <u>came</u> there

In this case, the parser analysed the partial noun phrase *greffuinnans gotze* ("the Countess' estate") as a direct object connected to *kom* ("came"). However, since the word *kom* is present in the valency dictionaries, we know that it is an intransitive verb that does not take a direct object. Hence, this complement can be removed. The valency dictionaries used for filtering are:

1. The Lexin dictionary, containing 3,550 verb lemmas with valency information.[2]

2. The Parole dictionary, containing 4,308 verb lemmas with valency information.[3]

3. An in-house machine translation dictionary, containing 2,852 verb lemmas with valency information.

## 4 Experimental Setup

### 4.1 Data

In order to evaluate the accuracy of our method, we have used ten texts from the period 1527–1737. The text types covered are court records

[1] http://maltparser.org/mco/swedish_parser/swemalt.html

[2] http://spraakbanken.gu.se/lexin/valens_lexikon.html

[3] http://spraakdata.gu.se/parole/lexikon/swedish.parole.lexikon.html

and documents related to the Church. In total, there are 444,075 tokens in the corpus, distributed as follows (number of tokens in parentheses):

Court records:

1. *Per Larssons dombok* (subset), 1638 (11,439)
2. *Hammerdals tingslag*, 1649–1686 (66,928)
3. *Revsunds tingslag*, 1649–1689 (101,020)
4. *Vendels socken*, 1615–45 (59,948)
5. *Vendels socken*, 1736–37 (55,780)
6. *Östra härads i Njudung*, 1602–1605 (34,956)

Documents related to the Church:

1. *Västerås recess*, 1527 (12,193)
2. *1571 års kyrkoordning* (49,043)
3. *Uppsala mötes beslut*, 1593 (26,969)
4. *1686 års kyrkolag* (25,799)

A gold standard of 40 randomly selected sentences from each text was compiled, i.e., in total 400 sentences. The gold standard was produced by manually annotating the sentences regarding verbs and complements. Because sentences are much longer in these texts than in contemporary texts, the 400 sentences together contain a total of 3,105 verbs. Each word form that was interpreted as a verb was annotated with the tag VB, and complements were enclosed in brackets labeled with their grammatical function. This is illustrated in Figure 1, which shows an annotated segment from the test corpus.

For comparison with contemporary text, we make use of a subset of the Stockholm-Umeå Corpus of contemporary Swedish text, SUC (Ejerhed and Källgren, 1997). This subset contains those segments in SUC that have been syntactically annotated and manually revised in the Swedish Treebank. In total, the subset includes approximately 20,000 tokens. Since the tagger used in the experiments on historical texts is trained on the whole of SUC, we had to slightly modify the extraction algorithm in order not to evaluate on the same data as the tagger has been trained. When testing the algorithm on contemporary text, we therefore trained a new model for the tagger, including all tokens in SUC except for the tokens reserved for evaluation.

| | |
|---|---|
| **Anklagadhes/VB**$_1$ | **Was accused/VB**$_1$ |
| [SS$_{vb1}$ | [SS$_{vb1}$ |
| ryttaren | the horse-rider |
| Hindrik | Hindrik |
| Hyldh | Hyldh |
| SS$_{vb1}$] | SS$_{vb1}$] |
| hwilken | who |
| [OO$_{vb2}$ | [OO$_{vb2}$ |
| mökrenkningh | rape |
| OO$_{vb2}$] | OO$_{vb2}$] |
| **giordt/VB**$_2$ | **done/VB**$_2$ |
| medh | with |
| en | a |
| gienta | girl |
| Elin | Elin |
| Eriksdotter | Eriksdotter |
| i | in |
| Sikås | Sikås |
| , | , |
| hwarföre | why |
| rätten | the Court |
| honnom | him |
| **tilspordhe/VB**$_3$ | **asked/VB**$_3$ |
| [OO$_{vb3}$ | [OO$_{vb3}$ |
| om | if |
| han | he |
| [OO$_{vb4}$ | [OO$_{vb4}$ |
| dhetta | this |
| OO $_{vb4}$] | OO $_{vb4}$] |
| **giordt/VB**$_4$ | **done/VB**$_4$ |
| **hafwer/VB**$_5$ | **has/VB**$_5$ |
| OO $_{vb3}$] | OO $_{vb3}$] |

Figure 1: Annotated segment in the test corpus.

### 4.2 Evaluation Metrics

In order to get a more fine-grained picture of the system's performance, we want to evaluate three different aspects:

1. Identification of verbs
2. Identification of complements
3. Identification of holistic verb constructions

The identification of verbs depends only on the part-of-speech tagger and can be evaluated using traditional precision and recall measures, comparing the tokens analysed as verbs by the tagger to the tokens analysed as verbs in the gold standard.

The identification of complements depends on both the tagger and the parser and can also be evaluated using precision and recall measures. In this case, every complement identified by the parser is compared to the complements annotated in the gold standard. Precision is the number of correct complements found by the parser divided by the total number of complements output by the parser, while recall is the number of correct complements found by the parser divided by the number of complements in the gold standard. We do not take the labels into account when assessing complements as correct or incorrect. The motivation for this is that the overall aim of the complement extraction is to present verb expressions to historians, for them to consider whether they are describing work activities or not. In this context, only textual strings will be of interest, and grammatical function labels are ignored. For example, assume that the gold standard is:

*lefverere [IO honom] [OO Sädh]*
deliver [IO him] [OO grain]

and that the system produces:

*lefverere [OO honom]*
deliver [OO him]

In this context, the complement *honom* ("him") will be regarded as correct, even though it has been analysed as a direct object instead of an indirect object. On the other hand, the evaluation of complement identification is strict in that it requires the complement found to coincide exactly with the complement in the gold standard. For example, assume the gold standard is:

*effterfrågat [OA om sinss manss dödh]*
asked [OA about her husband's death]

and that the system produces:

*effterfrågat [OA om sinss manss]*
asked [OA about her husband's]

In this case, the complement will not be regarded as correct because it does not cover exactly the same textual string as the gold standard annotation.

The identification of holistic verb constructions, that is, a verb and all its complements, depends on the identification of verbs and complements, as well as the optional filtering of complements using valency dictionaries. Here we want to evaluate the entire text segment extracted in a way that is relevant for the intended application of the system. First of all, this means that partially correct constructions should be taken into account. Consider again the earlier example:

*effterfrågat [OA om sinss manss dödh]*
asked [OA about her husband's death]

and assume that the system produces:

*effterfrågat [OA om sinss manss]*
asked [OA about her husband's]

As noted above, this complement would be considered incorrect in the precision/recall evaluation of complement extraction, even though only one word is missing as compared to the gold standard, and the output would probably still be valuable to the end-user. Secondly, we should consider the total segment extracted for a verb including all complements, rather than inspecting each complement separately.

In order to reflect partially correct complements and take the total segment extracted for each verb into account, we use a string-based evaluation method for the identification of holistic verb constructions. In this evaluation, all labels and brackets are removed before comparing the segments extracted to the segments in the text corpus and each extracted instance is classified as falling into one of the four following categories:

- Fully correct complement set (F)
- Partially correct complement set (P)
- Incorrect complement set (I)
- Missing complement set (M)

A complement set is regarded as fully correct if the output string generated by the system is identical to the corresponding gold standard string. Since labels and brackets have been removed, these analyses will be regarded as identical:

*lemnat [IO swaranden] [OO tid]*
given [IO the defendant] [OO time]

*lemnat [OO swaranden tid]*
given [OO the defendant time]

A complement set is regarded as partially correct if the output string generated by the system has a non-empty overlap with the corresponding gold standard string. For example, the following three sets of analyses will be considered as partially correct (gold standard top, system output bottom):

*lefverere [IO honom] [OO Sädh]*
deliver [IO him] [OO Grain]
*lefverere [OO honom]*
deliver [OO him]

*effterfrågat [OA om sinss manss dödh]*
asked [OA about her husband's death]
*effterfrågat [OA om sinss manss]*
asked [OA about her husband's]

*betale [PL åter] [IO här Mattz] [OO Rågen]*
pay [PL back] [IO mister Mattz] [OO the Rye]
*betale [OO åter här Mattz]*
pay [OO back mister Mattz]

A (non-empty) complement set is regarded as incorrect if the output string has no overlap with the gold standard string. Finally, a complement set is regarded as missing if the output string is empty but the gold standard string is not. It is worth noting that the four categories are mutually exclusive.

## 5 Results and Discussion

In this section, we evaluate the identification of verbs, complements and holistic verb constructions using the data and metrics described in the previous section.

### 5.1 Verbs

Results on the identification of verbs using part-of-speech tagging, with and without normalisation, are reported in Table 2. As can be seen, recall drastically increases when normalisation rules are applied prior to tagging, even though the normalisation rules used in this experiment are formulated based on a subset of one single 17th century text, and the test corpus contains samples of various text types ranging from 1527–1737. Normalisation also has a small positive effect on precision, and the best result for historical texts is 78.4% precision and 76.0% recall. This is slightly lower than the results presented by Pettersson and Nivre (2011) where only 17th century text was used for evaluation, indicating that the normalisation rules are somewhat biased towards 17th century text, and that the results could be improved if normalisation were adapted to specific time periods. It is also worth noting that the results are substantially lower for historical text than the results for contemporary text, with precision and recall at 99.1%, but still high enough to be useful in the intended context of application.

| | Precision | Recall | F-score |
|---|---|---|---|
| **Raw** | 75.4 | 60.0 | 66.9 |
| **Norm** | 78.4 | 76.0 | 77.2 |
| **SUC** | 99.1 | 99.1 | 99.1 |

Table 2: Identification of verbs by tagging. Raw = Unnormalised input text. Norm = Normalisation of input prior to tagging. SUC = Subset of Stockholm-Umeå corpus of contemporary Swedish texts, as described in section 4.1.

Tokens that are still erroneously analysed by the tagger include the following cases:

- tokens where the old spelling is identical to an existing, but different, word form in contemporary language; for example, the spelling *skal* would in contemporary language be considered a noun ("shell") but in the old texts this spelling is used for a word that is nowadays spelled *skall* ("shall/should") and should be regarded as a verb;
- ambiguous words; for example, past participles are often spelled the same way as the corresponding past tense verb, but participles are not regarded as verb forms in our experiments;[4]
- tokens that have not been normalised enough and thus do not correspond to a word form recognised by the tagger, e.g., the word form *lemnas* which in contemporary language should be spelled as *lämnas* ("be left").

[4] Participles are only used adjectivally in Swedish, as the perfect tense is formed using a distinct supine form of the verb.

| | Precision | Recall | F-score |
|---|---|---|---|
| **Raw** | 24.8 | 27.5 | 26.1 |
| **Norm** | 28.3 | 28.2 | 28.2 |
| **+Valency** | 33.1 | 25.5 | 28.8 |
| **SUC** | 68.2 | 70.7 | 69.5 |
| **+Valency** | 71.8 | 56.2 | 63.0 |

Table 3: Identification of complements by parsing. Raw = Unnormalised input text. Norm = Normalisation of input prior to tagging and parsing. +Valency = Adding valency filtering to the setting in the preceding row. SUC = Subset of Stockholm-Umeå corpus of contemporary Swedish texts, as described in section 4.1.

| | F | P | I | M |
|---|---|---|---|---|
| **Raw** | 32.6 | 20.3 | 29.3 | 17.8 |
| **Norm** | 34.5 | 19.5 | 25.2 | 20.8 |
| **+Valency** | 38.7 | 16.9 | 18.9 | 25.5 |
| **SUC** | 30.3 | 54.2 | 9.1 | 6.4 |
| **+Valency** | 30.8 | 47.9 | 6.8 | 14.6 |

Table 4: Identification of holistic verb constructions. F = Fully correct, P = Partially correct, I = Incorrect, M = Missing. Raw = Unnormalised input text. Norm = Normalisation of input prior to tagging and parsing. +Valency = Adding valency filtering to the setting in the preceding row. SUC = Subset of Stockholm-Umeå corpus of contemporary Swedish texts, as described in section 4.1.

## 5.2 Complements

Recall and precision for the identification of complements using parsing are presented in Table 3. In this case, normalisation has a smaller effect than in the case of tagging and affects precision more than recall. Adding a filter that eliminates unlikely complements based on the valency frame of the verb in existing dictionaries predictably improves precision at the expense of recall and results in a small F-score improvement.

Again, the best scores on the historical texts are much lower than the corresponding results for contemporary text, with an F-score of 28.8% in the former case and 69.5% in the latter, but it is worth remembering that precision and recall on exactly matching complements is a harsh metric that is not directly relevant for the intended application. Finally, it is worth noting that the valency filter has a large negative impact on recall for the modern texts, resulting in a decrease in the F-score, which indicates that the parser in this case is quite successful at identifying complements (in the wide sense) that are not covered by the valency dictionaries.

## 5.3 Verb Constructions

As argued in section 4.2, precision and recall measures are not sufficient for evaluating the extraction of holistic verb constructions. A more relevant assessment is made by counting the number of *fully correct*, *partially correct*, *incorrect* and *missing* complement sets for the verbs identified. Table 4 summarises the results in accordance with this metric.

First of all, we see that normalisation again has a rather small effect on overall results, increasing the number of fully correct constructions and decreasing the number of incorrect constructions, but also leading to an increase in the number of missing complements. Adding the valency filter to remove unlikely complements has a similar effect and increases the percentage of correctly extracted verb constructions to 38.7% while decreasing the share of incorrect constructions to 18.9%. However, it also increases the percentage of verbs with missing complement sets from 20.8% to 25.5%. This is partly due to the fact that some of the verbs are used in a slightly different way in historical text as compared to contemporary text, meaning that the valency frames are not as reliable. For example, the verb *avstå* ("refrain") in the historical corpus is used with a direct object, as in *Anders Andersson afstådt sitt skatte hemman* ("Anders Andersson refrained his homestead"), whereas in a contemporary context this verb would more likely be used with a prepositional complement, *avstå* **från** *någonting* ("refrain **from** something").

In total, 55.6% of the verbs are assigned a fully or partially correct set of complements. This is again lower than the result for contemporary texts (78.7%), but the difference is smaller than for the previous metrics, which is encouraging given that the evaluation in this section is most relevant for the intended application. Moreover, it is worth noting that the difference is mostly to be found in the category of partially correct constructions, where the best result for modern texts is 54.2%, to be compared to 16.9% for the historical texts. With respect to fully correct constructions, however, the results are actually better for the historical texts than for the modern texts, 38.7% vs. 30.8%, a rather surprising positive result.

## 6 Conclusion

We have presented a method for automatically extracting verbs and their complements from historical Swedish texts, more precisely texts from the Early Modern era (1550–1800), with the aim of providing language technology support for historical research. We have shown that it is possible to use existing contemporary NLP tools and dictionaries for this purpose, provided that the input text is first (automatically) normalised to a more modern spelling. With the best configuration of our tools, we can identify verbs with an F-score of 77.2% and find a partially or completely correct set of complements for 55.6% of the verbs. To the best of our knowledge, these are the first results of their kind.

In addition to presenting a method for the identification of verb constructions, we have also proposed a new evaluation framework for such methods in the context of information extraction for historical research. As a complement to standard precision and recall metrics for verbs and their complements, we have evaluated the text segments extracted using the categories *fully correct*, *partially correct*, *incorrect*, and *missing*. One important topic for future research is to validate this evaluation framework by correlating it to the perceived usefulness of the system when used by historians working on the Gender and Work Database. Preliminary experiments using a prototype system indicate that this kind of support can in fact reduce the time-consuming, manual work that is currently carried out by historians and other researchers working with older texts.

Another topic for future research concerns the variation in performance across time periods and text types. In the current evaluation, court records and papers related to the Church ranging from 1527 to 1737 have been sampled in the gold standard. It would be interesting to explore in more detail how the program performs on the oldest texts as compared to the youngest texts, and on court records as compared to the other genres.

## References


Maria Ågren, Rosemarie Fiebranz, Erik Lindberg, and Jonas Lindström. 2011. Making verbs count. The research project 'Gender and Work' and its methodology. *Scandinavian Economic History Review*, 59(3):271–291. Forthcoming.

Gösta Bergman. 1995. *Kortfattad svensk språkhistoria*. Prisma Magnum, Stockholm, 5th edition.

Thorsten Brants. 2000. TnT - a statistical part-of-speech tagger. In *Proceedings of the 6th Applied Natural Language Processing Conference (ANLP)*, Seattle, Washington, USA.

Nils Edling. 1937. *Uppländska domböcker*. Almqvist & Wiksells.

Eva Ejerhed and Gunnel Källgren. 1997. Stockholm Umeå Corpus. Version 1.0. Produced by Department of Linguistics, Umeå University and Department of Linguistics, Stockholm University. ISBN 91-7191-348-3.

Sofia Gustafson-Capková and Britt Hartmann. 2006. Manual of the Stockholm Umeå Corpus version 2.0. Technical report, December.

Péter Halácsy, András Kornai, and Csaba Oravecz. 2007. HunPos - an open source trigram tagger. In *Proceedings of the 45th Annual Meeting of the Association for Computational Linguistics*, pages 209–212, Prague, Czech Republic.

Beáta B. Megyesi. 2009. The open source tagger HunPos for Swedish. In *Proceedings of the 17th Nordic Conference on Computational Linguistics (NODALIDA)*.

Joakim Nivre, Johan Hall, and Jens Nilsson. 2006a. MaltParser: A data-driven parser-generator for dependency parsing. In *Proceedings of the 5th international conference on Language Resources and Evaluation (LREC)*, pages 2216–2219, Genoa, Italy, May.

Joakim Nivre, Jens Nilsson, and Johan Hall. 2006b. Talbanken05: A Swedish treebank with phrase structure and dependency annotation. In *Proceedings of the 5th international conference on Language Resources and Evaluation (LREC*, pages 24–26, Genoa, Italy, May.

Csaba Oravecz, Bálint Sass, and Eszter Simon. 2010. Semi-automatic normalization of Old Hungarian codices. In *Proceedings of the ECAI Workshop on Language Technology for Cultural Heritage, Social Sciences, and Humanities (LaTeCH)*, pages 55–59, Faculty of Science, University of Lisbon Lisbon, Portugal, August.

Marco Pennacchiotti and Fabio Massimo Zanzotto. 2008. Natural language processing across time: An empirical investigation on Italian. In *Advances in Natural Language Processing. GoTAL, LNAI*, volume 5221, pages 371–382.

Eva Pettersson and Joakim Nivre. 2011. Automatic verb extraction from historical Swedish texts. In *Proceedings of the 5th ACL-HLT Workshop on Language Technology for Cultural Heritage, Social Sciences, and Humanities*, pages 87–95, Portland, OR,

USA, June. Association for Computational Linguistics.

Vito Rocio, Mário Amado Alves, José Gabriel Lopes, Maria Francisca Xavier, and Graça Vicente. 1999. Automated creation of a partially syntactically annotated corpus of Medieval Portuguese using contemporary Portuguese resources. In *Proceedings of the ATALA workshop on Treebanks*, Paris, France.

Cristina Sánchez-Marco, Gemma Boleda, and Lluís Padró. 2011. Extending the tool, or how to annotate historical language varieties. In *Proceedings of the 5th ACL-HLT Workshop on Language Technology for Cultural Heritage, Social Sciences, and Humanities*, pages 1–9, Portland, OR, USA, June. Association for Computational Linguistics.

# A Classical Chinese Corpus with Nested Part-of-Speech Tags

**John Lee**
The Halliday Centre for Intelligent Applications of Language Studies
Department of Chinese, Translation and Linguistics
City University of Hong Kong
jsylee@cityu.edu.hk

## Abstract

We introduce a corpus of classical Chinese poems that has been word segmented and tagged with parts-of-speech (POS). Due to the ill-defined concept of a 'word' in Chinese, previous Chinese corpora suffer from a lack of standardization in word segmentation, resulting in inconsistencies in POS tags, therefore hindering interoperability among corpora. We address this problem with nested POS tags, which accommodates different theories of wordhood and facilitates research objectives requiring annotations of the 'word' at different levels of granularity.

## 1 Introduction

There has been much effort in enriching text corpora with linguistic information, such as parts-of-speech (Francis and Kučera, 1982) and syntactic structures (Marcus et al., 1993). The past decade has seen the development of Chinese corpora, mostly for Modern Chinese (McEnery & Xiao, 2004; Xue et al., 2005), but also a few for pre-modern, or "classical", Chinese (Wei et al. 97; Huang et al. 2006; Hu & McLaughlin 2007).

One common design issue for any corpus of Chinese, whether modern or classical, is word segmentation. Yet, no segmentation standard has emerged in the computational linguistics research community. Hence, two adjacent characters X1X2 may be considered a single word in one corpus, but treated as two distinct words $X_1$ and $X_2$ in another[1]; furthermore, the part-of-speech (POS) tag assigned to $X_1X_2$ in the first corpus may differ from the tag for $X_1$ and the tag for $X_2$ in the second. These inconsistencies have made it difficult to compare, combine or exploit Chinese corpora. This paper addresses this problem by proposing a new method for word segmentation and POS tagging for Chinese and applying it on a corpus of classical Chinese poems.

## 2 Research Objective

A Chinese character may either function as a word by itself, or combine with its neighbor(s) to form a multi-character word. Since the goal of part-of-speech (POS) tagging is to assign one tag to each word, a prerequisite step is word segmentation, i.e., drawing word boundaries within a string of Chinese characters. The general test for 'wordhood' is whether "the meaning of the whole is compositional of its parts"; in other words, $X_1X_2$ forms one word when the meaning of the characters $X_1X_2$ does not equal to the meaning of $X_1$ plus the meaning of $X_2$ (Feng, 1998). Consider the string 沙門 *sha men* 'Buddhist monk'. As a transliteration from Sanskrit, it bears no semantic relation with its constituent characters 沙 *sha* 'sand' and 門 *men* 'door'. The two characters therefore form one word.

From the point of view of corpus development, word segmentation has two consequences. First, it defines the smallest unit for POS analysis. It would be meaningless to analyze the POS of the individual characters as,

[1] This phenomenon can be compared with what is often known as multiword expressions (Sag et al., 2002) in other languages.

say, 沙/NN and 門/NN (see Table 1 for the list of POS tags used in this paper). Instead, the two characters *sha* and *men* together should be assigned one POS tag, 沙門/NN.

Second, word segmentation sets boundaries for automatic word retrieval. A simple string search for "*sha men*" on a non-segmented corpus might yield spurious matches, where *sha* is the last character of the preceding word, and *men* is the first character of the following one. In a word study on 本覺 *ben jue* 'original enlightenment' (Lancaster, 2010), based on a non-segmented corpus of the Chinese Buddhist Canon, the author needed to manually examine each of the 763 occurrences of the string *ben jue* in order to determine which of them are in fact the word in question, rather than accidental collocations of the two characters. Word boundaries resulting from word segmentation would have removed these ambiguities, expedited the search and enabled this kind of word studies to be performed on much larger scales.

There is not yet a scholarly consensus on a precise definition of 'wordhood' in Classical Chinese (Feng, 1998). Inevitably, then, treatment of word segmentation varies widely from corpus to corpus. Some did not perform word segmentation (Huang et al. 2006); others adopted their own principles (Wei et al. 1997; Hu & McLaughlin 2007). The lack of standardization not only hinders corpus interoperability, but also makes it difficult for any single corpus to cater to users with different assumptions about wordhood or different research objectives. What is regarded as one word for a user may be two words in the eyes of another. Consider two alternative analyses of the string 黃河 *huang he* 'Yellow River' in two research tasks. For retrieval of geographical references in a text, it should ideally be tagged as one single proper noun, 黃河/NR; to study parallelisms in poetry, however, it is better to be tagged as two separate words, 黃/JJ *huang* 'yellow' followed by 河/NN *he* 'river', in order not to obscure the crucial POS sequence 'adjective-noun' that signals parallelism in a couplet. To settle on any particular word segmentation criterion, then, is to risk omitting useful information.

We are not qualified to lay down any definitive criterion for word segmentation; rather, we advocate a theory-neutral approach through nested POS tags: characters are analyzed individually whenever possible, but annotated with hierarchical tags to recognize possible word boundaries.

## 3 Previous Work

In this section, we summarize previous practices in Chinese word segmentation (section 3.1) and part-of-speech tagging (section 3.2), then describe existing frameworks of multi-level tagging (section 3.3).

### 3.1 Word segmentation

As mentioned in Section 2, a common test for word segmentation is "compositionality of meaning". While there are clear-cut cases like *sha men*, many cases fall in the grey area. Indeed, even native speakers can agree on word boundaries in modern Chinese only about 76% of the time (Sproat et al., 1996). It is not surprising, then, that a myriad of guidelines for word segmentation have been proposed for various corpora of Modern Chinese (Liu et al., 1994; Chinese Knowledge Information Processing Group, 1996; Yu et al., 1998; Xia 2000; Sproat and Emerson, 2003). In the rest of this section, we first review the approaches taken in three classical Chinese corpora, developed respectively at Jiaotong University (Huang et al., 2006), University of Sheffield (Hu et al., 2005) and the Academia Sinica (Wei et al., 1997). We then describe in more detail a modern Chinese corpus, the Penn Chinese Treebank (Xue et al., 2005).

***Corpus at Jiaotong University***. This treebank consists of 1000 sentences of pre-Tsin classical Chinese. No word segmentation was performed. On the one hand, this decision may be supported by the fact that "in general the syllable, written with a single character, and the word correspond in Classical Chinese" (Pulleyblank, 1995). On the other hand, there are nonetheless a non-negligible number of strings for which it makes little sense to analyze their constituent characters. These include not only transliterations of foreign loanwords such as *sha men*, but also bound morphemes [2] and reduplications [3] (Pulleyblank, 1995). The lack of segmentation in this corpus also leads to the lack of word boundaries to support word retrieval.

---

[2] E.g., 然 ran, a suffix forming expressive adverbs such as 卒然 *cu ran* 'abruptly'

[3] E.g., 須 *xu* 'wait', which, via partial reduplication, derives 須臾 *xu yu* 'a moment'

***Academia Sinica Ancient Chinese Corpus***. With more than 500K characters, this is the largest word-segmented and POS-tagged corpus of classical Chinese. In the annotation process, a character is presumed to be a word in its own right; it is combined with other characters to form a word if they fall into one of the following categories: parallel and subordinating compounds; bisyllabic words; reduplications; and proper nouns. Two of these categories, namely, bisyllabic words and reduplications, are retained in our word segmentation criteria (see section 4.1). Proper nouns, as well as parallel and subordinating compounds, however, are treated differently (see section 4.2).

***Sheffield Corpus of Chinese***. This corpus has more than 109K characters of archaic Chinese and 147K characters of medieval Chinese. Word segmentation was performed by hand. Their criteria for word segmentation, unfortunately, do not seem to be publicly available.

***The Penn Chinese Treebank***. This widely used treebank of modern Chinese boasts an extensively documented word segmentation procedure (Xia, 2000), which rests on six principles. We follow their principle that complex internal structures should be segmented when possible (see section 4.2). We also retain a second principle that a bound morpheme forms a word with its neighbor[4], although morphemes in Classical Chinese are nearly always free forms (Feng, 1998).

A third criterion is the number of syllables. Consider a noun phrase $N_1N_2$ where the first noun ($N_1$) modifies the second ($N_2$). This noun phrase is considered one word if $N_2$ consists of one character, but two words if $N_2$ has two or more characters. For example, the string 北京大學 *bei jing da xue* 'Peking University' is segmented as two words *bei jing* 'Peking' and *da xue* 'university', since 'university' is made up of two characters; however, a similar string 北京市 *bei jing shi* 'Beijing City' is one word, since 'city' consists of just one character *shi*. Given the dominance of monosyllabic words in classical Chinese, a direct application of this principle would have resulted in a large number of multi-character words in our corpus.

Further, there are three linguistic tests. The "semantic compositionality" test has already been outlined in section 2 and is not repeated here. The "insertion test" asks whether another morpheme can be inserted between two characters $X_1$ and $X_2$; if so, then $X_1X_2$ is unlikely to be a word. The "XP-substitution test" asks if a morpheme can be replaced by a phrase of the same type; if not, then it is likely to be part of a word. Performing these tests requires intuition and familiarity with the language. Since no human is a native speaker of classical Chinese, we found it difficult to objectively and reliably apply these tests. Instead, we strive to accommodate different views of wordhood in our corpus.

[4] E.g., the morpheme 本 *ben* is bound to the character 人 *ren* 'person' in the word 本人 *ben ren* 'oneself'

### 3.2 Part-of-Speech Tagging

Following word segmentation, each word is assigned a part-of-speech (POS) tag. Most POS tagsets cover the major word categories, such as nouns, verbs, and adjectives; they differ in the more fine-grained distinctions within these categories. For examples, verbs may be further subdivided into transitive and intransitive; nouns may be further distinguished as common, proper or temporal; and so on. In general, a larger tagset provides more precise information, but may result in lower inter-annotator agreement, and hence reduced reliability.

Classical Chinese does not have inflectional morphology; this makes POS tags even more informative, but also makes inter-annotator agreement more challenging. As with other languages, the POS tagset is tailored to fit one's research objective, as reflected in the wide-ranging levels of granularity in different corpora, from 21 tags in (Huang et al., 2006), 26 in the Peking University corpus (Yu et al., 2002), 46 in the Academia Sinica Balanced Corpus (Chen et al., 1996), to 111 in the Sheffield Corpus of Chinese (Hu et al., 2005). Our tagset is based on that of the Penn Chinese Treebank, which lies towards the lower end of this spectrum, with 33 tags.

### 3.3 Multi-level Tagging

In principle, any text span may be annotated at an arbitrary number of levels using, for example, stand-off annotation. In practice, most effort has concentrated on identifying named entities, such as (Doddington et al., 2004). While our corpus does specify word boundaries of multi-character proper nouns, it tackles all other forms of compounds in general (section 4.2).

Turning to the Chinese language in particular, we are by no means the first to point out inconsistencies in word segmentation and POS tags among different corpora. Annotators of the Penn Chinese Treebank, among others, also recognized this issue (Xia, 2000). As a remedy, a two-level annotation method is used on a number of grammatical constructions. Suppose it is uncertain whether $X_1$ and $X_2$ should be considered two separate words or one word. Under this method, $X_1$ and $X_2$ are first tagged individually (say, as $pos_1$ and $pos_2$), then tagged as a whole (say, as *pos*), and finally grouped together with a pair of brackets, resulting in the final form ($X_1/pos_1$ $X_2/pos_2$)/*pos*. For instance, rather than simply tagging the string 走上來 *zou shang lai* 'walk up' as one verb 走上來/VV, the three-character word is further segmented internally as 走 *zou* 'walk' and 上來 *shang lai* 'come up', hence (走/VV 上來/VV)/VV. This method makes the interpretation more flexible: those who consider *zou shang lai* to be one word can simply ignore the details inside the brackets; others who view *zou* and *shang lai* as stand-alones can discard the brackets and retain their individual analyses.

This device is used in the Penn Chinese Treebank on only a narrow range of constructions to ensure compatibility with the Chinese Knowledge Information Processing Group (1996) and with (Liu et al., 1994). In contrast, it is generalized in our corpus as nested tags of arbitrary depth, and used systematically and extensively to mark alternate word boundaries.

| Tag | Part-of-Speech |
|---|---|
| AD | Adverb |
| CD | Cardinal number |
| DER | Resultative *de5* |
| DEV | Manner *de5* |
| FW | Foreign word |
| IJ | Interjection |
| JJ | Other noun modifier |
| LC | Localizer |
| NN | Other noun |
| NR | Proper noun |
| NT | Temporal noun |
| P | Preposition |
| PN | Pronoun |
| SP | Sentence-final particle |
| VV | Other verb |

Table 1: Part-of-speech tags of the Penn Chinese Treebank that are referenced in this paper. Please see (Xia, 2000) for the full list.

## 4 Corpus Design

This section describes our corpus at two levels, first the 'strings without internal structures' (section 4.1), which may be combined to form 'strings with internal structures' (section 4.2) and marked with nested brackets and tags.

### 4.1 Strings without internal structures

The lowest annotation layer marks the boundaries of what will be referred to as 'strings without internal structures'. These are roughly equivalent to 'words' in existing Chinese corpora.

***Segmentation criteria***. Following the practice of the Academia Sinica Ancient Chinese Corpus, each character is initially presumed to be a monosyllabic word. The annotator may then decide that it forms a multi-character word with its neighbor(s) under one of the categories listed in Table 2. This set of categories represents a more stringent segmentation criterion than those in most existing corpora, such that the number of multi-character words is relatively small in our target text (see section 6).

| Category | Example |
|---|---|
| Foreign loanwords | 匈奴 *xiong nu* 'the Xiongnu people'<br>e.g., 匈奴/NR 圍酒泉 'The Xiongnus surrounded the city of Jiuquan' |
| Numbers | 十五 *shi wu* 'fifteen', 十六 *shi liu* 'sixteen'<br>e.g., 少年十五/CD 十六/CD 時 'as a youth of 15 or 16 years of age' |
| Reduplications | 駸駸 *qin qin* 'quickly'<br>e.g., 車馬去駸駸/AD 'the chariots went quickly' |
| Bound morphemes | 油然 *you ran* 'spontaneously'<br>e.g., 天油然/AD 作雲 'the sky spontaneously makes clouds' |

Table 2: Categories of multi-character words that are considered 'strings without internal structures' (see Section 4.1). Each category is illustrated with one example from our corpus.

***Part-of-speech tagging***. Similar to the principle adopted by the Penn Chinese Treebank,

POS tags are assigned not according to the meaning of the word, but to syntactic distribution (Xia, 2000), i.e. the role the word plays in the sentence. Compared to modern Chinese, it is a much more frequent phenomenon in the classical language for a word to function as different parts-of-speech in different contexts. For example, it is not uncommon for nouns to be used as verbs or adverbs, and verbs as adverbs (Pulleyblank, 1995). Consider two nouns 鐘 *zhong* 'bell' and 雲 *yun* 'cloud'. The former is used as a verb 'to ring' in the verse 深山何處鐘/VV 'where in the deep mountain [is it] ringing'; the latter serves as an adverb 'in the manner of clouds' in the verse 倏忽雲/AD 散 'quickly disperses like clouds'. They are therefore tagged as a verb (VV) and an adverb (AD). Likewise, when the verb 盡 *jin* 'exhaust' has an adverbial sense 'completely', such as in 送君盡/AD 惆悵 'saying farewell to you, I am utterly sad', it is tagged as such.

We largely adopted the tagset of the Penn Chinese Treebank. As the standard most familiar to the computational linguistics community, their tagset has been used in annotating a large volume of modern Chinese texts, offering us the possibility of leveraging existing modern Chinese annotations as training data as we seek automatic methods to expand our corpus. For the most part, the Penn tagset can be adopted for classical Chinese in a straightforward manner. For example, the tag PN (pronoun) is used, instead of the modern Chinese pronouns 我 *wo* 'I' and 你 *ni* 'you', for the classical equivalents 吾 *wu* 'I' and 爾 *er* 'you'. Similarly, the tag SP (sentence-final particles) is applied, rather than to the modern Chinese particles 吧 *ba* or 呀 *a*, to their classical counterparts 耳 *er* and 也 *ye*. In other cases, we have identified roughly equivalent word classes in classical Chinese. To illustrate, although the classical language has no prepositions in the modern sense, the P (preposition) tag is retained for words known as coverbs (Pulleyblank, 1995). A few tags specific to modern Chinese are discarded; these include DER, DEV, and FW (see Table 1).

## 4.2 Strings with internal structures

Since our criteria for 'strings without internal structures' are intentionally strict, they disqualify many multi-character strings that may fail the "semantic compositionality" test and are therefore commonly deemed words. These include proper names with analyzable structures, as well as parallel or subordinating compounds, which are considered 'strings with internal structures' in our corpus, and are annotated with nested tags.

| Category | Example |
|---|---|
| Parallel compounds | |
| Similar meaning | 君王 *jun wang* 'king'<br>= 君 *jun* 'ruler' + 王 *wang* 'king'<br>(君/NN 王/NN)/NN |
| Related meaning | 骨肉 *gu rou* 'kin'<br>= 骨 *gu* 'bone' + 肉 *rou* 'flesh'<br>(骨/NN 肉/NN)/NN |
| Opposite meaning | 是非 *shi fei* 'rumors'<br>= 是 *shi* 'right' + 非 *fei* 'wrong'<br>(是/JJ 非/JJ)/NN |
| Subordinating compounds | |
| Verb-object | 識事 *shi shi* 'experience'<br>= 識 *shi* 'understand' + 事 *shi* 'affairs'<br>(識/VV 事/NN)/NN |
| Subject-verb | 日落 ri luo 'sunset'<br>= 日 *ri* 'sun' + 落 *luo* 'descend'<br>(日/NN 落/VV)/NN |
| Adjectival modifier | 少年 *shao nian* 'youth'<br>= 少 *shao* 'few' + 年 *nian* 'year<br>(少/JJ 年/NN)/NN |
| Noun modifier | 家食 *jia shi* 'household food'<br>= 家 *jia* 'house' + 食 *shi* 'food'<br>(家/NN 食/NN)/NN |

Table 3: Categories of multi-character words that are considered 'strings with internal structures' (see Section 4.2). Each category is illustrated with an example from our corpus. Both the individual characters and the compound they form receive a POS tag.

***Segmentation criteria.*** All parallel and subordinating compounds are considered to be 'strings with internal structures'. A parallel compound is a two-character noun, verb and adjective "in which neither member dominates the other" (Packard, 1998) and it refers to one meaning despite having two characters. For example, the noun compound 骨肉 *gu rou*, formed from from 骨 *gu* 'bone' and 肉 *rou* 'flesh', means simply 'kin' rather than 'bone and flesh'. In practice, in our corpus, two characters are considered to be a parallel compound when they are of the same POS, and have similar, related, or opposite meaning, as shown in Table 3. The individual characters are 'strings without internal structure' and receive their own POS tags, while the compound also receives its own tag.

Subordinating compounds refer to those where "one member (the modifier) is subordinate to and modifies the other (the head)" (Packard, 1998). For example, the compound 少年 *shao nian* is made up of an adjective 少 *shao* 'few' modifying a noun 年 *nian* 'year', but together has the specialized meaning 'youth'. In our corpus, two characters are considered to form a subordinating compound when they have the verb-object or subject-verb relationship, or a modifier-head relationship, including adjectival modifiers and noun modifiers.

Proper names can also have internal structures, whenever the grammatical structure of their constituent characters may be discerned. The most common such proper names in our corpus are geographical names, such as 黃河 *huang he* 'Yellow River', where the adjective *huang* 'yellow' modifies the noun *he* 'river'. Another frequent type is personal names with titles, such as 始興公 *shi xing gong* 'Duke Shixing', where one noun modifies another.

Our definition of 'strings with internal structures' is deliberately broad. As a result, some of these strings would not be considered to be a word or compound by all or even most linguists. Many verb-object combinations, for example, may well fail the 'semantic compositionality' test. This is intentional: rather than searching for the perfect segmentation policy that suits everyone [5], the nested annotations allow the user to decide which level of tags is suitable for the research objective at hand.

***Part-of-speech tagging***. The nested annotations of 'strings with internal structures' not only mark the possible word boundaries, but also assign a POS tag at every level, since that tag is not always predictable from the tags of the constituent characters. Consider the verse in Table 4. There are two possible segmentations for the string 晚來 *wan lai*. As two separate words, *wan* 'evening' and *lai* 'come' form a clause meaning 'as the evening comes'; the whole verse may be translated 'the weather turns chilly as the evening comes'. Alternatively, they can be taken as a two-character word, i.e., simply a temporal noun 晚來/NT *wan lai* 'evening'. In this case, the proper translation would be 'the weather turns chilly at evening'. Notice that the tag NT (temporal noun) cannot be predicted from the tags at the lower level, NN (noun) and VV (verb).

Further, these nested tags indicate alternatives for future syntactic analysis. In dependency grammar, for instance, the adjectival verb *qiu* 'chilly' would be the head of the verb *lai*, which is the verb in the subordinate clause; in the second interpretation, however, it would be the head of a temporal modifier, *wan lai* 'evening'.

<table>
<tr><td>天</td><td>氣</td><td>晚</td><td>來</td><td>秋</td></tr>
<tr><td>tian</td><td>qi</td><td>wan</td><td>lai</td><td>qiu</td></tr>
<tr><td colspan="2">'weather'</td><td>'night'</td><td>'come'</td><td>'chilly'</td></tr>
<tr><td colspan="2" rowspan="2">NN</td><td>NN</td><td>VV</td><td rowspan="2">JJ</td></tr>
<tr><td colspan="2">NT</td></tr>
</table>

Table 4: POS annotations of an example sentence with a string, *wan lai* 'evening', that has internal structure. See Section 4.2 for two possible translations, and Table 1 for the meaning of the POS tags.

<table>
<tr><td colspan="5">Verse 1</td></tr>
<tr><td>獨</td><td>樹</td><td>臨</td><td>關</td><td>門</td></tr>
<tr><td>du</td><td>shu</td><td>lin</td><td>guan</td><td>men</td></tr>
<tr><td>'only'</td><td>'tree'</td><td>'upon'</td><td>'pass'</td><td>'entrance'</td></tr>
<tr><td>JJ</td><td>NN</td><td>VV</td><td>NN</td><td>NN</td></tr>
<tr><td colspan="5">'a lone tree watches the entrance of the pass'</td></tr>
<tr><td colspan="5">Verse 2</td></tr>
<tr><td>黃</td><td>河</td><td>向</td><td>天</td><td>外</td></tr>
<tr><td>huang</td><td>he</td><td>Xiang</td><td>tian</td><td>wai</td></tr>
<tr><td>'yellow'</td><td>'river'</td><td>'face'</td><td>'sky'</td><td>'outside'</td></tr>
<tr><td>JJ</td><td>NN</td><td rowspan="2">VV</td><td rowspan="2">NN</td><td rowspan="2">LC</td></tr>
<tr><td colspan="2">NR</td></tr>
<tr><td colspan="5">'The Yellow River faces the outer sky'</td></tr>
</table>

Table 5: POS annotations of a couplet, i.e., a pair of two verses, in a classical Chinese poem. See Table 1 for the meaning of the POS tags.

One significant benefit of nested annotation, especially in classical Chinese poetry, is the preservation of the underlying parallelism. Two consecutive verses, called a *couplet*, always have the same number of characters. Moreover, two characters at the same position in the two verses

[5] The verb-object combination, for example, is "among the hardest cases for the word definition" (Xia, 2000).

often have the same or related POS. Consider the couplet in Table 5. The first two characters of each verse, 獨樹 *du shu* 'lone tree' and 黃河 *huang he* 'Yellow River', respectively, are parallel; both are noun phrases formed by a noun modified by the preceding adjective.

In most existing corpora, *huang he* would be simply considered one word and assigned one tag, namely, a proper noun 黃河/NR. This treatment would, first of all, result in one verse having four words and the other five, making it difficult to analyze character correspondences. It also obscures the parallelism between the noun phrases *du shu* and *huang he*: both are JJ-NN, i.e. 'adjective-noun'. In contrast, our corpus annotates *huang he* as a string with internal structures (黃/JJ 河/NN)/NR, as shown in Table 5. Its outer tag (NR) preserves the meaning and boundary of the whole proper noun *huang he*, facilitating word searches; the inner tags support automatic identification of parallel structures.

In all examples above of 'strings with internal structures', the nested annotations have only a depth of one. In theory, the depth can be arbitrary, although in practice, it rarely exceeds two. An example is the string 細柳營 *xi liu ying* 'Little Willow military camp'. At the coarsest level, the three characters may be considered to form one proper noun, referring to a camp at the ancient Chinese capital. The string obviously has 'internal structures', composed of 營 *ying* 'military camp' and its location, the place name 細柳 *xi liu* 'Xiliu'. Furthermore, this place name has an evocative meaning, 'little willow', made up of the adjective *xi* 'little' and the noun *liu* 'willow'. As shown in Table 6, this analysis results in a three-level, nested annotation ((細/JJ 柳/NN)/NR 營/NN)/NR.

Furthermore, these three characters are the last characters in the second verse of a couplet. Table 6 also shows the annotations for the corresponding characters in the first verse, 新豐市 *xin feng shi* 'Xinfeng city'. Taken together, the annotations reveal the perfect symmetry of both noun phrases at every level of analysis.

## 5 Data

Among the various literary genres, poetry enjoys perhaps the most elevated status in the classical Chinese tradition. The Tang Dynasty is considered the golden age of *shi*, one of the five subgenres of Chinese poetry. The *Complete Shi Poetry of the Tang* (Peng, 1960), originally compiled in 1705, consists of nearly 50,000 poems by more than two thousand poets.

Our method of word segmentation and POS tagging has been applied to the complete works by two Chinese poets in the 8th century CE, Wang Wei and Meng Haoran. Wang is considered one of the three most prominent Tang poets; Meng is often associated with Wang due to the similarity of his poems in style and content. Altogether, our corpus consists of about 32,000 characters in 521 poems.

<table>
<tr><td colspan="3">Noun Phrase in Verse 2</td></tr>
<tr><td>細</td><td>柳</td><td>營</td></tr>
<tr><td>xi</td><td>liu</td><td>ying</td></tr>
<tr><td>'little'</td><td>'willow'</td><td>'camp'</td></tr>
<tr><td colspan="3">'Little Willow camp'</td></tr>
<tr><td>JJ</td><td>NN</td><td rowspan="2">NN</td></tr>
<tr><td colspan="2">NR</td></tr>
<tr><td colspan="3">NR</td></tr>
<tr><td colspan="3">Noun Phrase in Verse 1</td></tr>
<tr><td>新</td><td>豐</td><td>市</td></tr>
<tr><td>xin</td><td>feng</td><td>shi</td></tr>
<tr><td>'new'</td><td>'abundance'</td><td>'city'</td></tr>
<tr><td colspan="3">'City of New Abundance'</td></tr>
<tr><td>JJ</td><td>NN</td><td rowspan="2">NN</td></tr>
<tr><td colspan="2">NR</td></tr>
<tr><td colspan="3">NR</td></tr>
</table>

Table 6: Part-of-speech annotations of the three-character strings 細柳營 *xi liu ying* 'Little Willow military camp' and 新豐市 *xin feng shi* 'Xinfeng city'. Both are 'strings with internal structures', with nested structures that perfectly match at all three levels. They are the noun phrases that end both verses in the couplet 忽過新豐市, 還歸細柳營.

## 6 Evaluation

Two research assistants, both of whom hold a Bachelor's degree in Chinese, have completed the annotations. To estimate inter-annotator agreement, the two annotators independently performed word segmentation and POS tagging on a 1,057-character portion of the poems of Wang. We measured their agreement on word segmentation, POS tags for 'strings without internal structures', and those for 'strings with internal structures'.

***Word segmentation***. This task refers to decisions on boundaries between 'strings without internal structure' (section 4.1). Given the rather stringent criteria, it is not surprising that only about 6.5% of the words in our texts contain more than one character. Among these, 75% consists of two characters.

Disagreement rate on the presence of word boundary between characters was only 1.7%. No comparable figure has been reported for classical Chinese word segmentation, but this rate compares favorably with past attempts for modern Chinese, e.g., an average of 76% inter-human agreement rate in (Sproat et al., 1996). This may be explained by the relatively small number of types of strings (see Table 2) that are considered to be multi-character words in our corpus.

***POS tagging on strings without internal structures***. We now consider the POS tags assigned at the lowest level, i.e. those assigned to strings without internal structures. After discarding characters with disputed word segmentation boundaries, the disagreement rate on POS tags was 4.9%. Three main areas of disagreement emerged.

One category is the confusion between verbs and adverbs, when the annotators do not agree on whether a verb has an adverbial force and should therefore be tagged as AD rather than VV. For example, the word 紆 *yu* 'bow' normally functions as a verb, but can also be used adverbially when referring to an attitude, 'respectfully', which is implied by bowing. When used in collocation with the word 顧 *gu* 'visit' in the verse 伏檻紆三顧 *fu jian yu san gu*, it can therefore mean 'prostrated on the threshold and respectfully (AD) paid visits three times' or 'prostrated on the threshold and bowed (VV) and paid visits three time'.

A second category is the confusion between measure word and a noun. The noun 簞 *dan* 'bowl' can collocate with the noun 食 *shi* 'food'. Taken together, *dan shi* can either mean 'a bowl of food' where *dan* is a measure word (M), or it can simply mean a specific kind of meal, in which case *dan* is a noun modifier (NN). Both interpretations have been supported by commentators.

The third is the confusion between adjective (JJ) and noun (NN), when the word in question modifies a noun that immediately follows. For example, for the noun phrase 命服 *ming fu* 'uniform with rank devices', it is clear that the first character 命 *ming* 'profession' modifies the second character 服 *fu* 'clothes'. The annotators did not agree, however, on whether *ming* is a noun modifier or an adjectival modifier. In the Penn Chinese Treebank POS guidelines (Xia, 2000), this question is resolved with the linguistic test: if the word is JJ, then it cannot be the head of a noun phrase. In practice, this test is difficult to apply for non-native speakers of a language. The annotator would have to decide whether he can compose a "good" classical Chinese that uses the word has an NP head.

***POS tagging on strings with internal structures***. Thirdly, we turn our attention to POS tags assigned at the higher levels of the nested structure. Of the 'strings with internal structures', about 73% consist of two characters; those longer than two characters are mostly proper names.

We measured inter-human agreement for the nested bracketing by taking each annotator in turn as 'gold', and calculated the precision and recall of the other. The average precision was 83.5%; the average recall also worked out to 83.5%. A significant source of error was disagreement over whether several characters form a proper name, and should therefore be bracketed and assigned the tag NR; these often involve knowledge of Chinese history and geography. In the remaining cases of discrepancies, the vast majority are direct consequences of differences in POS tagging. Lastly, among the strings with internal structures that have received identical bracketing, there was almost complete agreement between the annotators regarding their POS tags, except in a few isolated cases.

## 7 Conclusion

We have a described a novel method of word segmentation and POS tagging, tailored for the classical Chinese language, and designed to support interoperability between corpora. This method has been applied on about 32,000 characters, drawn from two well-known poets from the 8$^{th}$ century CE.

The corpus aspires to contribute to two areas of scholarly enquiry. First, it is expected to facilitate classical Chinese word studies by automating word retrieval (e.g., (Lancaster, 2010)), and will support investigations in other areas of classical Chinese philology, such as semantic and metaphorical coherence (Zhu & Cui, 2010), by supplying syntactic evidence. Second, it is intended to serve as training data for automatic POS taggers, to automate the analysis of the vast and growing digital collections of classical Chinese texts.

## Acknowledgments

We thank Tin Ho Chan, Yin Hei Kong and Cheuk Ho Wan for their assistance in annotating this corpus. This work was supported by a Strategic Research Grant (#7002549) from City University of Hong Kong.

## References

Pi-Chuan Chang, Michel Galley, and Chris Manning, 2008. Optimizing Chinese Word Segmentation for Machine Translation Performance. In *Proc. ACL 3rd Workshop on Statistical Machine Translation*.

Keh-Jiann Chen, Chu-Ren Huang, Li-Ping Chang, and Hui-Li Hsu, 1996. SINICA CORPUS: Design Methodology for Balanced Corpora. In *Proc. Language, Information and Computation (PACLIC)*.

Chinese Knowledge Information Processing Group, 1996. Shouwen Jiezi --- A study of Chinese Word Boundaries and Segmentation Standard for Information Processing (in Chinese). Technical Report, Academia Sinica, Taipei.

George Doddington, Alexis Mitchell, Mark Przybocki, Lance Ramshaw, Stephanie Strassel, and Ralph Weischedel, 2004. The Automatic Content Extraction (ACE) Program: Tasks, Data, and Evaluation. In *Proc. LREC*.

Shengli Feng, 1998. Prosodic Structure and Compound Words in Classical Chinese. In *New Approaches to Chinese Word Formation*, Jerome Packard (ed.), Mouton de Gruyter.

W. Nelson Francis and Henry Kučera, *1982. Frequency Analysis of English Usage: Lexicon and Grammar*. Houghton Mifflin.

Xiaolong Hu, N. Williamson and J. McLaughlin, 2005. Sheffield Corpus of Chinese for Diachronic Linguistic Study. In *Literary and Linguistic Computing* **20**(3):281---93.

Xiaoling Hu and Jamie McLaughlin, 2007. The Sheffield Corpus of Chinese. Technical Report, University of Sheffield, UK.

Liang Huang, Yinan Peng, Huan Wang and Zhengyu Wu, 2006. Statistical Part-of-Speech Tagging for Classical Chinese. In *Lecture Notes in Computer Science* **2448**:296-311.

Lewis Lancaster, 2010. Pattern Recognition and Analysis in the Chinese Buddhist Canon: A Study of "Original Enlightenment". In *Asia Pacific World* 3rd series **60**.

Yuan Liu, Qiang Tan, and Kun Xu Shen, 1994. *Segmentation Standard for Modern Chinese Information Processing and Automatic Segmentation Methodology*. Qinghua University Press, Beijing, China.

Mitchell P. Marcus, Mary Ann Marcinkiewicz, and Beatrice Santorini, 1993. Building a Large Annotated Corpus of English: the Penn Treebank. In *Computational Linguistics* **19**(2).

Anthony McEnery and Zhonghua Xiao, 2004. The Lancaster Corpus of Mandarin Chinese: a corpus for monolingual and contrastive language study. In *Proc. LREC*.

Jerome Lee Packard, 1998. New Approaches to Chinese Word Formation: Morphology, Phonology and the Lexicon in Modern and Ancient Chinese. In *Trends in Linguistics Studies and and Monographs*, Mouton de Gruyter.

Dingqiu Peng, 1960. *Quan Tang Shi* 全唐詩. Zhonghua Shuju, Beijing.

Edwin Pulleyblank, 1995. *Outline of Classical Chinese Grammar*. UBC Press, Vancouver, Canada.

Ivan A. Sag, Timothy Baldwin, Francis Bond, Ann Copestake, and Dan Flickinger, 2002. Multiword Expressions: A Pain in the Neck for NLP. In *Lecture Notes in Computer Science* 2276/2002:189—206.

Richard Sproat, Chilin Shih, William Gale and Nancy Chang, 1996. A Stochastic Finite-state Word-Segmentation Algorithm for Chinese. In *Computational Linguistics* **22**(3).

Richard Sproat and Thomas Emerson, 2003. The First International Chinese Word Segmentation Bakeoff. In *Proc. 2nd SIGHAN Workshop on Chinese Language Processing*.

Pei-chuan Wei, P. M. Thompson, Cheng-hui Liu, Chu-Ren Huang, Chaofen Sun, 1997. Historical Corpora for Synchronic and Diachronic Linguistics Studies. In *Computational Linguistics and Chinese Language Processing* **2**(1):131—145.

Fei Xia, 2000. *The Segmentation Guidelines for the Penn Chinese Treebank (3.0)*. University of Pennsylvania, PA.

Nianwen Xue, Fei Xia, Fu-Dong Chiou, and Martha Palmer, 2005. The Penn Chinese Treebank: Phrase structure annotation of a large corpus. In *Natural Language Engineering* **11**:207-238.

Shiwen Yu, Xuefeng Zhu, Hui Wang, and Yunyun Zhang, 1998. *The Grammatical Knowledgebase of Contemporary Chinese: A Complete Specification* (in Chinese). Tsinghua University Press, Beijing, China.

Shiwen Yu, Huiming Duan, Xuefeng Zhu, and Bin Sun, 2002. 北京大學現代漢語語料庫基本加工規範 *Beijing daxue xiandai hanyu yuliaoku jiben jiagong guifan*. 中文信息學報 *Zhongwen Xinxi Xuebao* **5**:49--64.

Chunshen Zhu and Ying Cui, 2010. Imagery Focalization and the Evocation of a Poetic World. In *Chinese Translators Journal*.

# Computing Similarity between Cultural Heritage Items using Multimodal Features

**Nikolaos Aletras**
Department of Computer Science
University of Sheffield
Regent Court, 211 Portobello
Sheffield, S1 4DP, UK
n.aletras@dcs.shef.ac.uk

**Mark Stevenson**
Department of Computer Science
University of Sheffield
Regent Court, 211 Portobello
Sheffield, S1 4DP, UK
m.stevenson@dcs.shef.ac.uk

## Abstract

A significant amount of information about Cultural Heritage artefacts is now available in digital format and has been made available in digital libraries. Being able to identify items that are similar would be useful for search and navigation through these data sets. Information about items in these repositories is often multimodal, such as pictures of the artefact and an accompanying textual description. This paper explores the use of information from these various media for computing similarity between Cultural Heritage artefacts. Results show that combining information from images and text produces better estimates of similarity than when only a single medium is considered.

## 1 Introduction and Motivation

In recent years a vast amount of Cultural Heritage (CH) artefacts have been digitised and made available on-line. For example, the Louvre and the British Museum provide information about exhibits on their web pages[1]. In addition, information is also available via sites that aggregate CH information from multiple resources. A typical example is Europeana[2], a web-portal to collections from several European institutions that provides access to over 20 million items including paintings, films, books, archives and museum exhibits.

However, online information about CH artefacts is often unstructured and varies by collection. This makes it difficult to identify information of interest in sites that aggregate information from multiple sources, such as Europeana, or to compare information across multiple collections (such as the Louvre and British Museum). These problems form a significant barrier to accessing the information available in these online collections. A first step towards improving access would be to identify similar items in collections. This could assist with several applications that are of interest to those working in CH including recommendation of interesting items (Pechenizkzy and Calders, 2007; Wang et al., 2008), generation of virtual tours (Joachims et al., 1997; Wang et al., 2009), visualisation of collections (Kauppinen et al., 2009; Hornbaek and Hertzum, 2011) and exploratory search (Marchionini, 2006; Amin et al., 2008).

Information in digital CH collections often includes multiple types of media such as text, images and audio. It seems likely that information from all of these types would help humans to identify similar items and that it could help to identify them automatically. However, previous work on computing similarity in the CH domain has been limited and, in particular, has not made use of information from multiple types of media. For example, Grieser et al. (2011) computed similarity between exhibits in Melbourne Museum by applying a range of text similarity measures but did not make use of other media. Techniques for exploiting information from multimedia collections have been developed and are commonly applied to a wide range of problems such as Content-based Image Retrieval (Datta et al., 2008) and image annotation (Feng and Lapata, 2010).

[1] http://www.louvre.fr/, http://www.britishmuseum.org/

[2] http://www.europeana.eu

This paper makes use of information from two media (text and images) to compute the similarity between items in a large collection of CH items (Europeana). A range of similarity measures for text and images are compared and combined. Evaluation is carried out using a set of items from Europeana with similarity judgements that were obtained in a crowdsourcing experiment. We find that combining information from both media produces better results than when either is used alone.

The main contribution of this paper is to demonstrate the usefulness of applying information from more than one medium when comparing CH items. In addition, it explores the effectiveness of different similarity measures when applied to this domain and introduces a data set of similarity judgements that can be used as a benchmark.

The remainder of this paper is structured as follows. Section 2 describes some relevant previous work. Sections 3, 4 and 5 describe the text and image similarity measures applied in this paper and how they are combined. Sections 6 describes the experiments used in this paper and the results are reported in Section 7. Finally, Section 8 draws the conclusions and provides suggestions for future work.

## 2 Background

### 2.1 Text Similarity

Two main approaches for determining the similarity between two texts have been explored: *corpus-based* and *knowledge-based* methods. Corpus-based methods rely on statistics that they learn from corpora while knowledge-based methods make use of some external knowledge source, such as a thesaurus, dictionary or semantic network (Agirre et al., 2009; Gabrilovich and Markovitch, 2007).

A previous study (Aletras et al., 2012) compared the effectiveness of various methods for computing the similarity between items in a CH collection based on text extracted from their descriptions, including both corpus-based and knowledge-based approaches. The corpus-based approaches varied from simple word counting approaches (Manning and Schutze, 1999) to more complex ones based on techniques from Information Retrieval (Baeza-Yates and Ribeiro-Neto, 1999) and topic models (Blei et al., 2003). The knowledge-based approaches relied on Wikipedia (Milne, 2007). Aletras et al. (2012) concluded that corpus-based measures were more effective than knowledge-based ones for computing similarity between these items.

### 2.2 Image Similarity

Determining the similarity between images has been explored in the fields such as Computer Vision (Szeliski, 2010) and Content-based Image Retrieval (CBIR) (Datta et al., 2008). A first step in computing the similarity between images is to transform them into an appropriate set of features. Some major feature types which have been used are colour, shape, texture or salient points. Features are also commonly categorised into global and local features.

Global features characterise an entire image. For example, the average of the intensities of red, green and blue colours gives an estimation of the overall colour distribution in the image. The main advantages of global features are that they can be computed efficiently. However, they are unable to represent information about elements in an image (Datta et al., 2008). On the other hand, local features aim to identify interesting areas in the image, such as where significant differences in colour intensity between adjacent pixels is detected.

Colour is one of the most commonly used global features and has been applied in several fields including image retrieval (Jacobs et al., 1995; Sebe and Michael S. Lew, 2001; Yu et al., 2002), image clustering (Cai et al., 2004; Strong and Gong, 2009), database indexing (Swain and Ballard, 1991) and, object/scene recognition (Schiele and Crowley, 1996; Ndjiki-Nya et al., 2004; Sande et al., 2008). A common method for measuring similarity between images is to compare the colour distributions of their histograms. A histogram is a graphical representation of collected counts for predefined categories of data. To create a histogram we have to specify the range of the data values, the number of dimensions and the bins (intervals into which ranges of values are combined). A colour histogram records the number of the pixels that fall in the interval of each bin. Schiele and Crowley (1996) describe several common metrics for comparing colour histograms including $\chi^2$, *correlation* and *intersection.*

### 2.3 Combining Text and Image Features

The integration of information from text and image features has been explored in several fields. In Content-based Image Retrieval image features are combined together with words from captions to retrieve images relevant to a query (La Cascia et al., 1998; Srihari et al., 2000; Barnard and Forsyth, 2001; Westerveld, 2002; Zhou and Huang, 2002; Wang et al., 2004). Image clustering methods have been developed to combine information from images and text to create clusters of similar images (Loeff et al., 2006; Bekkerman and Jeon, 2007). Techniques for automatic image annotation that generate models as a mixture of word and image features have also been described (Jeon et al., 2003; Blei and Jordan, 2003; Feng and Lapata, 2010).

### 2.4 Similarity in Cultural Heritage

Despite the potential usefulness of similarity in CH, there has been little previous work on the area. An exception is the work of Grieser et al. (2011). They computed the similarity between a set of 40 exhibits from Melbourne Museum by analysing the museum's web pages and physical layout. They applied a range of text similarity techniques (see Section 2.1) to the web pages as well as similarity measures that made use of Wikipedia. However, the Wikipedia-based techniques relied on a manual mapping between the items and an appropriate Wikipedia article. Although the web pages often contained images of the exhibits, Grieser et al. (2011) did not make use of them.

## 3 Text Similarity

We make use of various corpus-based approaches for computing similarity between CH items since previous experiments (see Section 2.1) have shown that these outperformed knowledge-based methods in a comparison of text-based similarity methods for the CH domain.

We assume that we wish to compute the similarity between a pair of items, $A$ and $B$, and that each item has both text and an image associated with it. The text is denoted as $A_t$ and $B_t$ while the images are denoted by $A_i$ and $B_i$.

### 3.1 Word Overlap

A common approach to computing similarity is to count the number of common words (Lesk, 1986). The text associated with each item is compared and the similarity is computed as the number of words (tokens) they have in common normalised by the combined total:

$$sim_{WO}(A, B) = \frac{|A_t \cap B_t|}{|A_t \cup B_t|}$$

### 3.2 N-gram Overlap

The Word Overlap approach is a bag of words method that does not take account of the order in which words appear, despite the fact that this is potentially useful information for determining similarity. One way in which this information can be used is to compare n-grams derived from a text. Patwardhan et al. (2003) used this approach to extend the Word Overlap measure. This approach identifies n-grams in common between the two text and increases the score by $n^2$ for each one that is found, where $n$ is the length of the n-gram. More formally,

$$sim_{ngram}(A, B) = \frac{\sum_{n \in n\text{-}gram(A_t, B_t)} n^2}{|A_t \cup B_t|}$$

where $n-gram(A_t, B_t)$ is the set of n-grams that occur in both $A_t$ and $B_t$.

### 3.3 TF.IDF

The word and n-gram overlap measures assign the same importance to each word but some are more important for determining similarity between texts than others. A widely used approach to computing similarity between documents is to represent them as vectors in which each term is assigned a weighting based on its estimated importance (Manning and Schutze, 1999). The vectors can then be compared using the cosine metric. A widely used scheme for weighting terms is tf.idf, which takes account of the frequency of each term in individual documents and the number of documents in a corpus in which it occurs.

### 3.4 Latent Dirichlet Allocation

Topic models (Blei et al., 2003) are a useful technique for representing the underlying content of documents. LDA is a widely used topic model that assumes each document is composed of a number of topics. For each document LDA returns a probability distribution over a set of topics that have been derived from an unlabeled corpus. Similarity between documents can be computed by converting these distributions into vectors and using the cosine metric.

## 4 Image Similarity

Two approaches are compared for computing the similarity between images. These are largely based on colour features and are more suitable for the images in the data set we use for evaluation (see Section 6).

### 4.1 Colour Similarity (RGB)

The first approach is based on comparison of colour histograms derived from images.

In the RGB (Red Green Blue) colour model, each pixel is represented as an integer in range of 0-255 in three dimensions (Red, Green and Blue). One histogram is created for each dimension. For grey-scale images it is assumed that the value of each dimension is the same in each pixel and a single histogram, called the luminosity histogram, is created. Similarity between the histograms in each colour channel is computed using the intersection metric. The *intersection* metric (Swain and Ballard, 1991) measures the number of corresponding pixels that have same colour in two images. It is defined as follows:

$$Inter(h_1, h_2) = \sum_I min(h_1(I), h_2(I))$$

where $h_i$ is the histogram of image $i$, $I$ is the set of histogram bins and $min(a, b)$ is the minimum between corresponding pixel colour values.

The final similarity score is computed as the average of the red, green and blue histogram similarity scores:

$$sim_{RGB}(A_i, B_i) = \frac{\sum_{i \in \{R,G,B\}} Inter(h_{A_i}, h_{B_i})}{3}$$

### 4.2 Image Querying Metric (imgSeek)

Jacobs et al. (1995) described an image similarity metric developed for Content-based Image Retrieval. It makes use of Haar wavelet decomposition (Beylkin et al., 1991) to create signatures of images that contain colour and basic shape information. Images are compared by determining the number of significant coefficients they have in common using the following function:

$$dist_{imgSeek}(A_i, B_i) = w_0 |C_{A_i}(0,0) - C_{B_i}(0,0)| + \sum_{i,j:\tilde{C}_{A_i}(i,j) \neq 0} w_{bin(i,j)} (\tilde{C}_{A_i}(i,j) \neq \tilde{C}_{B_i}(i,j))$$

where $w_b$ are weights, $C_I$ represents a single colour channel for an image $I$, $C_I(0, 0)$ are scaling function coefficients of the overall average intensity of the colour channel and $\tilde{C}_I(i, j)$ is the $(i, j)$-th truncated, quantised wavelet coefficient of image $I$. For more details please refer to Jacobs et al. (1995).

Note that this function measures the distance between two images with low scores indicating similar images and high scores dis-similar ones. We assign the negative sign to this metric to assign high scores to similar images. It is converted into a similarity metric as follows:

$$sim_{imgSeek}(A_i, B_i) = -dist_{imgSeek}(A_i, B_i)$$

## 5 Combining Text and Image Similarity

A simple weighted linear combination is used to combine the results of the text and image similarities, $sim_{img}$ and $sim_t$. The similarity between a pair of items is computed as follows

$$sim_{T+I}(A, B) = w_1 \cdot sim_t(A_t, B_t) + w_2 \cdot sim_{img}(A_i, B_i)$$

where $w_i$ are weights learned using linear regression (see Section 6.4).

## 6 Evaluation

This section describes experiments used to evaluate the similarity measures described in the previous sections.

### 6.1 Europeana

The similarity measures are evaluated using information from Europeana[3], a web-portal that provides access to information CH artefacts. Over 2,000 institutions through out Europe have contributed to Europeana and the portal provides access to information about over 20 million CH artefacts, making it one of the largest repositories

[3] http://www.europeana.eu

of digital information about CH currently available. It contains information about a wide variety of types of artefacts including paintings, photographs and newspaper archives. The information is in a range of European languages, with over 1 million items in English. The diverse nature of Europeana makes it an interesting resource for exploring similarity measures.

The Europeana portal provides various types of information about each artefact, including textual information, thumbnail images of the items and links to additional information available for the providing institution's web site. The textual information is derived from metadata obtained from the providing institution and includes title, description as well as details of the subject, medium and creator.

An example artefact from the Europeana portal is shown in Figure 1. This particular artefact is an image showing detail of an architect's office in Nottingham, United Kingdom. The information provided for this item is relatively rich compared to other items in Europeana since the title is informative and the textual description is of reasonable length. However, the amount of information associated with items in Europeana is quite varied and it is common for items to have short titles, which may be uninformative, or have very limited textual descriptions. In addition, the metadata associated with items in Europeana is potentially a valuable source of information that could be used for, among other things, computing similarity between items. However, the various providing institutions do not use consistent coding schemes to populate these fields which makes it difficult to compare items provided by different institutions. These differences in the information provided by the various institutions form a significant challenge in processing the Europeana data automatically.

### 6.2 Evaluation Data

A data set was created by selecting 300 pairs of items added to Europeana by two providers: Culture Grid[4] and Scran[5]. The items added to Europeana by these providers represent the majority that are in English and they contain different types of items such as objects, archives, videos and audio files. We removed five pairs that did not have any images associated with one of the items. (These items were audiofiles.) The resulting dataset consists of 295 pairs of items and is referred to as **Europeana295**.

Each item corresponds to a metadata record consisting of textual information together with a URI and a link to its thumbnail. Figure 1 shows an item taken from the Europeana website. The title, description and subject fields have been shown to be useful information for computing similarity (Aletras et al., 2012). These are extracted and concatenated to form the textual information associated with each item. In addition, the accompanying thumbnail image (or "preview") was also extracted to be used as the visual information. The size of these images varies from 7,000 to 10,000 pixels.

We have pre-processed the data by removing stop words and applying stemming. For the *tf.idf* and *LDA* the training corpus was a total of 759,896 Europeana items. We have filtered out all items that have no description and have a title shorter than 4 words, or have a title which has been repeated more than 100 times.

### 6.3 Human Judgements of Similarity

Crowdflower[6], a crowdsourcing platform, was used to obtain human judgements of the similarity between each pair of items. Participants were asked to rate each item pair using a 5 point scale where 4 indicated that the pair of items were highly similar or near-identical while 0 indicated that they were completely different. Participants were presented with a page containing 10 pairs of items and asked to rate all of them. Participants were free to rate as many pages as they wanted up to a maximum of 30 pages (i.e. the complete Europeana295 data set). To ensure that the annotators were not returning random answers each page contained a pair for which the similarity had been pre-identified as being at one end of the similarity scale (i.e. either near-identical or completely different). Annotations from participants that failed to answer correctly these questions or participants that have given same rating to all of their answers were removed. A total of 3,261 useful annotations were collected from 99 participants and each pair was rated by at least 10 participants.

The final similarity score for each pair was gen-

[4]http://www.culturegrid.org.uk/

[5]http://www.scran.ac.uk/

[6]http://crowdflower.com/

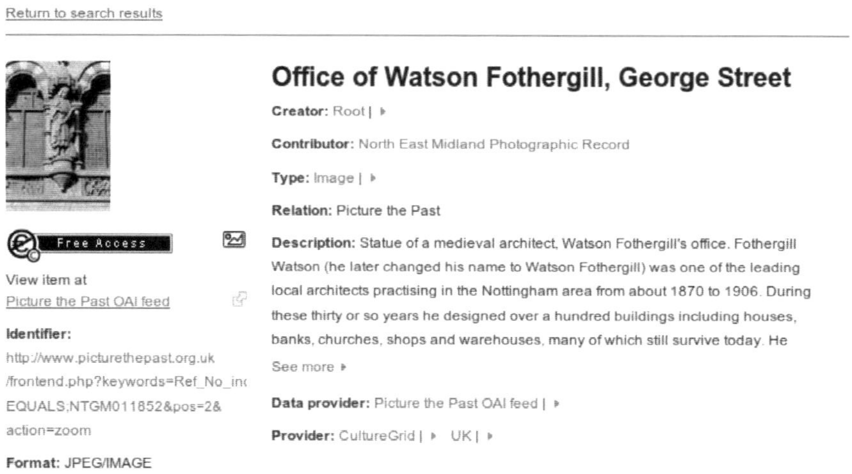


Figure 1: Example item from Europeana portal showing how both textual and image information are displayed. (Taken from http://www.europeana.eu/portal/)

erated by averaging the ratings. Inter-annotator agreement was computed as the average of the Pearson correlation between the ratings of each participant and the average ratings of the other participants, a methodology used by Grieser et al. (2011). The inter-annotator agreement for the data set was $\rho = +0.553$, which is comparable with the agreement score of $\rho = +0.507$ previously reported by Grieser et al. (2011).

### 6.4 Experiments

Experiments were carried out comparing the results of the various techniques for computing text and image similarity (Sections 3 and 4) and their combination (Section 5). Performance is measured as the Pearson's correlation coefficient with the gold-standard data.

The combination of text and image similarity (Section 5) relies on a linear combination of text and image similarities. The weights for this combination are obtained using a linear regression model. The input values were the results obtained for the individual text and similarity methods and the target value was the gold-standard score for each pair in the dataset. 10-fold cross-validation was used for evaluation.

## 7 Results

An overview of the results obtained is shown in Table 1. Results for the text and image similarity methods used alone are shown in the left and top part of the table while the results for their combination are in the main body.

| | | Image Similarity | |
|---|---|---|---|
| | | RGB | imgSeek |
| Text Similarity | | 0.254 | **0.370** |
| Word Overlap | **0.487** | 0.450 | **0.554** |
| tf.idf | 0.437 | 0.426 | 0.520 |
| N-gram overlap | 0.399 | 0.384 | 0.504 |
| LDA | 0.442 | 0.419 | 0.517 |

Table 1: Performance of similarity measures applied to Europeana295 data set (Pearson's correlation coefficient).

The best performance for text similarity (0.487) is achieved by Word Overlap and the lowest by N-gram Overlap (0.399). The results are surprising since the simplest approach produces the best results. It is likely that the reason for these results is the nature of the textual data in Europeana. The documents are often short, in some cases the description missing or the subject information is identical to the title.

For image similarity, results using imgSeek are higher than RGB (0.370 and 0.254 respectively). There is also a clear difference between the performance of the text and image similarity methods and results obtained from both image similarity measures is lower than all four that are based on text. The reason for these results is the nature of the Europeana images. There are a large number of black-and-white image pairs which means that colour information cannot be obtained from many of them. In addition, the images are low resolution, since they are thumbnails, which limits the amount of shape information that can be derived from them, restricting the effectiveness of imgSeek. However, the fact that performance is better for imgSeek and RGB suggests that it is still possible to obtain useful information about shape from these images.

When the image and text similarity measures are combined the highest performance is achieved by the combination of the Word Overlap and imgSeek (0.554), the best performing text and image similarity measures when applied individually. The performance of all text similarity measures improves when combined with imgSeek. All results are above 0.5 with the highest gain observed for N-gram Overlap (from 0.399 to 0.504), the worst performing text similarity measure when applied individually. On the other hand, combining text similarity measures with RGB consistently leads to performance that is lower than when the text similarity measure is used alone.

These results demonstrate that improvements in similarity scores can be obtained by making use of information from both text and images. In addition, better results are obtained for the text similarity methods and this is likely to be caused by the nature of the images which are associated with the items in our data set. It is also important to make use of an appropriate image similarity method since combing text similarity methods with RGB reduces performance.

## 8 Conclusion

This paper demonstrates how information from text and images describing CH artefacts can be combined to improve estimates of the similarity between them. Four corpus-based and two image-based similarity measures are explored and evaluated on a data set consisting of 295 manually-annotated pairs of items from Europeana. Results showed that combing information from text and image similarity improves performance and that imgSeek similarity method consistently improves performance of text similarity methods.

In future work we intend to make use of other types of image features including the low-level ones used by approaches such as Scale Invariant Feature Transformation (SIFT) (Lowe, 1999; Lowe, 2004) and the bag-of-visual words model (Szeliski, 2010). In addition we plan to apply these approaches to higher resolution images to determine how the quality and size of an image affects similarity algorithms.

## Acknowledgments

The research leading to these results was carried out as part of the PATHS project (`http://paths-project.eu`) funded by the European Community's Seventh Framework Programme (FP7/2007-2013) under grant agreement no. 270082.

## References

Eneko Agirre, Enrique Alfonseca, Keith Hall, Jana Kravalova, Marius Pasca, and Aitor Soroa. 2009. A study on similarity and relatedness using distributional and wordnet-based approaches. In *Proceedings of Human Language Technologies: The 2009 Annual Conference of the North American Chapter of the Association for Computational Linguistics (NAACL '09)*, pages 19–27, Boulder, Colorado.

Nikolaos Aletras, Mark Stevenson, and Paul Clough. 2012. Computing similarity between items in a digital library of cultural heritage. *Submitted.*

Alia Amin, Jacco van Ossenbruggen, Lynda Hardman, and Annelies van Nispen. 2008. Understanding Cultural Heritage Experts' Information Seeking Needs. In *Proceedings of the 8th ACM/IEEE-CS Joint Conference on Digital Libraries*, pages 39–47, Pittsburgh, PA.

Ricardo Baeza-Yates and Berthier Ribeiro-Neto. 1999. *Modern Information Retrieval.* Addison Wesley Longman Limited, Essex.

Kobus Barnard and David Forsyth. 2001. Learning the Semantics of Words and Pictures. *Proceedings Eighth IEEE International Conference on Computer Vision (ICCV '01)*, 2:408–415.

Ron Bekkerman and Jiwoon Jeon. 2007. Multi-modal clustering for multimedia collections. In *IEEE Conference on Computer Vision and Pattern Recognition (CVPR '07)*, pages 1–8.

Gregory Beylkin, Ronald Coifman, and Vladimir Rokhlin. 1991. Fast Wavelet Transforms and Numerical Algorithms I. *Communications on Pure and Applied Mathematics*, 44:141–183.

David M. Blei and Michael I. Jordan. 2003. Modeling Annotated Data. *Proceedings of the 26th annual international ACM SIGIR conference on Research and Development in Information Retrieval (SIGIR '03)*, pages 127–134.

David M. Blei, Andrew Y. Ng, and Michael I. Jordan. 2003. Latent Dirichlet Allocation. *Journal of Machine Learning Research*, 3:993–1022.

Deng Cai, Xiaofei He, Zhiwei Li, Wei-Ying Ma, and Ji-Rong Wen. 2004. Hierarchical Clustering of WWW Image Search Results Using Visual, Textual and Link Information. *Proceedings of the 12th annual ACM international conference on Multimedia (MULTIMEDIA '04)*, pages 952–959.

Ritendra Datta, Dhiraj Joshi, Jia Li, and James Z. Wang. 2008. Image Retrieval: Ideas, Influences, and Trends of the New Age. *ACM Computing Surveys*, 40(2):1–60.

Yansong Feng and Mirella Lapata. 2010. Topic Models for Image Annotation and Text Illustration. In *Proceedings of Human Language Technologies: The 2010 Annual Conference of the North American Chapter of the Association for Computational Linguistics*, pages 831–839, Los Angeles, California, June.

Evgeniy Gabrilovich and Shaul Markovitch. 2007. Computing semantic relatedness using wikipedia-based explicit semantic analysis. In *Proceedings of the International Joint Conference on Artificial Intelligence (IJCAI '07)*, pages 1606–1611.

Karl Grieser, Timothy Baldwin, Fabian Bohnert, and Liz Sonenberg. 2011. Using Ontological and Document Similarity to Estimate Museum Exhibit Relatedness. *Journal on Computing and Cultural Heritage (JOCCH)*, 3(3):10:1–10:20.

Kasper Hornbaek and Morten Hertzum. 2011. The notion of overview in information visualization. *International Journal of Human-Computer Studies*, 69:509–525.

Charles E. Jacobs, Adam Finkelstein, and David H. Salesin. 1995. Fast multiresolution image querying. In *Proceedings of the 22nd annual conference on Computer Graphics and Interactive Techniques (SIGGRAPH '95)*, pages 277–286, New York, NY, USA.

Jiwoon Jeon, Victor Lavrenko, and Raghavan Manmatha. 2003. Automatic image annotation and retrieval using cross-media relevance models. In *Proceedings of the 26th annual international ACM SIGIR Conference on Research and Development in Information Retrieval (SIGIR '03)*, pages 119–126, New York, NY, USA.

Thorsten Joachims, Dayne Freitag, and Tom Mitchell. 1997. Webwatcher: A tour guide for the world wide web. In *Proceedings of the International Joint Conference on Artificial Intelligence (IJCAI '97)*, pages 770–777.

Tomi Kauppinen, Kimmo Puputti, Panu Paakkarinen, Heini Kuittinen, Jari Väätäinen, and Eero Hyvönen. 2009. Learning and visualizing cultural heritage connections between places on the semantic web. In *Proceedings of the Workshop on Inductive Reasoning and Machine Learning on the Semantic Web (IRMLeS2009) and the 6th Annual European Semantic Web Conference (ESWC2009)*, Heraklion, Crete, Greece.

Marco La Cascia, Sarathendu Sethi, and Stan Sclaroff. 1998. Combining textual and visual cues for content-based image retrieval on the world wide web. In *IEEE Workshop on Content-Based Access of Image and Video Libraries*, pages 24–28.

Michael Lesk. 1986. Automatic Sense Disambiguation using Machine Readable Dictionaries: how to tell a pine cone from an ice cream cone. In *Proceedings of the ACM Special Interest Group on the Design of Communication Conference (SIGDOC '86)*, pages 24–26, Toronto, Canada.

Nicolas Loeff, Cecilia Ovesdotter Alm, and David A. Forsyth. 2006. Discriminating image senses by clustering with multimodal features. In *Proceedings of the COLING/ACL on Main Conference Poster Sessions (COLING-ACL '06)*, pages 547–554, Stroudsburg, PA, USA.

David G. Lowe. 1999. Object Recognition from Local Scale-invariant Features. *Proceedings of the Seventh IEEE International Conference on Computer Vision*, pages 1150–1157.

David G. Lowe. 2004. Distinctive Image Features from Scale-Invariant Keypoints. *International Journal of Computer Vision*, 60(2):91–110.

Christopher D. Manning and Hinrich Schutze. 1999. *Foundations of Statistical Natural Language Processing*. The MIT Press.

Gary Marchionini. 2006. Exploratory Search: from Finding to Understanding. *Communications of the ACM*, 49(1):41–46.

David Milne. 2007. Computing Semantic Relatedness using Wikipedia Link Structure. In *Proceedings of the New Zealand Computer Science Research Student Conference.*

Patrick Ndjiki-Nya, Oleg Novychny, and Thomas Wiegand. 2004. Merging MPEG 7 Descriptors for Image Content Analysis. In *Proceedings of IEEE International Conference on Acoustics, Speech, and Signal Processing (ICASSP '04)*, pages 5–8.

Siddhard Patwardhan, Satanjeev Banerjee, and Ted Pedersen. 2003. Using Measures of Semantic Relatedness for Word Sense Disambiguation. In *Proceedings of the 4th International Conference on Intelligent Text Processing and Computational Linguistics*, pages 241–257.

Mykola Pechenizkzy and Toon Calders. 2007. A framework for guiding the museum tours personalization. In *Proceedings of the Workshop on Personalised Access to Cultural Heritage (PATCH '07)*, pages 11–28.

Koen E.A. Sande, Theo Gevers, and Cees G. M. Snoek. 2008. Evaluation of Color Descriptors for Object and Scene Recognition. In *Proceedings of the IEEE Computer Society Conference on Computer Vision and Pattern Recognition (CVPR '08)*, pages 1–8.

Bernt Schiele and James L. Crowley. 1996. Object recognition using multidimensional receptive field histograms. In *Proceedings of the 4th European Conference on Computer Vision (ECCV '96)*, pages 610–619, London, UK.

Nicu Sebe and Michael S. Lew. 2001. Color-based Retrieval. *Pattern Recognition Letters*, 22:223–230, February.

Rohini K. Srihari, Aibing Rao, Benjamin Han, Srikanth Munirathnam, and Xiaoyun Wu. 2000. A model for multimodal information retrieval. In *Proceedings of the IEEE International Conference on Multimedia and Expo (ICME '00)*, pages 701–704.

Grant Strong and Minglun Gong. 2009. Organizing and Browsing Photos using Different Feature Vectors and their Evaluations. *Proceedings of the ACM International Conference on Image and Video Retrieval (CIVR '09)*, pages 3:1–3:8.

Michael J. Swain and Dana H. Ballard. 1991. Color indexing. *International Journal of Computer Vision*, 7:11–32.

Richard Szeliski. 2010. *Computer Vision: Algorithms and Applications*. Springer-Verlag Inc. New York.

Xin-Jing Wang, Wei-Ying Ma, Gui-Rong Xue, and Xing Li. 2004. Multi-model similarity propagation and its application for web image retrieval. In *Proceedings of the 12th annual ACM International Conference on Multimedia (MULTIMEDIA '04)*, pages 944–951, New York, NY, USA.

Yiwen Wang, Natalia Stash, Lora Aroyo, Peter Gorgels, Lloyd Rutledge, and Guus Schreiber. 2008. Recommendations based on semantically-enriched museum collections. *Journal of Web Semantics: Science, Services and Agents on the World Wide Web*, 6(4):43–50.

Yiwen Wang, Lora Aroyo, Natalia Stash, Rody Sambeek, Schuurmans Yuri, Guus Schreiber, and Peter Gorgels. 2009. Cultivating personalized museum tours online and on-site. *Journal of Interdisciplinary Science Reviews*, 34(2):141–156.

Thijs Westerveld. 2002. Probabilistic multimedia retrieval. In *Proceedings of the 25th Annual International ACM SIGIR Conference on Research and Development in Information Retrieval (SIGIR '02)*, pages 437–438, New York, NY, USA.

Hui Yu, Mingjing Li, Hong-Jiang Zhang, and Jufu Feng. 2002. Color Texture Moments for Content-based Image Retrieval. In *Proceedings of the IEEE International Conference on Image Processing (ICIP '02)*, pages 929–932.

Xiang Sean Zhou and Thomas S. Huang. 2002. Unifying keywords and visual contents in image retrieval. *IEEE Multimedia*, 9(2):23 –33.

# Enabling the Discovery of Digital Cultural Heritage Objects through Wikipedia


**Mark M Hall**
**Paul D Clough**
Information School
Sheffield University
Sheffield, UK
m.mhall@shef.ac.uk
p.d.clough@shef.ac.uk

**Oier Lopez de Lacalle**[1,2]
[1]IKERBASQUE
Basque Foundation for Science
Bilbao, Spain
[2]School of Informatics
University of Edinburgh
Edinburgh, UK

**Aitor Soroa**
**Eneko Agirre**
IXA NLP Group
University of the Basque Country
Donostia, Spain
a.soroa@ehu.es
e.agirre@ehu.es

oier.lopezdelacalle@gmail.es



## Abstract

Over the past years large digital cultural heritage collections have become increasingly available. While these provide adequate search functionality for the expert user, this may not offer the best support for non-expert or novice users. In this paper we propose a novel mechanism for introducing new users to the items in a collection by allowing them to browse Wikipedia articles, which are augmented with items from the cultural heritage collection. Using Europeana as a case-study we demonstrate the effectiveness of our approach for encouraging users to spend longer exploring items in Europeana compared with the existing search provision.


## 1 Introduction

Large amounts of digital cultural heritage (CH) information have become available over the past years, especially with the rise of large-scale aggregators such as Europeana[1], the European aggregator for museums, archives, libraries, and galleries. These large collections present two challenges to the new user. The first is discovering the collection in the first place. The second is then discovering what items are present in the collection. In current systems support for item discovery is mainly through the standard search paradigm (Sutcliffe and Ennis, 1998), which is well suited for CH professionals who are highly familiar with the collections, subject areas, and have specific search goals. However, for new users who do not have a good understanding of what is in the collections, what search keywords to use, and have vague search goals, this method of access is unsatisfactory as this quote from (Borgman, 2009) exemplifies:

> "So what use are the digital libraries, if all they do is put digitally unusable information on the web?"

Alternative item discovery methodologies are required to introduce new users to digital CH collections (Geser, 2004; Steemson, 2004). Exploratory search models (Marchionini, 2006; Pirolli, 2009) that enable switching between collection overviews (Hornb[Pleaseinsertintopreamble]k and Hertzum, 2011) and detailed exploration within the collection are frequently suggested as more appropriate.

We propose a novel mechanism that enables users to discover an unknown, aggregated collection by browsing a second, known collection. Our method lets the user browse through Wikipedia and automatically augments the page(s) the user is viewing with items drawn from the CH collection, in our case Europeana. The items are chosen to match the page's content and enable the user to acquire an overview of what information is available for a given topic. The goal is to introduce new users to the digital collection, so that they can then successfully use the existing search systems.

## 2 Background

Controlled vocabularies are often seen as a promising discovery methodology (Baca, 2003). However, in the case of aggregated collections such as Europeana, items from different providers are frequently aligned to different vocabularies, requiring an integration of the two vocabularies in

[1] http://www.europeana.eu

order to present a unified structure. (Isaac et al., 2007) describe the use of automated methods for aligning vocabularies, however this is not always successfully possible. A proposed alternative is to synthesise a new vocabulary to cover all aggregated data, however (Chaudhry and Jiun, 2005) highlight the complexities involved in then linking the individual items to the new vocabulary.

To overcome this automatic clustering and visualisations based directly on the meta-data have been proposed, such as 2d semantic maps (Andrews et al., 2001), automatically generated tree structures (Chen et al., 2002), multi-dimensional scaling (Fortuna et al., 2005; Newton et al., 2009), self-organising maps (Lin, 1992), and dynamic taxonomies (Papadakos et al., 2009). However none of these have achieved sufficient success to find widespread use as exploration interfaces.

Faceted search systems (van Ossenbruggen et al., 2007; Schmitz and Black, 2008) have arisen as a flexible alternative for surfacing what meta-data is available in a collection. Unlike the methods listed above, faceted search does not require complex pre-processing and the values to display for a facet can be calculated on the fly. However, aggregated collections frequently have large numbers of potential facets and values for these facets, making it hard to surface a sufficiently large fraction to support resource discovery.

Time-lines such as those proposed by (Luo et al., 2012) do not suffer from these issues, but are only of limited value if the user's interest cannot be focused through time. A user interested in examples of pottery across the ages or restricted to a certain geographic area is not supported by a time-line-based interface.

The alternative we propose is to use a second collection that the user is familiar with and that acts as a proxy to the unfamiliar collection. (Villa et al., 2010) describe a similar approach where Flickr is used as the proxy collection, enabling users to search an image collection that has no textual meta-data.

In our proposed approach items from the unfamiliar collection are surfaced via their thumbnail images and similar approaches for automatically retrieving images for text have been tried by (Zhu et al., 2007; Borman et al., 2005). (Zhu et al., 2007) report success rates that approach the quality of manually selected images, however their approach requires complex pre-processing, which

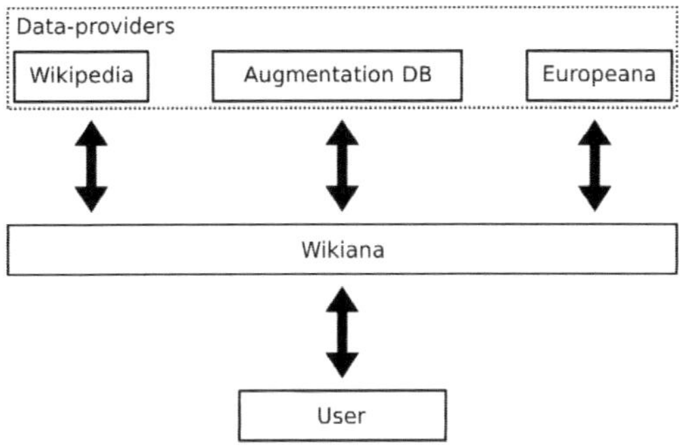


Figure 1: Architectural structure of the Wikiana system

the dynamic nature of discovery prohibits.

Wikipedia was chosen as the discovery interface as it is known to have good content coverage and frequently appears at the top of search results (Schweitzer, 2008) for many topics, its use has been studied (Lim, 2009; Lucassen and Schraagen, 2010), and it is frequently used as an information source for knowledge modelling (Suchanek et al., 2008; Milne and Witten, 2008), information extraction (Weld et al., 2009; Ni et al., 2009), and similarity calculation (Gabrilovich and Markovitch, 2007).

## 3 Discovering Europeana through Wikipedia

As stated above our method lets users browse Wikipedia and at the same time exposes them to items taken from Europeana, enabling them to discover items that exist in Europeana.

The Wikipedia article is augmented with Europeana items at two levels. The article as a whole is augmented with up to 20 items that in a pre-processing step have been linked to the article and at the same time each paragraph in the article is augmented with one item relating to that paragraph.

Our system (Wikiana, figure 1) sits between the user and the data-providers (Wikipedia, Europeana, and the pre-computed article augmentation links). When the user requests an article from Wikiana, the system fetches the matching article from Wikipedia and in a first step strips everything except the article's main content. It then queries the augmentation database for Europeana items that have been linked to the article and selects the top 20 items from the results, as detailed below. It then processes each paragraph and uses

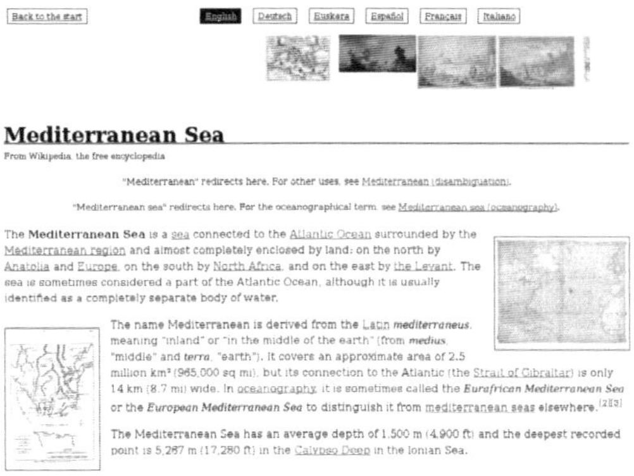


Figure 2: Screenshot of the augmented article "Mediterranean Sea" with the pre-processed article-level augmentation at the top and the first two paragraphs augmented with items as returned by the Europeana API.

keywords drawn from the paragraphs (details below) to query Europeana's OpenSearch API for items. A random item is selected from the result-set and a link to its thumbnail image inserted into the paragraph. The augmented article is then sent to the user's browser, which in turn requests the thumbnail images from Europeana's servers (fig. 2).

The system makes heavy use of caching to speed up the process and also to reduce the amount of load on the backend systems.

### 3.1 Article augmentation

To create the article-level augmentations we first create a Wikipedia "dictionary", which maps strings to Wikipedia articles. The mapping is created by extracting all anchor texts from the inter-article hyperlinks[2] and mapping these to the articles they link to. For instance, the string "roman coin" is used as an anchor in a link to the Wikipedia article `Roman_currency`[3]. Where the same string points to multiple articles we select the most frequent article as the target. In the case of ties an article is selected arbitrarily.

In a second step, we scan the subset of Europeana selected for a European project, which comprises SCRAN and Culture Grid collections for English. The items in this sub-set are then linked to Wikipedia articles. The sub-set of Europeana that was processed followed the Europeana Semantic Elements (ESE) specifications[4]. Figure 3 shows an example of an ESE record describing a photograph of a Roman coin belonging to the Kirklees Image Archive. We scan each ESE record and try to match the "dc:title" field with the dictionary entries. In the example in figure 3, the item will be mapped to the Wikipedia article `Roman_currency` because the string "roman coins" appears in the title.

```
<record>
  <dc:identifier>http://www.kirkleesimage...</dc:identifier>
  <dc:title>Roman Coins found in 1820..., Lindley</dc:title>
  <dc:source>Kirklees Image Archive OAI Feed</dc:source>
  <dc:language>EN-GB</dc:language>
  <dc:subject>Kirklees</dc:subject>
  <dc:type>Image</dc:type>
</record>
```

Figure 3: Example of an ESE record, some fields have been omitted for clarity.

As a result, we create a many-to-many mapping between Wikipedia articles and Europeana items. The Wikiana application displays at most 20 images per article, thus the Europeana items need to be ranked. The goal is to rank interesting items higher, with "interestingness" defined as how unusual the items are in the collection. This metric is an adaption of the standard inverse-document-frequency formula used widely in Information Retrieval and is adapted to identify items that have meta-data field-values that are infrequent in the collection. As in original IDF we diminish the weight of values that occur very frequently in the collection, the non-interesting items, and increases the weight of values that occur rarely, the interesting items. More formally the interestingness $\alpha_i$ of an item $i$ is calculated as follows:

$$\alpha_i = \frac{\#\{\text{title}_i\}}{\mu_{\text{title}}} \log \frac{N_{\text{title}}}{c(\text{title}_i)+1} + \frac{\#\{\text{desc}_i\}}{\mu_{\text{desc}}} \log \frac{N_{\text{desc}}}{c(\text{desc}_i)+1} + \frac{\#\{\text{subj}_i\}}{\mu_{\text{subj}}} \log \frac{N_{\text{subj}}}{c(\text{subj}_i)+1}$$

where $\#\{\text{field}_i\}$ is the length in words of the field of the given item i, $\mu_{\text{field}}$ is the average length in words of the field in the collection, $N_{\text{field}}$ is the total number of items containing that field in the

[2] We used the 2008 Wikipedia dump to construct the dictionary.

[3] http://en.wikipedia.org/wiki/Roman_currency

[4] http://version1.europeana.eu/web/guest/technical-requirements

The Roman Empire (**Latin**: Imperium Romanum) was the post-**Republican** period of the **ancient Roman civilization**, characterised by an **autocratic** form of government and large territorial holdings in Europe and around the Mediterranean.

| | |
|---|---|
| "Latin language" OR "Roman Republic" OR "Ancient Rome" or "Autocracy" |  |

Figure 4: Example paragraph with the Wikipedia hyperlinks in bold. Below the search keywords extracted from the hyperlinks and the resulting thumbnail image.

entire collection, and $c(\text{field}_i)$ is the frequency of the value in that field.

Items are ranked by descending $\alpha_i$ and the for the top 20 items, the thumbnails for the items are added to the top of the augmented page.

### 3.2 Paragraph augmentation

The items found in the article augmentation tend to be very focused on the article itself, thus to provide the user with a wider overview of available items, each paragraph is also augmented. This augmentation is done dynamically when an article is requested. As stated above the augmentation iterates over all paragraphs in the article and for each article determines its core keywords. As in the article augmentation the Wikipedia hyperlinks are used to define the core keywords, as the inclusion of the link in the paragraph indicates that this is a concept that the author felt was relevant enough to link to. For each paragraph the Wikipedia hyperlinks are extracted, the underscores replaced by spaces and these are then used as the query keywords. The keywords are combined using "OR" and enclosed in speech-marks to ensure only exact phrase matches are returned and then submitted to Europeana's OpenSearch API (fig. 4). From the result set an item is randomly selected and the paragraph is augmented with the link to the item, the item's thumbnail image and its title. If there are no hyperlinks in a paragraph or the search returns no results, then no augmentation is performed for that paragraph.

## 4 Evaluation

The initial evaluation focuses on the paragraph augmentation, as the quality of that heavily depends on the results provided by Europeana's API and on a log-analysis looking at how users coming to Europeana from Wikiana behave.

| Question | Yes | No |
|---|---|---|
| *Familiar* | 18 | 18 |
| *Appropriate* | 9 | 27 |
| *Supports* | 4 | 32 |
| *Visually interesting* | 13 | 23 |
| *Find out more* | 3 | 33 |

Table 1: Evaluation experiment results reduced from the 5-point Likert-like scale to a yes/no level.

### 4.1 Paragraph augmentation evaluation

For the paragraph augmentation evaluation 18 wikipedia articles were selected from six topics (Place, Person, Event, Time period, Concept, and Work of Art). From each article the first paragraph and a random paragraph were selected for augmentation, resulting in a total set of 36 augmented paragraphs. In the experiment interface the participants were shown the text paragraph, the augmented thumbnail image, and five questions ("How familiar are you with the topic?", "How appropriate is the image?", "How well does the image support the core ideas of the paragraph?", "How visually interesting is the image?", and "How likely are you to click on the image to find out more?"). Each question used a five-point Likert-like scale for the answers, with 1 as the lowest score and 5 the highest. Neither the topic nor the paragraph selection have a statistically significant influence on the results. To simplify the analysis the results have been reduced to a yes/no level, where an image is classified as "yes" for that question if more than half the participants rated the image 3 or higher on that question (table 1).

Considering the simplicity of the augmentation approach and the fact that the search API is not under our control, the results are promising. 9 out of 36 (25%) of the items were classified as *appropriate*. The non-appropriate images are currently being analysed to determine whether there are shared characteristics in the query structure or item meta-data that could be used to improve the query or filter out non-appropriate result items.

The difficulty with automatically adding items taken from Europeana is also highlighted by the fact that only 13 of the 36 (36%) items were classified as *interesting*. While no correlation could be found between the two *interest* and *appro-*

| Category | Sessions | 1st q. | Med | 3rd q. |
|---|---|---|---|---|
| Wikiana | 88 | 6 | 11 | 15.25 |
| All users | 577642 | 3 | 8 | 17 |

Table 2: Summary statistics for the number of items viewed in per session for users coming from our system (Wikiana) and for all Europeana users.

*priate* results, only one of the 23 uninteresting items was judged *appropriate*, while 8 out of 9 of the *appropriate* items were also judged to be *interesting*. We are now looking at whether the item meta-data might allow filtering uninteresting items, as they seem unlikely to be appropriate.

Additionally the approach taken by (Zhu et al., 2007), where multiple images are shown per paragraph, is also being investigated, as this might reduce the impact of non-appropriate items.

### 4.2 Log analysis

Although the paragraph augmentation results are not as good as we had hoped, a log analysis shows that the system can achieve its goal of introducing new users to an unknown CH collection (Europeana). The system has been available online for three months, although not widely advertised, and we have collected Europeana's web-logs for the same period. Using the referer information in the logs we can distinguish users that came to Europeana through our system from all other Europeana users. Based on this classification the number of items viewed per session were calculated (table 2). To prevent the evaluation experiment influencing the log analysis only logs acquired before the experiment date were used.

Table 2 clearly shows that users coming through our system exhibit different browsing patterns. The first quartile is higher, indicating that Wikiana users do not leave Europeana as quickly, which is further supported by the fact that 30% of the general users leave Europeana after viewing three items or less, while for Wikiana users it is only 19%. At the same time the third quartile is lower, showing that Wikiana users are less likely to have long sessions on Europeana. The difference in the session length distributions has also been validated using a Kolmogorov-Smirnov test ($p = 0.00287$, $D = 0.1929$).

From this data we draw the hypothesis that Wikiana is at least in part successfully attracting users to Europeana that would normally not visit or not stay and that it successfully helps users overcome that first hurdle that causes almost one third of all Europeana users to leave after viewing three or less items.

## 5 Conclusion and Future Work

Recent digitisation efforts have led to large digital cultural heritage (CH) collections and while search facilities provide access to users familiar with the collections there is a lack of methods for introducing new users to these collections. In this paper we propose a novel method for discovering items in an unfamiliar collection by browsing Wikipedia. As the user browses Wikipedia articles, these are augmented with a number of thumbnail images of items taken from the unknown collection that are appropriate to the article's content. This enables the new user to become familiar with what is available in the collection without having to immediately interact with the collection's search interface.

An early evaluation of the very straightforward augmentation process revealed that further work is required to improve the appropriateness of the items used to augment the Wikipedia articles. At the same time a log analysis of Europeana browsing sessions showed that users introduced to Europeana through our system were less likely to leave after viewing less than three items, providing clear indication that the methodology proposed in this paper is successful in introducing new users to a large, aggregated CH collection.

Future work will focus on improving the quality of the augmentation results by including more collections into the article-level augmentation and by introducing an "interestingness" ranking into the paragraph augmentation. We will also look at evaluating the system in a task-based setting and with existing, comparable systems.

## Acknowledgements

The research leading to these results has received funding from the European Community's Seventh Framework Programme (FP7/2007-2013) under grant agreement n° 270082. We acknowledge the contribution of all project partners involved in PATHS (see: `http://www.paths-project.eu`).

## References


Keith Andrews, Christian Gutl, Josef Moser, Vedran Sabol, and Wilfried Lackner. 2001. Search result visualisation with xfind. In *uidis*, page 0050. Published by the IEEE Computer Society.

Murtha Baca. 2003. Practical issues in applying metadata schemas and controlled vocabularies to cultural heritage information. *Cataloging & Classification Quarterly*, 36(3–4):47–55.

Christine L. Borgman. 2009. The digital future is now: A call to action for the humanities. *Digital humanities quarterly*, 3(4).

Andy Borman, Rada Mihalcea, and Paul Tarau. 2005. Picnet: Augmenting semantic resources with pictorial representations. In *Knowledge Collection from Volunteer Contributors: Papers from the 2005 Spring Symposium*, volume Technical Report SS-05-03. American Association for Artificial Intelligence.

Abdus Sattar Chaudhry and Tan Pei Jiun. 2005. Enhancing access to digital information resources on heritage: A case of development of a taxonomy at the integrated museum and archives system in singapore. *Journal of Documentation*, 61(6):751–776.

Chaomei Chen, Timothy Cribbin, Jasna Kuljis, and Robert Macredie. 2002. Footprints of information foragers: behaviour semantics of visual exploration. *International Journal of Human-Computer Studies*, 57(2):139 – 163.

Blaz Fortuna, Marko Grobelnik, and Dunja Mladenic. 2005. Visualization of text document corpus. *Informatica*, 29:497–502.

Evgeniy Gabrilovich and Shaul Markovitch. 2007. Computing semantic relatedness using wikipedia-based explicit semantic analysis. In *Proceedings of the 20th international joint conference on Artifical intelligence*, IJCAI'07, pages 1606–1611, San Francisco, CA, USA. Morgan Kaufmann Publishers Inc.

Guntram Geser. 2004. Resource discovery - position paper: Putting the users first. *Resource Discovery Technologies for the Heritage Sector*, 6:7–12.

Kasper Hornbæk and Morten Hertzum. 2011. The notion of overview in information visualization. *International Journal of Human-Computer Studies*, 69(7-8):509 – 525.

Antoine Isaac, Stefan Schlobach, Henk Matthezing, and Claus Zinn. 2007. Integrated access to cultural heritage resources through representation and alignment of controlled vocabularies. *Library Review*, 67(3):187–199.

Sook Lim. 2009. How and why do college students use wikipedia? *Journal of the American Society for Information Science and Technology*, 60(11):2189–2202.

Xia Lin. 1992. Visualization for the document space. In *Proceedings of the 3rd conference on Visualization '92*, VIS '92, pages 274–281, Los Alamitos, CA, USA. IEEE Computer Society Press.

Teun Lucassen and Jan Maarten Schraagen. 2010. Trust in wikipedia: how users trust information from an unknown source. In *Proceedings of the 4th workshop on Information credibility*, WICOW '10, pages 19–26, New York, NY, USA. ACM.

Dongning Luo, Jing Yang, Milos Krstajic, William Ribarsky, and Daniel A. Keim. 2012. Eventriver: Visually exploring text collections with temporal references. *Visualization and Computer Graphics, IEEE Transactions on*, 18(1):93 –105, jan.

Gary Marchionini. 2006. Exploratory search: From finding to understanding. *Communications of the ACM*, 49(4):41–46.

David Milne and Ian H. Witten. 2008. Learning to link with wikipedia. In *Proceedings of the 17th ACM conference on Information and knowledge management*, CIKM '08, pages 509–518, New York, NY, USA. ACM.

Glen Newton, Alison Callahan, and Michel Dumontier. 2009. Semantic journal mappiong for search visualization in a large scale article digital library. In *Second Workshop on Very Large Digital Libraries at ECDL 2009*.

Xiaochuan Ni, Jian-Tao Sun, Jian Hu, and Zheng Chen. 2009. Mining multilingual topics from wikipedia. In *Proceedings of the 18th international conference on World wide web*, WWW '09, pages 1155–1156, New York, NY, USA. ACM.

Panagiotis Papadakos, Stella Kopidaki, Nikos Armenatzoglou, and Yannis Tzitzikas. 2009. Exploratory web searching with dynamic taxonomies and results clustering. In Maristella Agosti, José Borbinha, Sarantos Kapidakis, Christos Papatheodorou, and Giannis Tsakonas, editors, *Research and Advanced Technology for Digital Libraries*, volume 5714 of *Lecture Notes in Computer Science*, pages 106–118. Springer Berlin / Heidelberg.

Peter Pirolli. 2009. Powers of 10: Modeling complex information-seeking systems at multiple scales. *Computer*, 42(3):33–40.

Patrick L Schmitz and Michael T Black. 2008. The delphi toolkit: Enabling semantic search for museum collections. In *Museums and the Web 2008: the international conference for culture and heritage on-line*.

Nick J. Schweitzer. 2008. Wikipedia and psychology: Coverage of concepts and its use by undergraduate students. *Teaching of Psychology*, 35(2):81–85.

Michael Steemson. 2004. Digicult experts seek out discovery technologies for cultural heritage. *Resource Discovery Technologies for the Heritage Sector*, 6:14–20.

Fabian M. Suchanek, Gjergji Kasneci, and Gerhard Weikum. 2008. Yago: A large ontology from wikipedia and wordnet. *Web Semantics: Science, Services and Agents on the World Wide Web*, 6(3):203 – 217. World Wide Web Conference 2007Semantic Web Track.

Alistair Sutcliffe and Mark Ennis. 1998. Towards a cognitive theory of information retrieval. *Interacting with Computers*, 10:321–351.

Jacco van Ossenbruggen, Alia Amin, Lynda Hardman, Michiel Hildebrand, Mark van Assem, Borys Omelayenko, Guus Schreiber, Anna Tordai, Victor de Boer, Bob Wielinga, Jan Wielemaker, Marco de Niet, Jos Taekema, Marie-France van Orsouw, and Annemiek Teesing. 2007. Searching and annotating virtual heritage collections with semantic-web technologies. In *Museums and the Web 2007*.

Robert Villa, Martin Halvey, Hideo Joho, David Hannah, and Joemon M. Jose. 2010. Can an intermediary collection help users search image databases without annotations? In *Proceedings of the 10th annual joint conference on Digital libraries*, JCDL '10, pages 303–312, New York, NY, USA. ACM.

Daniel S. Weld, Raphael Hoffmann, and Fei Wu. 2009. Using wikipedia to bootstrap open information extraction. *SIGMOD Rec.*, 37:62–68, March.

Xiaojin Zhu, Andrew B. Goldberg, Mohamed Eldawy, Charles A. Dyer, and Bradley Strock. 2007. A text-to-picture synthesis system for augmenting communication. In *The integrated intelligence track of the 22nd AAAI Conference on Artificial Intelligence (AAAI-07)*.

# Adapting Wikification to Cultural Heritage

**Samuel Fernando** and **Mark Stevenson**
Department of Computer Science
Regent Court
211 Portobello
Sheffield, S1 4DP
s.fernando@shef.ac.uk
m.stevenson@dcs.shef.ac.uk

## Abstract

Large numbers of cultural heritage items are now archived digitally along with accompanying metadata and are available to anyone with internet access. This information could be enriched by adding links to resources that provide background information about the items. Techniques have been developed for automatically adding links to Wikipedia to text but the methods are general and not designed for use with cultural heritage data. This paper explores a range of methods for adapting a system for adding links to Wikipedia to cultural heritage items. The approaches make use of the structure of Wikipedia, including the category hierarchy. It is found that an approach that makes use of Wikipedia's link structure can be used to improve the quality of the Wikipedia links that are added.

## 1 Introduction

Cultural heritage (CH) items are now increasingly being digitised and stored online where they can be viewed by anyone with a web browser. These items are usually annotated with metadata which gives the title of the item, subject keywords, descriptions and so on. However such metadata can often be very limited, with some items having very little metadata at all. This paper examines methods to enrich such metadata with inline links to Wikipedia. These links allow users to find interesting background information on the items and related topics, and provides a richer experience especially where the metadata is limited. Additionally the links may also help to categorise and organise the collections using the Wikipedia category hierarchy.

CH items from Europeana[1] are used for the evaluation. Europeana is a large online aggregation of cultural heritage collections from across Europe. The WikiMiner software (Milne and Witten, 2008) is used to automatically enrich the Europeana items collections with Wikipedia links. Two methods are used to improve the quality of the links. The first makes use of the Wikipedia category hierarchy. Top-level categories of interest are selected and articles close to these categories are used as training data for WikiMiner. The second method uses existing links from Wikipedia as evidence to find useful links for the CH items.

## 2 Background

Mihalcea and Csomai (2007) first addressed the task of automatically adding inline Wikipedia links into text and coined the term Wikification for the process. Their procedure for wikification used two stages. The first stage was *detection*, which involved identifying the terms and phrases from which links should be made. The most accurate method for this was found to be using link probability, defined as the number of Wikipedia articles that use the term as an anchor, divided by the number of Wikipedia articles that mention it at all. The next stage, *disambiguation* ensure that the detected phrases link to the appropriate article. For example the term *plane* usually links to an article about fixed wing aircraft. However it sometimes points to a page describing the mathematical concept of a theoretical surface, or of the tool for flattening wooden surfaces. To find the correct destination a classifier is trained using features from the context. Although the quality of re-

[1] http://www.europeana.eu

sults obtained is very good, a large amount of preprocessing is required, since the entire Wikipedia encyclopedia must be parsed.

Milne and Witten (2008) build upon this previous work with the WikiMiner program. The software is trained on Wikipedia articles, and thus learns to disambiguate and detect links in the same way as Wikipedia editors. Disambiguation of terms within the text is performed first. A machine-learning classifier is used with several features. The main features used are commonness and relatedness, as in Medelyan et al. (2008). The commonness of a target sense is defined by the number of times it is used a destination from some anchor text e.g. the anchor text 'Tree' links to the article about the plant more often than the mathematical concept and is thus more common. Relatedness gives a measure of the similarity of two articles by comparing their incoming and outgoing links. The performance achieved using their approach is currently state of the art for this task. The WikiMiner software is freely available[2], and has been used as the basis for the approaches presented here.

Recent work on named entity linking and wikification makes use of categories and link information (Bunescu and Pasca, 2006; Dakka and Cucerzan, 2008; Kulkarni et al., 2009). Wikification has also been applied to the medical domain (He et al., 2011). Wikipedia categories and links have been used previously to find the similarity between CH items (Grieser et al., 2011). The category retraining approach presented here differs in that it only makes use of the top-level categories.

## 3 Methods

Three approaches to improving the quality of Wikipedia links added by WikiMiner were developed. The first two make use of Wikipedia's category structure while the third uses the links between Wikipedia articles.

### 3.1 Wikipedia Categories

Almost all articles in Wikipedia are manually assigned to one or more categories. For example the page ALBERT EINSTEIN belongs to the categories Swiss physicists, German-language philosophers and several others. The category pages thus group together articles of interest. Furthermore, each category may itself be a sub-category of one or more categories. So for example Swiss physicists is a sub-category of the categories Swiss scientists, Physicists by nationality etc.

The categories give a general indication of the topic of the article and we assume that articles relevant to Cultural Heritage items are likely to be closely associated with certain categories.

### 3.2 Retraining using Categories

The first approach is to retrain WikiMiner using articles associated with particular categories. Three top-level categories manually judged to indicate articles that are relevant to cultural heritage were selected: Culture, Arts and Humanities. All articles within 2 links of these selected categories were found and used as training data for WikiMiner. (We also explored using different numbers of links but found that fewer than 2 links produced a very small number of articles while more than 2 generated very large numbers which would be prohibitively expensive for retraining.) The same approach was also tested with categories which are unlikely to be related to cultural heritage (Computers, Mathematics and Science) in order to test the effect of using different categories.

### 3.3 Filtering using Categories

This approach uses the category information to filter articles after WikiMiner has been run. Each article added by WikiMiner is examined and any which are more than a certain distance from a top-level category which has been identified as being relevant to cultural heritage is removed. The assumption behind this approach is that relevant articles are much more likely to be closely associated with these categories than ones which are not relevant.

### 3.4 Exploiting Wikipedia's Link Structure

The final method makes use of Wikipedia's link structure rather than the category hierarchy and is similar to the previous method since it filters the links added by WikiMiner to identify those which are relevant to a particular article.

The first stage is to run the item through WikiMiner to detect suitable links. This is done with 2 parameter settings, each returning a set of links. The aim of the first run is to find as many

[2] http://wikipedia-miner.cms.waikato.ac.nz/

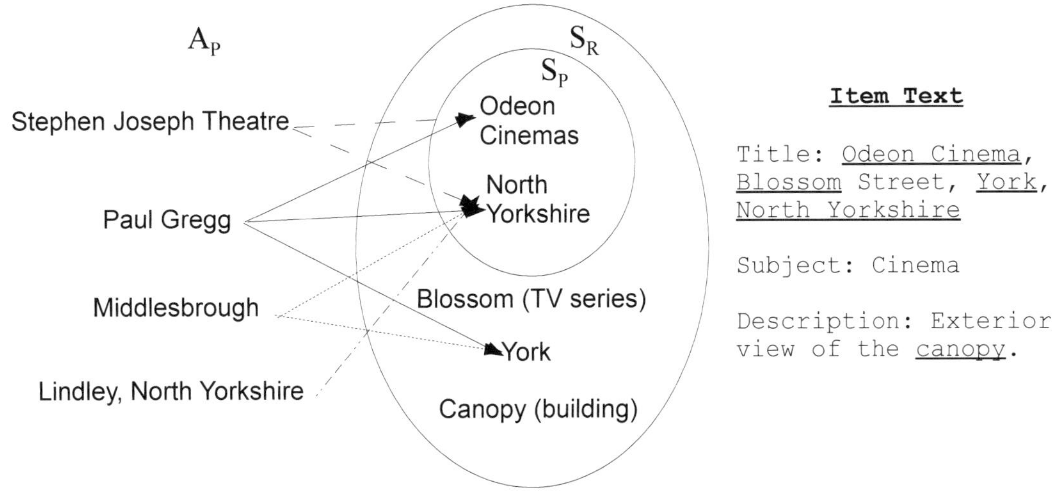


Figure 1: Example illustrating the method, where articles (on the left) which link to the high precision articles ($S_P$) are used to find good links in the high recall set ($S_R$).

potential links in the text as possible, for example by using a low confidence threshold. This give a set of links $S_R$ which is high recall (because most links are included), but low precision, since many incorrect or irrelevant links are also present. The aim of the second run is to find a smaller set of links which are likely to be of good quality, for example by setting a high confidence threshold. The resulting set $S_P$ is high precision but lower recall since good links may be discarded.

The result set of links is initialised with the high precision articles $R = S_P$. The aim is then to try to find additional good links within $S_R$. This is done by finding a list of articles $A_P$ which contain links to 1 or more of the articles in $S_P$. Let $O(a)$ be the set of outlinks from an article $a$. Each article in $A_P$ is then scored on how many links are shared with $S_P$:

$$\forall a \in A_P : score(a) = |O(a) \cap S_P| \qquad (1)$$

The $N$ top scoring articles in $A_P$ are then used to find further good links with within $S_R$. For each of these articles $a$:

$$R := R \cup (O(a) \cap S_R) \qquad (2)$$

Figure 1 gives an example illustrating how the method works on an Europeana item about an old Odeon Cinema in York. The article on Paul Gregg links to the articles in the $S_P$ set {Odeon Cinemas, North Yorkshire}. Since it also links to the York article in the $S_R$ set, the method takes this as evidence that York might also be a good article to link to, and so this would be added to the result set $R$.

## 4 Annotation

To evaluate the quality of the Wikipedia links, a sample of CH items was manually annotated. The sample of 21 items was randomly selected from Europeana. When run through WikiMiner with no probability threshold (i.e. including all possible links), a total of 366 potential links were identified. A further 16 links were manually added which the WikiMiner software had missed, giving a total of 381 links.

Web surveys were created to allow the annotators to judge the links. For each item in the survey users were presented with a picture of the item, the metadata text, and the set of possible links (with the anchor text identified). The annotators were then given a binary choice for each link to decide if it should be included or not.

Two separate surveys were taken by three fluent English speakers. The first was to determine if each link was correctly disambiguated within the context of the item (regardless of whether the link was useful or appropriate for that item). For each link the majority decision was used to judge if the link was indeed correct or not. Out of the 381 links, 70% were judged to be correct and 30% as incorrect. For 80% of the links the judgement was unanimous with all 3 annotators agreeing on the correctness of the links. The remaining 20% were 2-to-1 judgements. This gives an overall inter-annotator agreement of 93.4%.

The second survey was to determine which of the correct links were useful and appropriate for the corresponding items. As before each of the 21 items was presented to the annotators, but this time only with the 267 links that had been judged as correct within the previous survey. Again, three annotators completed the survey. Out of the 267 correct links, 49.8% were judged to be useful/appropriate and 50.2% as not. For 67.7% of the links the judgement was unanimous. The remaining 32.2% were 2-1 judgements. This gives an inter-annotator agreement of 89.3%. The 133 links judged to be correct, useful and appropriate were then used as the gold standard to evaluate the automatic methods.

As an example, the links and judgements for the following text are shown in Table 1:

Title: Odeon Cinema, Blossom Street, York, North Yorkshire
Subject: Cinema
Description: Exterior view of the canopy.

| Link | Correct | Useful |
|---|---|---|
| Odeon Cinemas | Yes | Yes |
| Blossom (TV series) | No | N/A |
| York | Yes | Yes |
| North Yorkshire | Yes | No |
| Cinema | Yes | No |
| Canopy | Yes | Yes |

Table 1: Examples of links and judgements

## 5 Experiments

The methods from Section 3 were used to identify links in the items from Europeana. The results were evaluated against the gold standard manually annotated data that was described in Section 4. For all experiments the standard metrics of precision, recall and F-measure are used to measure the performance of the methods.

Milne and Witten (2008) noted that training using articles with a similar length and link density to the target documents can improve WikiMiner's performance. The descriptions associated with Europeana items are relatively short so further experiments were carried out in which WikiMiner was retrained with different sets of articles. The best results were obtained using a set of articles between 100 and 500 words that contained a minimum of five links to other articles. (Results for experiments comparing other configurations are not reported here for brevity.) Table 2 shows results obtained using the default model, when WikiMiner is run 'off the shelf', and when it has been retrained. These results demonstrate that retraining WikiMiner improves performance. Precision improves to over 50% and, although there is a drop in recall, F-measure is also higher. Results using the retrained model are used as a baseline against which alternative approaches are compared.

| Model | P | R | F |
|---|---|---|---|
| Default | 34.0 | **91.7** | 49.6 |
| Retrained | **56.6** | 77.4 | **65.4** |

Table 2: Results obtained using WikiMiner using default model and after retraining

### 5.1 Category retraining

The category retraining approach (Section 3.2) was applied using all articles within two links of selected categories as training data for WikiMiner. The results are shown in Table 3 and show that precision is improved over the baseline for all categories. However the results do not fit the hypothesis, with Science giving the best F-measure overall, a statistically significant improvement over the baseline ($p < 0.05$, t-test). This may be for various reasons. Firstly the category hierarchy in Wikipedia is often messy with articles assigned to many different categories, and each category can contain a diverse sets of articles which may not be very useful. Secondly it may be that the topics of the articles are not so important for the training, but rather factors like the length of the articles and the link densities. However it is interesting that using articles close to the top level categories does appear to improve performance.

| Method | P | R | F |
|---|---|---|---|
| Baseline | 56.6 | **77.4** | 65.4 |
| Culture | 65.5 | 71.4 | 68.3 |
| Arts | 69.6 | 65.4 | 67.4 |
| Humanities | 71.9 | 65.4 | 68.5 |
| Mathematics | 72.9 | 58.6 | 65.0 |
| Science | 72.4 | 69.1 | **70.8** |
| Computers | **76.7** | 59.4 | 66.9 |

Table 3: Retraining using top level categories.

### 5.2 Category filtering

The category filtering approach (Section 3.3) was applied. Articles within a distance of 1 to 4 links from selected top level categories are kept and all others are discarded. The following combinations of categories were used: C (Culture), CHA (Culture, Humanities and Arts), and CHAGSE (Culture, Humanities, Arts, Geography, Society and Education).

Results are shown in Table 4 and are surprisingly low. Both precision and recall drop significantly when category filtering is applied. This may be because the articles within categories are often very diverse and do not capture many of the possible topics found within cultural heritage items.

| Method | Precision | Recall | F |
|---|---|---|---|
| Baseline | **56.6** | **77.4** | **65.4** |
| C | 35.1 | 19.5 | 25.1 |
| CHA | 27.4 | 27.8 | 27.6 |
| CHAGSE | 24.5 | 34.6 | 28.7 |

Table 4: Filtering using top level categories.

### 5.3 Using Wikipedia links

The final experiment explores the link filtering approach described in Section 3.4. The high precision $S_P$ set is chosen to be those returned by the retrained WikiMiner model ("Retrained" in Table 2) while the high recall $S_R$ set is the default model ("Default" in Table 2). Experiments were performed varying $N$, the number of top scoring articles used (using the score metric defined in Equation 1).

| No. of similar articles | P | R | F |
|---|---|---|---|
| Baseline | 56.6 | **77.4** | 65.4 |
| 1 | **74.0** | 53.4 | 62.0 |
| 2 | 70.7 | 61.7 | 65.9 |
| 3 | 68.5 | 63.9 | 66.1 |
| 4 | 67.4 | 68.4 | 67.9 |
| 5 | 66.9 | 69.9 | **68.4** |
| 6 | 66.2 | 70.6 | **68.4** |
| 7 | 66.2 | 70.7 | **68.4** |
| 8 | 65.5 | 71.4 | 68.3 |
| 9 | 65.1 | 71.4 | 68.1 |
| 10 | 63.9 | **72.9** | 68.1 |

Table 5: Filtering using Wikipedia's link structure

The results are shown in Table 5 and show a clear improvement in precision for N from 1 to 10. The F-measure peaks when 5-7 related articles are used. The improvement in the F-measure over the baseline is statistically significant ($p < 0.05$ t-test).

## 6 Conclusions and future work

This paper explores a variety of methods for improving the quality of Wikipedia links added by the WikiMiner software when applied to the cultural heritage domain. Approaches that make use of the Wikipedia category hierarchy and link structure were compared and evaluated using a data set of manual judgements created for this study.

The approaches based on the category hierarchy appeared to be less promising than those which used the link structure. Improvements were obtained by retraining WikiMiner using articles associated with particular categories. However the results were unexpected, with categories such as Science giving better performance as training data than categories such as Culture or Arts. Although a higher score was obtained using this method than the link approach, this may be due to factors such as document length and link density rather than the topic of the articles.

Results obtained using a novel method based on existing links within Wikipedia suggest this approach is promising. The method is fully unsupervised so it can be easily applied to domains other than cultural heritage.

Information from both categories and links could be combined in a similar way to that suggested by Grieser et al. (2011). Enriching cultural heritage data with Wikipedia links should improve the experience for users while they browse the data. In addition the links themselves may be useful to categorise, cluster and find similar items. Further work will investigate these possibilities.

## Acknowledgments

The research leading to these results was carried out as part of the PATHS project (`http://paths-project.eu`) funded by the European Community's Seventh Framework Programme (FP7/2007-2013) under grant agreement no. 270082.

## References


Razvan Bunescu and Marius Pasca. 2006. Using Encyclopedic Knowledge for Named Entity Disambiguation. In *Proceedings of European Chapter of the Association of Computational Linguistics (EACL)*, volume 6, pages 9–16.

Wisam Dakka and Silviu Cucerzan. 2008. Augmenting Wikipedia with Named Entity Tags. In *Proceedings of The Third International Joint Conference on Natural Language Processing (IJCNLP)*.

Karl Grieser, Timothy Baldwin, Fabian Bohnert, and Liz Sonenberg. 2011. Using Ontological and Document Similarity to Estimate Museum Exhibit Relatedness. *Journal on Computing and Cultural Heritage (JOCCH)*, 3(3):10.

Jiyin He, Maarten de Rijke, Maarten de Rijke, Rob van Ommering, and Yuechen Qian. 2011. Generating Links to Background Knowledge: A Case Study Using Narrative Radiology Reports. In *20th ACM Conference on Information and Knowledge Management (CIKM)*, pages 1867–1876, Glasgow.

Sayali Kulkarni, Amit Singh, Ganesh Ramakrishnan, and Soumen Chakrabarti. 2009. Collective Annotation of Wikipedia Entities in Web Text. In *Proceedings of the 15th ACM SIGKDD International Conference on Knowledge Discovery and Data Mining*, pages 457–466.

Olena Medelyan, Ian H. Witten, and David Milne. 2008. Topic Indexing with Wikipedia. In *Proceedings of the Association for the Advancement of Artificial Intelligence (AAAI) WikiAI workshop*.

Rada Mihalcea and Andras Csomai. 2007. Wikify!: Linking Documents to Encyclopedic Knowledge. In *ACM Sixteenth Conference on Information and Knowledge Management (CIKM)*, volume 7, pages 233–242.

David Milne and Ian H. Witten. 2008. Learning to Link with Wikipedia. In *Proceeding of the 17th ACM conference on Information and Knowledge Management*, pages 509–518.

# Natural Language Inspired Approach for Handwritten Text Line Detection in Legacy Documents*

**Vicente Bosch Campos**
Inst. Tec. de Informática
Univ. Politécnica Valencia
Valencia - Spain
vbosch@iti.upv.es

**Alejandro Héctor Toselli**
Inst. Tec. de Informática
Univ. Politécnica Valencia
Valencia - Spain
ahector@iti.upv.es

**Enrique Vidal**
Inst. Tec. de Informática
Univ. Politécnica Valencia
Valencia - Spain
evidal@iti.upv.es

## Abstract

Document layout analysis is an important task needed for handwritten text recognition among other applications. Text layout commonly found in handwritten legacy documents is in the form of one or more paragraphs composed of parallel text lines. An approach for handwritten text line detection is presented which uses machine-learning techniques and methods widely used in natural language processing. It is shown that text line detection can be accurately solved using a formal methodology, as opposed to most of the proposed heuristic approaches found in the literature. Experimental results show the impact of using increasingly constrained "vertical layout language models" in text line detection accuracy.

## 1 Introduction

Handwritten text transcription is becoming an increasingly important task, in order to provide historians and other researchers new ways of indexing, consulting and querying the huge amounts of historic handwritten documents which are being published in on-line digital libraries.

Transcriptions of such documents are currently obtained with solutions that range from the use of systems that aim at fully automatic handwritten text recognition (Bazzi et al., 1999)

(HTR), to computer assisted transcription (CATTI), were the users participate interactively in the proper transcription process (Toselli et al., 2009).

*Work supported under the MIPRCV "Consolider Ingenio 2010" program (CSD2007-00018), MITTRAL (TIN2009-14633-C03-01) and also Univ. Politécnica Valencia (PAID-05-11)

The basic input to these systems consists of text line images. Hence, text line detection and extraction from a given document page image becomes a necessary preprocessing step in any kind of transcription systems. Furthermore the quality of line segmentation directly influences the final accuracy achieved by such systems.

Detection of handwritten text lines in an image entails a greater difficulty, in comparison with printed text lines, due to the inherent properties of handwritten text: variable inter-line spacing, overlapping and touching strokes of adjacent handwritten lines, etc.

The difficulty is further increased in the case of ancient documents, due to common problems appearing in them: presence of smear, significant background variations and uneven illumination, spots due to the humidity, and marks resulting from the ink that goes through the paper (generally called "bleed-through").

Among the most popular state-of-the art methods involved in handwritten text line detection we find four main families: based on (vertical) projection profiles (Likforman-Sulem et al., 2007), on the Hough transform (Likforman-Sulem et al., 1995), the repulsive-attractive network approach (Öztop et al., 1999) and finally the so-called stochastic methods (Vinciarelli et al., 2004), which combine probabilistic models such as Hidden Markov Models (HMMs) along with dynamic programming techniques (e.g. Viterbi algorithm) to derive optimal paths between overlapping text lines.

It is worth noting that, most of the mentioned approaches somewhat involve heuristic adjustments of their parameters, which have to be properly tuned according to the characteristics of each task in order to obtain adequate results.

In this work, the text line detection problem in legacy handwritten documents is approached by using machine-learning techniques and methods which are widely used in natural language processing (NLP).

It is shown that the text line detection problem can be solved by using a formal methodology, as opposed to most of the currently proposed heuristic based approaches found in the literature.

## 2 Statistical Framework for Text Line Detection

For the work presented in this paper, we assume that the input image (of a page or selected region) contains one or more paragraphs of single-column parallel text with no images or diagram figures. Additionally, we assume that the input image has been properly preprocessed so as to ensure that their text lines are roughly horizontal. These assumptions are reasonable enough for most legacy handwritten documents.

Similarly to how the statistic framework of automatic speech recognition (ASR) is established, the handwritten text line detection problem can be also formulated as the problem of finding the most likely text lines sequence, $\hat{\mathbf{h}} = \langle h_1, h_2, \ldots, h_n \rangle$, for a given handwritten page image represented by a sequence of observations[1] $\mathbf{o} = \langle o_1, o_2, \ldots, o_m \rangle$, that is:

$$\hat{\mathbf{h}} = \arg\max_{h} P(\mathbf{h} \mid \mathbf{o}) \tag{1}$$

Using the Bayes' rule we can decompose the probability $P(\mathbf{h} \mid \mathbf{o})$ into two terms:

$$\hat{\mathbf{h}} = \arg\max_{h} P(\mathbf{o} \mid \mathbf{h}) \cdot P(\mathbf{h}) \tag{2}$$

In the jargon of NLP these probabilities represent the morphological and syntactic knowledge levels, respectively. As it happens in ASR, $P(\mathbf{o} \mid \mathbf{h})$ is typically approximated by HMMs, which model vertical page regions, while $P(\mathbf{h})$ by a "language model" (LM), which restricts how those regions are composed in order to form an actual page. In what follows, a detailed description of this modelling scheme is given.

[1] Henceforward, in the context of this formal framework, each time it is mentioned image of *page or selected text*, we are implicitly referring to the input feature vector sequence "**o**" describing it.

### 2.1 Modelling

In our line detection approach four different kinds of vertical regions are defined:

**Blank Line-region (BL):** Large rectangular region of blank space usually found at the start and the end of a page (top and bottom margins).

**Normal text Line-region (NL):** Region occupied by the main body of a normal handwritten text line.

**Inter Line-region (IL):** Defined as the region found within two consecutive normal text lines, characterized by being crossed by the ascenders and descenders belonging to the adjacent text lines.

**Non-text Line-region (NT):** Stands for everything which does not belong to any of the other regions.

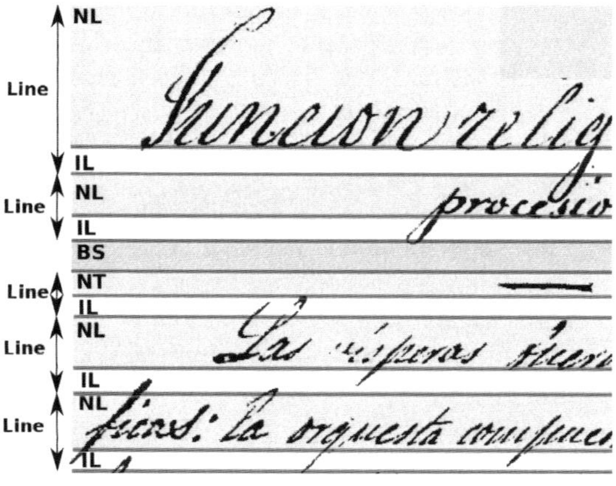


Figure 1: Examples of the different kind of line-regions.

We model each of these regions by an HMM which is trained with instances of such regions. Basically, each line-region HMM is a stochastic finite-state device that models the succession of feature vectors extracted from instances of this line-region image. In turn, each HMM state generates feature vectors following an adequate parametric probabilistic law; typically, a mixture of Gaussian densities. The adequate number of states and Gaussians per state may be conditioned by the available amount of training data.

Once an HMM "topology" (number of states and structure) has been adopted, the model parameters can be easily trained from instances (sequences of features vectors) of full images containing a sequence of line-regions (without any kind of segmentation) accompanied by the reference labels of these images into the corresponding sequence of line-region classes. This training process is carried out using a well known instance of the EM algorithm called forward-backward or Baum-Welch re-estimation (Jelinek, 1998).

The syntactic modelling level is responsible for the way that the different line regions are composed in order to produce a valid page structure. For example we can force that NL and NT line regions must always be followed by IL inter-line regions: NL+IL and NT+IL. We can also use the LM to impose restrictions about the minimum or maximum number of line-regions to be detected. The LM for our text line detection approach, consists in a stochastic finite state grammar (SFSG) which recognizes valid sequences of elements (line regions): NL+IL, NT+IL and BL.

Both modelling levels, morphological and syntactical, which are represented by finite-state automaton, can be integrated into a single global model on which Eq. (2) is easily solved; that is, given an input sequence of raw feature vectors, an output string of recognized sequence of line-region labels is obtained. In addition the vertical position of each detected line and and line-region is obtained as a by-product.

## 3 System Architecture

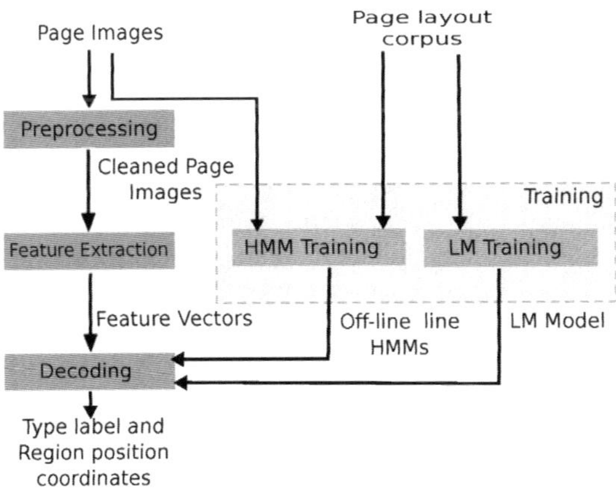


Figure 2: Global scheme of the handwritten text line detection process.

The flow diagram of Fig. 2 displays the overall process of the proposed handwritten text line detection approach. It is composed of four different phases: image preprocessing, feature extraction, HMMs and LM training and decoding. Next we will overview the first two phases, preprocessing and feature extraction, since the rest has already been covered in the preceding section.

### 3.1 Preprocessing Phase

Initially performing background removal and noise reduction is carried out by applying a bi-dimensional median filter on them. The resulting image skew is corrected by applying vertical projection profile and RLSA (Wong and Wahl, 1982), along with standard techniques to calculate the skew angle.

### 3.2 Feature Extraction Phase

As our text line detection approach is based on HMMs, each preprocessed image must be represented as a sequence of feature vectors.This is done by dividing the already preprocessed image (from left-to-right) into $D$ non-overlapping rectangular regions with height equal to the image-height (see Fig. 3).

In each of these rectangular regions we calculate the vertical grey level histogram. RLSA is applied to obtain a more emphasized vertical projection profile. Finally, to eliminate local maxima on the obtained vertical projection profiles, they are smoothed with a rolling median filter (Manmatha and Srimal, 1999) (see Fig. 3) . In this way,

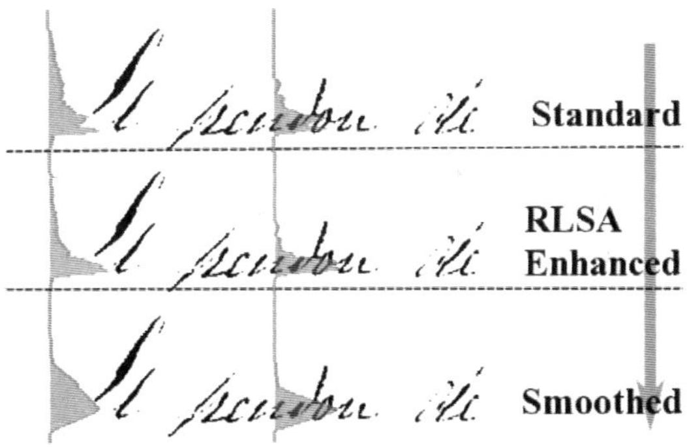


Figure 4: Review of the impact of the RLSA and rolling media filter on the histogram calculation of a sample line.

a $D$-dimensional feature vector is constructed for each page/block image pixels row, by stacking the $D$ projection profile values corresponding to that row. Hence, at the end of this process, a sequence of $L$ $D$-dimensional feature vectors is obtained, where $L$ is the image height.

## 4 Experimental Setup and Results

In order to study the efficacy of the line detection approach proposed in this paper, different experiments were carried out. We are mainly interested in assessing the impact upon final text line detec-

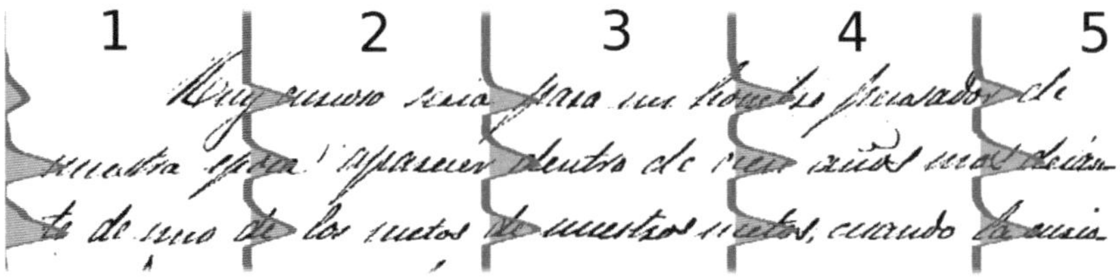


Figure 3: Partial page image visualization of 5 ($D = 5$) rectangular regions across over 3 handwritten text lines. For each region, its vertical projection profile is also plotted.

tion accuracy of employing increasingly restrictive LMs.

### 4.1 Corpus Description

Experiments are carried out with corpus compiled from a XIX century Spanish manuscript identified as "Cristo-Salvador" (CS), which was kindly provided by the *Biblioteca Valenciana Digital* (BiVaLDi)[2]. This is a rather small document composed of 53 colour images of text pages, scanned at 300 dpi and written by a single writer. Some page images examples are shown in Fig. 5.

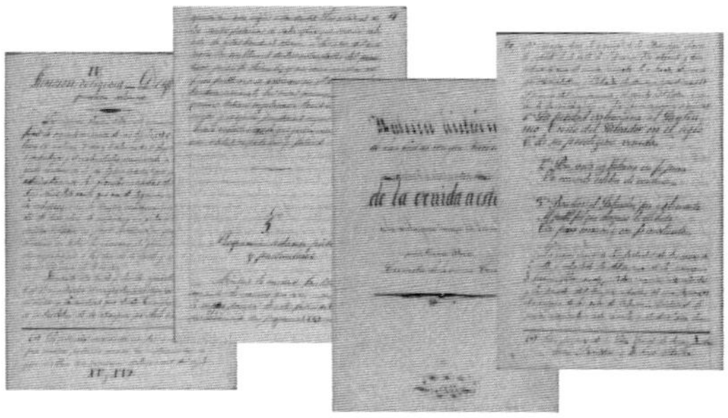

Figure 5: Examples of pages images from CS corpus.

In this work we employ the so-called *book* partition, which has been defined for this data-set (Romero et al., 2007). Its test set contains the last 20 page images were as the training set is composed of the 33 remaining pages. Table 1 summarizes the relevant information of this partition.

Table 1: Basic statistics of the Cristo-Salvador corpus partition.

| Number of: | Training | Test | Total |
|---|---|---|---|
| Pages | 33 | 20 | 53 |
| Normal-text lines (NL) | 685 | 497 | 1 182 |
| Blank Lines (BL) | 73 | 70 | 143 |
| Non-text Lines (NT) | 16 | 8 | 24 |
| Inter Lines (IL) | 701 | 505 | 1 206 |

Each page was annotated with a succession of reference labels (NL, NT, BL and IL) indicating the kind of line-regions that composed it. Such references were generated by executing standard methods for text line detection based on vertical projection profiles, which were afterwards manually labelled, verified, adjusted and/or rectified by a human operator to ensure correctness.

### 4.2 Evaluation Measures

We measure the quality of the text line detection by means of the "line error rate" (LER) which is performed by comparing the sequences of automatically obtained region labels with the corresponding reference label sequences. The LER is computed in the same way as the well known WER, with equal costs assigned to deletions, insertions and substitutions (McCowan et al., 2004).

### 4.3 Experiments and Results

A series of experiments were performed on the CS corpus using a simple hold-out validation as per the CS "book" partition. Initially some parameters were set up: feature extraction dimension $D$, HMM topology (number of states and Gaussians),number of Baum-Welch iterations, and decoding grammar scale factor (GSF) and word insertion penalty (WIP). After some informal experimentation, adequate values were found for several of them: feature vectors dimension of 2, left-to-right HMMs with 4 states topology, 32 Gaussian mixtures per state trained by running 3 cycles of Baum-Welch re-estimation algorithm. The remaining parameters, all related with the decoding process itself, were tuned to obtain the best figures for each of the two following language models: the *prior* and *conditional* represented by topologically different SFSGs. The *prior* model transition probabilities are estimated from the training set as the fraction of the number of appearances of each vertical region label over the whole count of labels. The conditional model also considers the previous label in order to perform the estimation. These estimates resemble the uni-gram and

[2] http://bv2.gva.es.

bi-gram LMs calculations, except no smoothing strategy is implemented here.

Additionally, it is defined for each test page a *line-number constrained* LM which uses the *conditional* probabilities to populate the model but enforces a total number of possible line-regions to detect as per the number of reference line-region labels of that test page. Table 2 reports the obtained LER results for each of these LMs.

Table 2: Best detection LER(%) obtained for each kind of language model: Prior, Conditional and Line-Number Constrained.

| LM | WIP | GSF | LER(%) |
|---|---|---|---|
| Prior | -32 | 8 | 0.86 |
| Conditional | -8 | 16 | 0.70 |
| LN-Constrained | -128 | 1 | 0.34 |

As can be seen, the more restrictive the LM is, the better accuracy is achieved. Concerning the *line-number constrained*, they are really conceived for its utilization in (parts of) documents or document collections with homogeneous numbers of lines per page.

## 5 Conclusions

We have presented a new approach for text line detection by using a statistical framework similar to that already employed in many topics of NLP. It avoids the traditional heuristics approaches usually adopted for this task.

The accuracy of this approach is similar to or better than that of current state of the art solutions found in the literature. We find that the detected baselines provided by our approach are of better quality (visually closer to the actual line) than current heuristic methods as can be seen in 6.

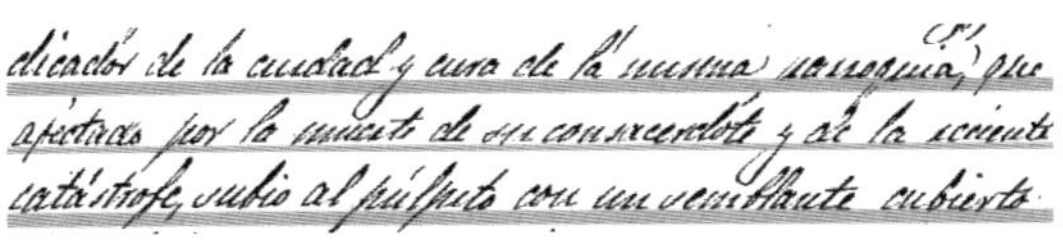

Figure 6: Image shows the difference between our proposed method (upper side of each coloured region ) and the histogram projection method (lower side)

In the future we will extend this approach not only to detect, but also to classify line-region types in order to determine for example titles, short lines, beginning and and end of paragraphs, etc. Furthermore, it is envisioned that the proposed stochastic framework serves as a cornerstone to implementing interactive approaches to line detection similar to those used for handwritten text transcription used in (Toselli et al., 2009).

## References


Issam Bazzi, Richard Schwartz, and John Makhoul. 1999. An omnifont open-vocabulary OCR system for English and Arabic. *IEEE Transactions on Pattern Analysis and Machine Intelligence*, 21(6):495–504.

Frederick Jelinek. 1998. *Statistical methods for speech recognition.* MIT Press.

Laurence Likforman-Sulem, Anahid Hanimyan, and Claudie Faure. 1995. A hough based algorithm for extracting text lines in handwritten documents. *Document Analysis and Recognition, International Conference on*, 2:774.

Laurence Likforman-Sulem, Abderrazak Zahour, and Bruno Taconet. 2007. Text line segmentation of historical documents: a survey. *International Journal on Document Analysis and Recognition*, 9:123–138, April.

Raghavan Manmatha and Nitin Srimal. 1999. Scale space technique for word segmentation in handwritten documents. In *Proceedings of the Second International Conference on Scale-Space Theories in Computer Vision*, SCALE-SPACE '99, pages 22–33, London, UK. Springer-Verlag.

Iain A. McCowan, Darren Moore, John Dines, Daniel Gatica-Perez, Mike Flynn, Pierre Wellner, and Hervé Bourlard. 2004. On the use of information retrieval measures for speech recognition evaluation. Idiap-RR Idiap-RR-73-2004, IDIAP, Martigny, Switzerland, 0.

Verónica Romero, Alejandro Héctor Toselli, Luis Rodríguez, and Enrique Vidal. 2007. Computer Assisted Transcription for Ancient Text Images. In *International Conference on Image Analysis and Recognition (ICIAR 2007)*, volume 4633 of *LNCS*, pages 1182–1193. Springer-Verlag, Montreal (Canada), August.

Alejandro Héctor Toselli, Verónica Romero, Moisés Pastor, and Enrique Vidal. 2009. Multimodal interactive transcription of text images. *Pattern Recognition*, 43(5):1824–1825.

Alessandro Vinciarelli, Samy Bengio, and Horst Bunke. 2004. Off-line recognition of unconstrained handwritten texts using hmms and statistical language models. *IEEE Transactions on Pattern Analysis and Machine Intelligence*, 26(6):709–720, june.

Kwan Y. Wong and Friedrich M. Wahl. 1982. Document analysis system. *IBM Journal of Research and Development*, 26:647–656.

Erhan Öztop, Adem Y. Mülayim, Volkan Atalay, and Fatos Yarman-Vural. 1999. Repulsive attractive network for baseline extraction on document images. *Signal Processing*, 75(1):1 – 10.

# Language Classification and Segmentation of Noisy Documents in Hebrew Scripts

**Nachum Dershowitz**
School of Computer Science
Tel Aviv University
Ramat Aviv, Israel
nachumd@tau.ac.il

**Alex Zhicharevich**
School of Computer Science
Tel Aviv University
Ramat Aviv, Israel
alex.zhicharevich@gmail.com

## Abstract

Language classification is a preliminary step for most natural-language related processes. The significant quantity of multilingual documents poses a problem for traditional language-classification schemes and requires segmentation of the document to monolingual sections. This phenomenon is characteristic of classical and medieval Jewish literature, which frequently mixes Hebrew, Aramaic, Judeo-Arabic and other Hebrew-script languages. We propose a method for classification and segmentation of multi-lingual texts in the Hebrew character set, using bigram statistics. For texts, such as the manuscripts found in the Cairo Genizah, we are also forced to deal with a significant level of noise in OCR-processed text.

## 1. Introduction

The identification of the language in which a given test is written is a basic problem in natural-language processing and one of the more studied ones. For some tasks, such as automatic cataloguing, it may be used stand-alone, but, more often than not, it is just a preprocessing step for some other language-related task. In some cases, even English and French, the identification of the language is trivial, due to non-identical character sets. But this is not always the case. When looking at Jewish religious documents, we often find a mixture of several languages, all with the same Hebrew character set. Besides Hebrew, these include Aramaic, which was once the lingua franca in the Middle East, and Judeo-Arabic, which was used by Jews living all over the Arab world in medieval times.

Language classification has well-established methods with high success rates. In particular, character n-grams, which we dub *n-chars*, work well. However, when we looked at recently digitized documents from the Cairo Genizah, we found that a large fraction contains segments in different languages, so a single language class is rather useless. Instead, we need to identify monolingual segments and classify them. Moreover, all that is available is the output of mediocre OCR of handwritten manuscripts that are themselves of poor quality and often seriously degraded. This raises the additional challenge of dealing with significant noise in the text to be segmented and classified.

We describe a method for segmenting documents into monolingual sections using statistical analysis of the distribution of n-grams for each language. In particular, we use cosine distance between character unigram and bigram distributions to classify each section and perform smoothing operations to increase accuracy.

The algorithms were tested on artificially produced multilingual documents. We also artificially introduced noise to simulate mistakes made in OCR. These test documents are similar in length and language shifts to real Genizah texts, so similar results are expected for actual manuscripts.

## 2 Related Work

Language classification is well-studied, and is usually approached by character-distribution methods (Hakkinen and Tian, 2001) or dictionary-based ones. Due to the lack of appropriate dictionaries for the languages in question and their complex morphology, the dictionary-based approach is not feasible. The poor quality of the results of OCR also precludes using word lists.

Most work on text segmentation is in the area of topic segmentation, which involves semantic features of the text. The problem is a simple case of structured prediction (Bakir, 2007). Text tiling (Hearst, 1993) uses a sliding-window approach.

Similarities between adjacent blocks within the text are computed using vocabularies, counting new words introduced in each segment. These are smoothed and used to identify topic boundaries via a cutoff function. This method is not suitable for language segmentation, since each topic is assumed to appear once, while languages in documents tend to switch repeatedly. Choi (2000) uses clustering methods for boundary identification.

## 3. Language Classification

Obviously, different languages, even when sharing the same character set, have different distribution of character occurrences. Therefore, gathering statistics on the typical distribution of letters may enable us to uncover the language of a manuscript by comparing its distribution to the known ones. A simple distribution of letters may not suffice, so it is common to employ n-chars (Hakkinen and Tian, 2001).

Classification entails the following steps: (1) Collect n-char statistics for relevant languages. (2) Determine n-char distribution for the input manuscript. (3) Compute the distance between the manuscript and each language using some distance measure. (4) Classify the manuscript as being in the language with the minimal distance.

The characters we work with all belong to the Hebrew alphabet, including its final variants (at the end of words). The only punctuation we take into account is inter-word space, because different languages can have different average word lengths (shorter words mean more frequent spaces), and different languages tend to have different letters at the beginnings and ends of words. For instance, a human might look for a prevalence of words ending in *alef* to determine that the language is Aramaic. After testing, bigrams were found to be significantly superior to unigrams and usually superior to trigrams, so bigrams were used throughout the classification process. Moreover, in the segmentation phase, we deal with very short texts on which trigram probabilities will be too sparse.

We represent the distribution function as a vector of probabilities. The language with smallest cosine distance between vectors is chosen, as this measure works well in practice.

## 4. Language Segmentation

For the splitting task, we use only n-char statistics, not presuming the availability of useful wordlists. We want the algorithm to work even if the languages shift frequently, so we do not assume anything about the minimal or maximal length of segments. We do not, of course, consider a few words in another language to constitute a language shift. The algorithm comprises four major steps: (1) Split text into arbitrary segments. (2) Calculate characteristics of each segment. (3) Classify each. (4) Refine classifications and output final results.

### 4.1 Splitting the Text

Documents are not always punctuated into sentences or paragraphs. So, splitting is done in the naïve way of breaking the text into fixed-size segments. As language does not shift mid-word (except for certain prefixes), we break the text between words. If sentences are delineated and one ignores possible transitions mid-sentence, then the breaks should be between sentences.

The selection of segment size should depend on the language shift frequency. Nonetheless, each segment is classified using statistical properties, so it has to be long enough to have some statistical significance. But if it is too long, the language transitions will be less accurate, and if a segment contains two shifts, it will miss the inner one. Because the post-processing phase is computationally more expensive, and grows proportionally with segment length, we opt for relatively short initial segments.

### 4.2 Feature Extraction

The core of the algorithm is the initial classification of segments. Textual classification is usually reduced to vector classification, so there each segment is represented as a vector of features. Naturally, the selection of features is critical for successful classification, regardless of classification algorithm. Several other features were tried such as hierarchical clustering of segments and classification of the clusters (Choi, 2000) but did not yield significant improvement.

**N-char distance** – The first and most obvious feature is the classification of the segment using the methods described in Section 3. However, the segments are significantly smaller than the usual documents, so we expect lower accuracy than usual for language classification. The features are the cosine distance from each language model. This is rather natural, since we want to preserve the distances from each language model in order to combine it with other features later on. For each segment $f$ and language $l$, we compute $Distance_1 = Dist(l, f)$, the cosine distance of their bigram distributions.

**Neighboring segments language** – We expect that languages in a document do not shift too frequently, since paragraphs tend to be monolingual and at least several sentences in a row will be in the same language to convey some idea. Therefore, if we are sure about one segment, there is a high chance that the next segment will be in the same language. One way to express such dependency is by post-processing the results to reduce noise. Another way is by combining the classification results of neighboring segments as features in the classification of the segment. Of course, not only neighboring segments can be considered, but all segments within some distance can help. Some parameter should be estimated to be the threshold for the distance between segments under which they will be considered neighbors. We denote by (negative or positive) $Neighbor(f,i)$ the $i$-th segment before/after $f$. If $i$=0, $Neighbor(f,i) = f$. For each segment $f$ and language $l$, we compute $NDist_{l,f}(i) = Dist(l, Neighbor(f, i))$.

**Whole document language** - Another feature is the cosine distance of the whole document from each language model. This tends to smooth and reduce noise from classification, especially when the proportion of languages is uneven. For a monolingual document, the algorithm is expected to output the whole document as one correctly-classified segment.

### 4.3 Post-processing

We refine the segmentation procedure as follows: We look at the results of the splitting procedure and recognize all language shifts. For each shift, we try to find the place where the shift takes place (at word granularity). We unify the two segments and then try to split the segment at N different points. For every point, we look at the cosine distance of the text before the point from the class of the first segment, and at the distance of the text after the point to the language of the second segment. For example, suppose a segment $A_1 \ldots A_n$ was classified as Hebrew and segment $B_1 \ldots B_m$, which appeared immediately after was classified Aramaic. We try to split $A_1 \ldots A_n, B_1 \ldots B_m$ at any of N points, N=2, say. First, we try $F_1 = A_1 \ldots A_{(n+m)/3}$ and $F_2 = A_{(n+m)/3+1} \ldots B_m$ (supposing $(n+m)/3 < n$). We look at cosine distance of $F_1$ to Hebrew and of $F_2$ to Aramaic. Then, we look at $F_1 = A_1 \ldots A_{2(n+m)/3}$ and $F_2 = A_{2(n+m)/3+1} \ldots B_m$. We choose the split with the best product of the two cosine distances. The value of N is a tradeoff between accuracy and efficiency. When N is larger, we check more transition points, but for large segments it can be computationally expensive.

### 4.4 Noise Reduction

OCR-processed documents display a significant error rate and classification precision should be expected to drop. Relying only on n-char statistics, we propose probabilistic approaches to the reduction of noise. Several methods (Kukich, 1992) have been proposed for error correction using n-chars, using letter-transition probabilities. Here, we are not interested in error correction, but rather in adjusting the segmentation to handle noisy texts.

To account for noise, we introduce a $ sign, meaning "unknown" character, imagining a conservative OCR system that only outputs characters with high probability. There is also no guarantee that word boundaries will not be missed, so $ can occur instead of a space.

**Ignoring unrecognized n-chars** – We simply ignore n-chars containing $ in the similarity measures. We assume there are enough bigrams left in each segment to successfully identify its language.

**Error correction** – Given an unknown character, we could try correcting it using trigrams, looking for the most common trigram of the form a$b. This seems reasonable and enhances the statistical power of the n-char distribution, but does not scale well for high noise levels, since there is no solution for consecutive unknowns.

**Averaging n-char probabilities** – When encountering the $, we can use averaging to estimate the probability of the n-char containing it. For instance, the probability of the bigram $x will be the average probability of all bigrams starting with $x$ in a certain language. This can of course scale to longer n-chars and integrates the noisy into the computation.

**Top n-chars** – When looking at noisy text, we can place more weight on corpus statistics, since they are error free. Therefore, we can look only at the N most common n-chars in the corpus for edit distance computing.

**Higher n-char space** – So far we used bigrams, which showed superior performance. But when the error rate rises, trigrams may show a higher success rate.

## 5. Experimental Results

We want to test the algorithm with well-defined parameters and evaluation factors. So, we created artificially mixed documents, containing segments from pairs of different languages (Hebrew/Aramaic, which is hard, Hebrew/Judeo-Arabic, where classification is easy and segmentation is the main challenge, or a mix of all three). The segments are produced using two parameters: The desired document length $d$ and the average monolingual segment length $k$. Obviously, $k < d$. We iteratively take a random number in the range [$k$–20:$k$+20] and take a substring of that length from a corpus, rounded to whole words. We cycle through the languages until the text is of size $d$. The smaller $k$, the harder to segment.

### 5.2 Evaluation Measures

Obviously splitting will not be perfect and we cannot expect to precisely split a document. Given that, we want to establish some measures for the quality of the splitting result. We would like the measure to produce some kind of score to the algorithm output, using which we can indicate whether a certain feature or parameter in the algorithm improves it or not. However, the result quality is not well defined since it is not clear what is more important: detecting the segment's boundaries accurately, classifying each segment correctly or even split the document to the exact number of segments. For example, given a long document in Hebrew with a small segment in Aramaic, is it better to return that it actually is a long document in Hebrew with Aramaic segment but misidentify the segment's location or rather recognize the Aramaic segment perfectly but classify it as Judeo-Arabic. There are several measures for evaluating text segmentation (Lamprier et al., 2007).

**Correct word percentage** – The most intuitive measure is simply measuring the percentage of the words classified correctly. Since the "atomic" block of the text is words (or sentences in some cases described further), which are certainly monolingual, this measure will resemble the algorithm accuracy pretty good for most cases. It is however not enough, since in some cases it does not reflect the quality of the splitting. Assume a long Hebrew document with several short sentences in Aramaic. If the Hebrew is 95% of the text, a result that classifies the whole text as Hebrew will get 95% but is pretty useless and we may prefer a result that identifies the Aramaic segments but errs on more words.

**Segmentation error (SE)** estimates the algorithm's sensitivity to language shifts. It is the difference between the correct number and that returned by the algorithm, divided by correct number. Obviously, SE is in the range [−1:1]. It will indeed resemble the problem previously described, since, if the entire document is classified as Hebrew, the SE score will be very low, as the actual number is much greater than 1.

### 5.3 Experiments

**Neighboring segments** – The first thing we tested is the way a segment's classification is affected by neighboring segments. We begin by checking if adding the distance of the closest segments enhances performance. Define $Score_{f,l} = Dist(l,f) + a\left(NDist_{l,f}(1) + NDist_{l,f}(-1)\right)$. For the test we set $a$=0.4.

From Figures 1 and 2, one can see that neighboring segments improve classification of short segments, while on shorter ones classification without the neighbors was superior. It is not surprising that when using neighbors the splitting procedure tends to split the text to longer segments, which has good effect only if segments actually are longer. We can also see from Figure 3 that the SE measure is now positive with $k$=100, which means the algorithm underestimates the number of segments even when each segment is 100 characters long. By further experiments, we can see that the $a$ parameter is insignificant, and fix it at 0.3.

As expected, looking at neighboring segments can often improve results. The next question is if farther neighbors also do. Let: $Score_{f,l} = Dist(l,f) + \sum_{k=1}^{N}\left(\frac{a}{k}\right)\left(NDist_{l,f}(k1) + NDist_{l,f}(-k)\right)$. Parameter $N$ stands for the longest distance of neighbors to consider in the score. Parameter $a$ is set to 0.3.

We see that increasing $N$ does not have a significant impact on algorithm performance, and on shorter segment lengths performance drops with $N$. We conclude that there is no advantage at looking at distant neighbors.

**Post-processing** – Another thing we test is the post-processing of the splitting results to refine the initial segment choice. We try to move the transition point from the original position to a more accurate position using the technique described above. We note is cannot affect the SE measure, since we only move the transition points without changing the classification. As shown in Figure 4, it does improve the performance for all values of $l$.

**Noise reduction –** To test noise reduction, we artificially added noise, randomly replacing some letters with $. Let P denote the desired noise rate and replace each letter independently with $ with probability P. Since the replacements of character is mutually independent, we can expect a normal distribution of error positions, and the correction phase described above does not assume anything about the error creation process. Error creation does not assign different probabilities for different characters in the text unlike natural OCR systems or other noisy processing.

Not surprisingly, Figure 5 illustrates that the accuracy reduces as the error rate rises. However, it does not significantly drop even for a very high error rate, and obviously we cannot expect that the error reducing process will perform better then the algorithm performs on errorless text. Figure 6 illustrates the performance of each method. It looks like looking at most common n-chars does not help, nor trying to correct the unrecognized character. Ignoring the unrecognized character, using either bigrams or trigrams, or estimating the missing unrecognized bigram probability show the best and pretty similar results.

## 6. Conclusion

We have described methods for classifying texts, all using the same character set, into several languages. Furthermore, we considered segmented multilingual texts into monolingual components. In both cases, we made allowance for corrupted texts, such as that obtained by OCR from handwritten manuscripts. The results are encouraging and will be used in the Friedberg Genizah digitization project (www.genizah.org).

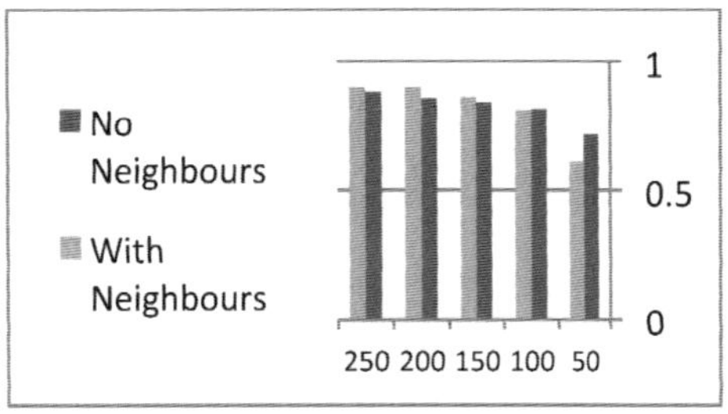


Figure 1: Correct word percentage considering neighbors and not, as a function of segment length $k$ (document length was 1500).

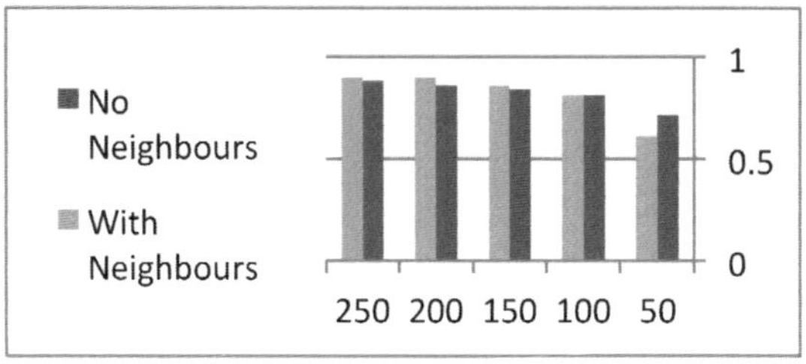


Figure 2: Segmentation error considering neighbors or not ($k$ =1500).

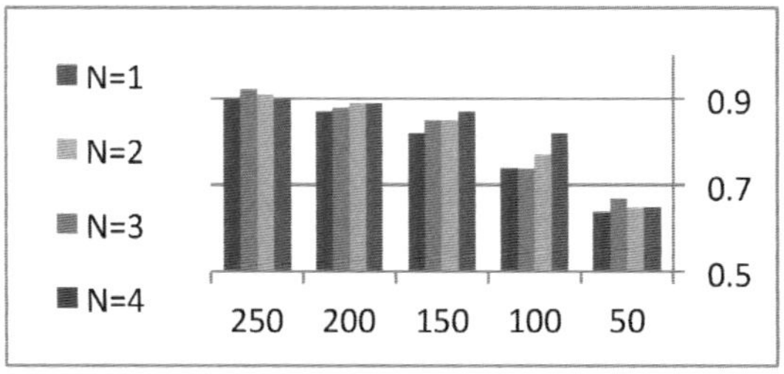


Figure 3: Correct word percentage for various resplitting values N as a function of $k$.

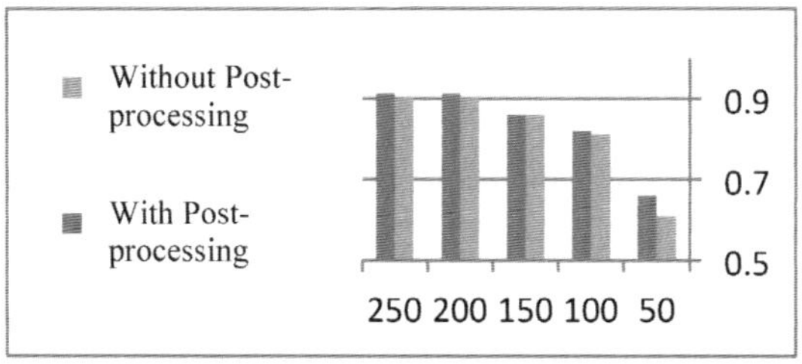


Figure 4: Correct word percentage with and without post-processing.

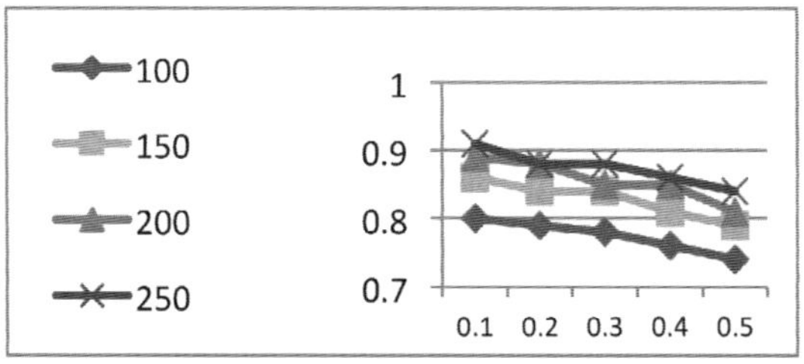


Figure 5: Word accuracy as a function of noise.

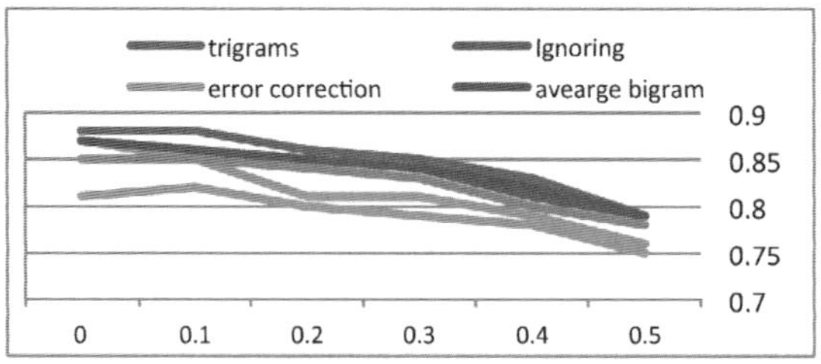


Figure 6: The performance of suggested correction methods for each error rate.

## Acknowledgement

We thank the Friedberg Genizah Project for supplying data to work with and for their support.

## References

Gökhan Bakır. 2007. *Predicting Structured Data.* MIT Press, Cambridge, MA.

Freddy Y. Y. Choi. 2000. Advances in domain independent linear text segmentation. *Proc. 1st North American Chapter of the Association for Computational Linguistics Conference,* pp. 26-33.

Juha Häkkinen and Jilei Tian. 2001. *N*-gram and decision tree based language identification for written words. *Proc. Automatic Speech Recognition and Understanding (ASRU '01),* Italy, pp. 335-338.

Marti A. Hearst. 1993. TextTiling: A quantitative approach to discourse segmentation. Technical Report, Sequoia 93/24, Computer Science Division.

Sylvain Lamprier, Tassadit Amghar, Bernard Levrat, and Frédéric Saubion. 2007. On evaluation methodologies for text segmentation algorithms. *Proc. 9th IEEE International Conference on Tools with Artificial Intelligence (ICTAI),* volume 2, pp. 19-26.

Karen Kukich. 1992. Techniques for automatically correcting words in text. *ACM Computing Surveys* 24(4): 377-439.

# Author Index